RHINO Presents

THE GREATEST ROCK & ROLL STORIES

By ART FEIN

The Most Outrageous, Magical
And Scandalous Events In
The History Of Rock & Roll!

GENERAL PUBLISHING GROUP
Los Angeles

Publisher: W. Quay Hays
Editors: Richard Foos, Harold Bronson
Managing Editor: Colby Allerton
Cover Design: Kurt Wahlner and Chitra Sekhar
Design: Chitra Sekhar
Production Director: Trudihope Schlomowitz
Color and Prepress Manager: Bill Castillo
Production Artist: Gaston Moraga
Production Assistant: Tom Archibeque
Copy Editor: Dianne Woo
Editorial Assistance: Stephen Motika

Picture credits: Art Fein: 20 (series on right), 33, 80, 81, 83, 85, 139, 171, 217,
220, 223; Warner Brothers: 65, 68, 69, 86, 91, 122, 154, 156, 164, 167;
Jim Marshall: 54, 108-109, 157, 180, 189, 207, 221; AP/Wide World: 39, 101, 150,
159, 187; Frank Driggs Collection: 10, 11, 31, 176, 198; Rhino/Atlantic: 34, 101, 132;
Rhino: 36, 45, 76; Michael Ochs Archive: 26, 116; Mike Reisbord Collection: 37, 38;
PBS: 56, 141; Beth Gwynn: 61 (left), 136; Karen Bystedt Hardy: 63, 71 (right); MCA:
13, 52; Jeffrey Mayer Photography: 44; Electra: 49; Retna: 182; Star File: 120.

Very special thanks to Jon and Jason Moch, David "Schollie" Schollenbarger,
David Gowing, Ron Tracey, Mike Dimkitch (and Jack), Jason Wizelman,
Mitch Tobias, Dave Levison, John Boyle, Phil Dupuoy,
Mike Reisbord and the Isley Brothers—"It's Your Thing."

For Information:
General Publishing Group, Inc.
2701 Ocean Park Boulevard, Suite 140
Santa Monica, CA 90405

Library of Congress Catalog Card Number 96-077582

ISBN 1-881649-75-X

Printed in the USA
10 9 8 7 6 5 4 3 2 1

General Publishing Group
Los Angeles

CONTENTS

ACKNOWLEDGMENTS

As in past projects, it is impossible to salute everyone's specific contributions, so their names are simply listed below alphabetically. However, the MOST important person has been singled out—and the name is circled in red.

Mary Katherine Aldin; Colby Allerton ("Ed."); Jimmy Angel ("thank you for keeping the '50s alive"); James Austin; Cary Baker; Ken Barnes; Lew Bedell; Kent Benjamin (#31, 54, 55, 81); Dick Blackburn; Paul Body; Donna Boni; Bruce Bromberg; Harold Bronson; G. Brown; Denny Bruce; Bug Music; Cliff Burnstein; Charlie Burton; Flash Cadillac; Randy California; Chris Carter; Susan Clary; Jason Cohen; Larry and Lorrie Collins; Richard Creamer; Marshall Crenshaw; Richard Cromelin; Saul Davis; Jim Dawson; Taisco Del Ray (Dan Forte); Pam Des Barres; Jim Dickinson; Henry Diltz; Swamp Dogg; Brad Elterman; Todd Everett; Tav Falco; Steve Farber; Pat Faulstich; Doug Fieger (#33, 79, 95); Harvey Sid Fisher; Richard Foos; Kim Fowley; Odel Franklin; David Fricke; Steve Gaydos; Sam Graham; Paul Grein; Sid Griffin; Paul Hampton; Barry Hansen (Dr. Demento); Bill Holdship; Peter Holsapple; Carl Hungness; Lindsay Hutton; Howard Kaylan; Elliot Kendall; Tom Kenny; Alexander King; Cub Koda; Harvey Kubernik; Fred Labour; Alan Larman; Byron Laursen; Robert Leslie; Mark Leviton; Bill Liebowitz; Lisa Lindstrom (#87); Greg Loescher; Toby Mamis; Hudson Marquez; Dave Marsh; Jimmy Lee Maslon; Rip Masters; Bob Merlis; Dr. Millar; Don Misraje; Mr. Morrison; Brendan Mullen; Michael Ochs; Ed Odel; Mats Olsson; Earl Palmer; Freddie Patterson; Jennifer Pelphrey; Dan Perloff; Tom Popson; Domenic Priore (#90); Heidi Robinson; Steve Roeser; Ric Ross; Mark Rubenstein; Andrew Sandoval; Rob Santos; Sue Sawyer; Sharon Sheeley; Scott Schinder; Kathe Schreyer; Andy Schwartz; Gene Sculatti; Joel Selvin; Lewis Shiner (#93, 94); David Skepner; P.F. Sloan; Chris & Frank Sprague; Mike Stax; Gary Stewart; Billy Swan; Malcom Tent; Lynn Van Matre; Rich Victor; Don Waller; Ian Whitcomb; Alan White; Timothy White; David Wild; Mike Willard; Paul Williams; John Wolfe; Kent Wolgamott.
("#" indicates special help, or full authorship!)

INTRODUCTION

The Greatest Rock & Roll Stories?

What do you mean, "Greatest"?, I asked myself at the outset of this journey. Great, like ironic? Great like big? Great like with happy endings, you know, uplifting?

After a lot of wrangling and soul-searching I elected to put the most **famous** stories that came up, the classics. And some others.

"Pretend nobody's ever heard a rock & roll story," said the Rhino guy, and with that signpost I headed down the road forthrightly with a smile and the steel gaze of a man with a purpose.

Some years ago, Michael Ochs was all hepped up about the book he and his friend Lester Bangs were going to write.

"It's going to be firsthand stories from rock and blues guys," he said.

I was less than enthused.

"But those guys by their nature don't remember things," I said. "They get stuff wrong. And they lie. Details are for guys like us."

That book never got written because of the death of one of the authors, and so I now continue with a fuzzy variation on that shaky theme.

The assignment was to write the greatest **stories**. So what's a story?— JFK got shot, the Mets won the World Series in 1969? Those are stories. What about Paul Bunyan, OJ's alibi? Stories too. So, then, I didn't feel encumbered by facts (though striving to keep things accurate when checkable), and felt free to explore what people <u>said</u> happened.

And I don't necessarily mean the people involved.

Also, many of these entries contain lists that were cut off by time restraints. If I cite three rock & roll stage deaths, you probably know three more. If I salute great musical moments in films, you probably have other favorites.

Well, write them in the margins—this is an interactive book! With its inevitable shortcomings in YOUR favorite areas, you fill in the blanks and make it YOUR book, not mine.

(Heck, gather 'em together and send 'em to me, and we'll write some more books!)

We rock fans (I am not a rock critic)[1] face the world of rock history daily, and see un-truths or half-truths find their way into history.

Take the BBC radio interview I heard with the Bobbettes ("Mr. Lee," 1957), where they said Elvis Presley rode with them on a bus touring the south in 1957. Maybe it was Paul Anka fooling them with sideburns and maybe their memory got a little fuzzy in 40 years, but Elvis didn't do any bus tours with the Bobbettes in 1957. Similarly, on the 1995 PBS **Rock & Roll** documentary series, the Shirelles gave the old excuse, "We were doing all right 'til the Beatles came along, then you had to be English." We've heard this from countless musicians whose time ran its course. The Shirelles' hit string stopped in late 1962: by early '63 they were just nudging the bottom of the charts, and then—natural oblivion.

Historians WAIT to hear that story, both for its sameness and its variations. Tell it to the Beach Boys and Dionne Warwick and the Righteous Brothers and Sonny & Cher and Roger Miller and the Four Seasons and Johnny Rivers and the Supremes and the Temptations and the Four Tops and…

Likewise, books tell tales that are gathered from original sources that are wrong. I've read that Jimi Hendrix was yanked off the Monkees 1967 U.S. tour because his sexuality offended the Daughters of the American Revolution. Truth be told, his manager Chas Chandler concocted that story to get him off the tour—Hendrix was getting popular enough to be a headliner, and the Monkees wished him godspeed. (Both the Monkees and Herman's Hermits had a hand in launching rock gods—the Monkees with Hendrix, and Herman's Hermits with the Who.) In March 1994, newspapers reported that Kurt Cobain accidentally overdosed in his hotel room in Rome, but later events revealed the truth. When people "remember" John Lennon's misbehavior in Los Angeles in early 1974, they often truncate two stories, one when he went into the Troubadour with a Kotex on his forehead during an Ann Peebles show, and another when he was thrown out, with Harry Nilsson, for disrupting a Smothers Brothers appearance. That happens. History compresses things.

So it depends on where, and from when, you get your information.

Stories from the past ten years—oh, let's say fifteen, the MTV era—are hard to get. Whether it's because rock stars are more tightly managed, or because their idea of "doing something" involves doing it on TV, it was hard to reap many great ones from today's performers.

Don't get me wrong—they're great in their way and have millions of fans. But I wrestled with what to say about U2—they pretended to be the Beatles on an LA rooftop? Spraypainted a sculpture in San Francisco? Made a video in Las Vegas? None of what I uncovered added up to much, other than they are fabulously popular and widely beloved. How about the Red Hot Chili Peppers' "socks-on-cocks" business? It's funny as all get-out, but apparently didn't raise an eyebrow, judging from the lack of reporting in newspaper files. Madonna's antics? Where does one begin, and how to choose one over the others?

I inquired of Gen-X writers, and they told me essentially the same thing: Today's rock stars aren't as interesting as yesteryear's. (They die of drug abuse at about the same rate, but I disdained that.) One young major-label promotion man told me, "The Foo Fighters deal with Capitol gives them a huge percentage." It was an echo of an industry veteran's observation, "Today's band stories are how they're getting 85% on their overseas royalties rather than 75%." (I've stayed pretty much away from "business" stories in this book. Who needs 'em?)

Rolling Stone's year-end wrap-ups are depressing because they dwell on the whole media mix. Highlights of the year are often ceremonious, when a film star hugs a rock star, or Sting gives an award to Peter Gabriel— it becomes obvious that the year's "news" is photo-driven. And too often, TV itself makes an event significant! Did the Beastie Boys say "poo-poo" on an awards show? Did Madonna say "fuck" on the David Letterman show? None of this would matter if it were not on TV.

I take a lot of shots at MTV in this book. TV has twice ruined rock & roll. Dick Clark and American Bandstand spread rock & roll to the nation in 1957, but once they realized their power they manipulated it to their ends and killed off the best stuff (even if you say pop pushed out rock & roll naturally without them, it wouldn't have happened so fast). Now MTV, a hideous behemoth, dictates that visuals accompany music, which is madness on two levels:

(1) The "picture stories" that now accompany songs are silent movies made for 10-year-olds. None has ever made a song better! Most could have a different song attached without a loss. Which leads to: (2) Music stands on its own. It's a hearing experience that goes directly to your soul, a process that MUST NOT BE DERAILED by visual gobbledygook.

And finally, some people will find this book's style of:
(a) story
and
(b) lengthy footnotes
to be annoying and possibly megalomaniacal—
The writer says something, and then comments on what he's said!

This unfair typecasting of a Gemini—supposedly we have two personalities, which would lead to this alleged bifurcation—has plagued me all my life.

I don't even believe in astrology.
And neither do I.

Art Fein
Hollywood, CA, 1996

---

[1] In Balzac's *Lost Illusions*, published in 1847, the theater critic sells extra tickets supplied by the promoter, and the book critic keeps books he reviews sealed so they can be "clean" when he sells them to a bookstore.

Of course, this was 150 years ago. Things were different then.

There was no record industry.

Alan Freed Presents the World's First Rock & Roll Show

Before there was Rock & Roll, there was nothing…

…but the pop sounds of Perry Como, Eddie Fisher, Doris Day: Fine artists, but remnants of a bygone time, the Big Band era.

In the early 1950s, though, in big cities and small towns alike, **adventurous kids started turning to black radio stations**[1] to hear new, soulful rhythm & blues by the Clovers, the Dominoes and the Midnighters. Most adults were not aware of this mysterious and, if they had known, alarming[2] trend until mid-1951, when Alan Freed, a Cleveland disc jockey, seized the moment and began broadcasting these records on heretofore white radio.

It was a move that rocked the world.

Though he knew he already had a black audience for the black-made music, Freed soon noticed he had a white audience, too. *But he had no idea who was really listening* until he put on a live show at the Cleveland Armory in March 1952. The hall normally held 10,000 people, but twice as many, both black and white, showed up to see Ruth Brown, Screamin' Jay Hawkins, the Dominoes and the Buddy Johnson Band perform.

The racial mix and the large turnout shocked the music world. All over the country, promoters and disc jockeys realized there was a new sound that appealed to a new generation.

Rock & roll was on its way.

Freed went on to achieve bigger fame in New York City, where he introduced rock and roll—a term that he and a business partner tried unsuccessfully to copyright despite its decades-old lineage—to the Big Apple and ruled the airwaves. He also appeared in several rock-exploitation movies. See Marshall Crenshaw's *Hollywood Rock* (Harper, 1994) for an overview of Freed's and other rock movies.

But Freed's business conduct was not always tip-

top. He added his name as writer on several records ("Sincerely" and "Maybellene" to name two[3]) in exchange for airing them and took other forms of payola, not illegal at the time.

In 1958, Freed's reputation took a nosedive when a show he was presenting in Boston was halted by police, sparking a riot[4] and leading, precipitously, to his downfall. **He soon became *persona non grata*** at venues across America and lost his exalted standing in radio. In 1959, government payola investigations (prompted by the theory that if rock & roll is popular, it must be the work of criminals) further blackened Freed's name,[5] and he spent his final years deejaying in smaller markets. He died of alcoholism in 1965.

[1] Veteran Memphis producer Jim Dickinson said it well: "Kids today don't understand what it was like back then. The first time you heard a rock & roll record, it was like a miracle. You couldn't believe such a wonderful thing could happen. Then a month later you heard a *second* rock & roll record, and you had to pinch yourself to be sure you weren't dreaming. You know, you had no idea there would *be* another one."

[2] All of America was racially segregated in the 1950s, whether there were laws dictating so or not.

[3] In 1972—years before the full story was out—Charlie Gillett wrote an excellent rock-history book, *Sound of the City*, in which he naively praised Freed's songwriting.

[4] Then as now, cops were nervous about teenagers gathering together. And rock & roll itself was viewed as bad, just as punk music was in the '70s and rap in the '90s. So whether it was the image of Jerry Lee Lewis whipping the crowd into hysteria, as Myra Gale Lewis writes in her book, *Great Balls of Fire*, or a white girl lusting for a black singer's groin, as hysterically reported by Ed Ward in *Rock of Ages* (Summit, 1988) *something* prompted the cops to pull the plug. Freed allegedly egged on the crowd by saying words to the effect of "Hey, I guess the police don't like your music." He was arrested and charged with riot incitement.

[5] That Freed "knew names" but refused to divulge them made him a pariah in the eyes of America. Dick Clark, who faced similar charges, came out of the payola hearings squeaky clean, hailed by his accusers as an upright, honorable young man. Maybe it was because, unlike Freed, he could honestly say he didn't own any rock & roll records.

1956 "Rock Around the Clock" Causes Riots in Theaters

The movie *Blackboard Jungle* was about a schoolteacher in a New York slum. It was intended to be a commentary on violence in school. Trouble was, teenage movie fans identified not with the embattled teacher, but with the sneering, gum-chewing, knife-wielding students who disrupted class and generally screwed off.[1]

That feeling of **anarchy was intensified** tenfold by the song heard over the film's opening credits. As Bill Haley and the Comets belted out "Rock Around The Clock," teenagers let loose and acted as arrogant and antagonistic as the ones in the movie, dancing in the aisles, tearing up seats, getting in fights. The song may or may not sound a little tame today (depending on who you ask), but it contained everything—driving drums, electric guitar, pulsating slap-bass, honking sax—to drive a kid in the mid-fifties to ecstasy…or mayhem.

Consequently, **audiences rioted[2] when Bill Haley and the Comets made personal appearances.** Haley was an unlikely hero,[3] a stout 30-year-old singer with squinty eyes (because only one was real), a bow tie and a spit-curl in the center of his receding hairline. (This was before MTV.)

Haley had strong "straight" roots. As a western Pennsylvania country singer, he'd had novelty hits— actually, the first rock & roll hits, the country-boogie "Rock the Joint" and "Crazy Man Crazy"—in the early '50s. His "rock" band, often dressed in checkered sportcoats and bow ties, was *très* square and contained the one instrument that is anathema to rock & roll, an accordion[4] (actually, *two* unfashionable instruments: The other was a steel guitar!). Decca Records' Milt Gabler, who produced "Rock Around the Clock" at a union hall in New York City, had for the previous dozen years produced records for the stylistically similar black entertainer Louis Jordan.

Haley died on February 9, 1981, at age 55, somewhat mentally enfeebled. Dave Alvin's tribute to him, "Haley's Comet," appears on Alvin's *Blue Blvd.* album (HighTone HCD 8029).

---

[1] The film, and the book on which it was based, may have reflected actu-

al values of the teenagers of its day, but it doesn't sit well with history. In a scene that still brings tears to record collectors' eyes, the student-hoodlums smash rare 78s by Louis Armstrong and Bunk Johnson, demanding Italian crooners Tony Bennett and Julius La Rosa!

It might've been accurate, but it sure is weird.

[2] In famous newsreel footage of the October 26, 1958, Haley concert in Berlin, kids hurled chairs and dismantled the stage until the cops moved in.

[3] There is a touching story attributed to Haley. Arriving at a train station in London in 1956, he saw thousands of screaming fans and wondered what famous person was on the train.

[4] Accordions have always been reviled in rock & roll. Watch Teddy Randazzo, with the Chuckles, play one in the 1956 film *The Girl Can't Help It* and see how inappropriate it was: Teddy sang and snapped his fingers while this big cow udder swayed against his movements. Tony Bellus played one on the utterly forgotten 1959 semi-hit (#25) "Robbin' the Cradle." The instrument—a cordo-vox—next popped up in 1965 in the decidedly unhip Gary Lewis & the Playboys band, but Lewis soon scotched it. Later, an accordion was used to provide a Mediterranean touch on such songs as the Stones' "Backstreet Girl," the Rascals' "How Can I Be Sure," Peter Sarstedt's "Where Do You Go to My Lovely," and Jack Bonus' incredible "Sweet Mehidabelle." It was never used as a lead instrument, except in odd turns such as the Dave Edmunds' "Ju Ju Man" and Dave Allen's swamp-pop rendering of Chuck Berry's "Promised Land" (a 1965 non-hit that was reissued in England in 1975 and went to #1!). Truly, the accordion never got any respect until Garth Hudson played one in The Band (1968), and its next appearance wasn't until the 1980s, when U2 picked one up. (Comedians "Weird Al" Yankovic and Judy Tenuta did nothing to boost accordion-lovers' morale.)

1956 Screamin' Jay Hawkins Gets Locked in His Coffin

Jalacy Hawkins of Cleveland, Ohio, **wanted to be an opera singer.**

Instead, as Screamin' Jay Hawkins,[1] his song "I Put a Spell on You" and his look—a dark black, wide-eyed turbanned man with a bone in his nose and holding a skull on a stick—made him the embodiment of everything America feared about the encroaching rock & roll culture. He had 30 suits in shocking pink and stupefying chartreuse, and *traveled in a zebra-skin station wagon followed by a hearse.*

"Spell" was voodoo-rock. He says everyone in the room was drunk when they recorded it at a New York studio in 1956, and the resulting song, a list of revenges the singer will take on his departing lover, ends with spine-chilling, half-animal growls that surely put parents of the day in a dither, thinking, *This is music?*

"I built my career on it," says Jay, who as of 1996 was enjoying a prosperous musical career in Europe.[2]

But every moment wasn't grand for Jay. The most memorable *bad* moment of his career came when he was playing an R&B revue at the Apollo Theater in New York City. Jay's stage act opened with him climbing out of a closed coffin. One night, some of his fellow performers from the Drifters locked Jay inside it as a joke. When his musical cue came, he pushed and shoved but no dice.

"I soiled myself," he says today ruefully. The joke may have been funny to the handful of people who knew about it, but to Jay it was a moment he never wants to relive.

The threat of suffocation is rarely funny to the victim.

I Put a Spell on You" was Hawkins' only major hit.[3] The song has been kept alive to this day through numerous cover recordings, including an important jazz-inflected one by Nina Simone, a cover by the Animals (and one by ex-Animal Alan Price), Audience's interesting progressive-rock version and the much-played, big-selling Creedence Clearwater version. And the song was given big play in the oddball 1984 hit movie *Stranger Than Paradise*, directed and written by Jim Jarmusch. In 1989 Jay played a hotel-keep in *Mystery Train*, another Jarmusch film.

[1] Asked whence came his colorful moniker, Jay says, "From a fat old drunk lady in Nitro, West Virginia. I was emceeing a show there, and they wanted a singer, so I sat at the piano and hollered. This fat woman kept shouting, 'Scream, Jay, scream!' and I kinda liked the sound of that. I decided if I'm gonna make it in this business I'm gonna be a screamer, and I've been destroying songs ever since."

[2] A Cleveland native, Screamin' Jay was on the bill at the big Alan Freed rock & roll show in March 1952 (see "Alan Freed Presents...", page 10).

[3] And it never even made the charts! But his 1966 recording,

"Constipation Blues," a musical vamp with a lot of pained grunting, got a lot of play on FM underground stations in the '60s—and was a big hit in Japan!

January 28, 1956 — Elvis Presley appears on TV

Elvis Presley was the first TV-born rock star.[1]
Elvis was just 21 years old and variously called the Memphis Flash, *the Hillbilly Cat and the Atomic-Powered Singer* when he made his national TV debut in 1956. The previous year he'd made big noise in the South and Southwest with raw, often suggestive records

Elvis in 1956 (Below) at RCA recording studio NYC and appearing on the Dorsey Show (Inset).

such as "Baby Let's Play House" and "Good Rockin' Tonight" that mixed country, pop, and rhythm & blues. To boot, he had a wiggling stage presence that was unheard of for a male.[2] When RCA Records bought his contract from Sun Records in November 1955, the record industry was agog at the unprecedented price tag of $35,000[3] for a rookie. **After all, he could be just a flash in the pan**!

January 28, 1956, a cold, rainy night in New York, Elvis proved the naysayers wrong. Booked on the *Stage Show*,[4] a lead-in to Jackie Gleason's popular *Honeymooners* and hosted by the waning big-band brothers Tommy and Jimmy Dorsey, Presley exploded like an atom bomb.

Swaggering onstage with otherworldly confidence and a sneer, his appearance was startling. He had a handsome face with deep-black eyes (later it would be revealed that he used eye shadow, an affectation since high school!), thick black[5] hair combed back, a pompadour in front and sideburns. Under his suit he sported a black shirt and a white tie.

For his first appearance before Mom and Pop America, he dressed like a gangster in makeup! "Shake, Rattle and Roll" mixed with "Flip, Flop and Fly" set the fuse burning. Elvis' message seemed urgent, like God-on-high commanding the universe to rock! One moment **his eyes burned holes in the camera,** a second later his eyebrows arched up pleadingly and his eyes squeezed shut in rapture. Perhaps he was a messenger from Below! His shoulders twitched, his legs buckled in and out, he moved like he was riding a horse and slapped his guitar like he was punishing it.

The audience applauded and smiled at the seeming madman; was he kidding?[6] He wasn't. At the song's midpoint the guitarist broke loose, the bass player leaned in and the newcomer took flight. His legs jerked frantically, his eyes flashed, his guitar swung to the side and **he**

made pelvic movements that were likened by his critics—and there were many—to those of a female stripper.

Three weeks later on February 18, during his third Dorsey appearance, the die was irreversibly cast. For his second song he did the newly recorded "Heartbreak Hotel." He was backed up, as ever, by his trio of guitarist Scotty Moore, bassist Bill Black and drummer D.J. Fontana. In the middle of the song a Dorsey band horn man took a solo where the guitar break belonged.[7] It was a coarse, desperate sound akin to a dying animal's last bleat, which in fact it was—the final sound of the Swing era, the birth of the new.

Rock & roll had been lying nascent in the bones and souls of teenagers around the world.

When Elvis arrived, these feelings awakened, and the world was never the same.[8]

[1] Ricky Nelson was the second, but that's another story.

[2] Plenty of black male performers wiggled suggestively, especially R&B favorite Wynonie Harris, who influenced Elvis. But they never got on TV.

[3] Ahmet Ertegun desperately tried to sign him but couldn't come up with the money. Imagine if Elvis had recorded for Atlantic! But Colonel Parker, Elvis' manager, probably still would have chosen RCA, where Parker was already known from having managed country singers Eddy Arnold and Hank Snow.

[4] Elvis' TV debut is often thought of as being on the *Ed Sullivan Show*. In fact, he made his mark on the Dorsey Brothers, Milton Berle and Steve Allen shows before Sullivan belatedly and reluctantly booked him in October 1956.

[5] He darkened his light-brown hair (some call it blond, but I'll fight them) to look more like Tony Curtis. It wasn't till his second movie, *Loving You*, in 1957 that he sported the jet-black dye job that became his permanent color.

[6] Audiences in 1951 also reacted to emotionally charged Johnnie Ray with "Is he kidding?" Ironically, Ray's reaction to Presley was, "Is he kidding?"

[7] So you see, Paul Shaffer's isn't the first TV band to "horn in" on an established group's music.

[8] Many people, from '60s radicals Abbie Hoffman and Eldridge Cleaver to historian David Halberstam, consider Elvis' arrival to be one of the pivotal events of the 20th century. The fictitious college in Don De Lillo's hilarious 1985 novel, *White Noise*, boasts a Department of Elvis Studies. It was absurd then….

1957 Jerry Lee Lewis Sets Piano on Fire

First Steve Allen appearance in 1957 (Above) and still a rockin' muthahumper at LA's Palomino in 1977 (Right).

Jerry Lee Lewis is surely an egotist: He has said that his greatest regret is that he has never sat in an audience and enjoyed a Jerry Lee Lewis show.

So it's not hard to believe that at one Alan Freed stage show, after Jerry Lee lost a coin toss and had to go on before Chuck Berry, he vowed to put on a show that *nobody* could follow. After playing his usual manic, hair-tossing, piano-stool kicking, microphone-strangling, shirt-tearing set, *he reached up under the piano lid, tossed in a bunch of paper and threw a match in after it!* In seconds the instrument was an inferno, causing Freed to laugh, the promoter to tear out his hair and the audience to shriek in appreciation.

Berry, waiting in the wings, was not amused.

But then, there's no substantiation of this story, despite its immortalization in the fictional Alan Freed film biography *American Hot Wax* and the fanciful but enjoyable Lewis biopic *Great Balls of Fire*. No Chuck Berry book, Jerry Lee book or rock history tome mentions this incident as fact.

Supposedly, when it was all over, Jerry Lee swaggered past Berry and said **"Follow that, Killer."** Legend, which is what writers invent to make history more colorful, is that Jerry Lee said, "Follow that, Nigger." Rock writers are, by and large, white middle class and Northern (rock scribes Robert Palmer and Robert Gordon notwithstanding), so they lean toward colorful portrayals of Southerners' racism. But in the Atlantic Video history of the Animals, Eric Burdon relates that when they were traveling 'round the United States on a bus with Jerry Lee and Chuck, Jerry Lee would constantly provoke Chuck with "nigger" comments.

Whether Jerry Lee said that, or whether he truly did set the piano aflame, remains a mystery. Ask Jerry Lee, and he might say anything.

In another racial note, inventive music writer Nick Tosches asserted in *Country: The Biggest Music in America* (Stein & Day, 1977) that Warren Smith, on his 1956 Sun record "Ubangi Stomp," utters the line, "I seen them niggers doin' an odd-lookin' skip."[1]

That's bunk: the word is "natives." Just listen to it on the Rhino *Sun Story*, R2 75884, or the Rhino *Sun Records Collection*, R2 71780.[2]

Finally, there's a little-known, shocking[3] bit of racism on page 13 of the booklet accompanying the 1979 MCA six-record set *The Complete Buddy Holly*. In a letter to his mother dated July 30, 1957, Cricket drummer Jerry Allison, not yet 18, shares this impression of New

York: "So the negroes play like they are just as good as us here, they can do anything we can except say they're white."

Surely Allison matured out of this silliness; at the time, the Crickets' "That'll Be the Day" had not yet been released. Elsewhere in the letter, Allison complains of the rigors of traveling and says, *"I'm so confused I can't really think."* These should be seen as the words of a confused, frightened boy.

[1] A misapprehension corrected in the 1985 edition of *Country*, but echoed in later editions of Greil Marcus' *Mystery Train*.

[2] Or check Jerry Lee's Sun version. Or check Alice Cooper's version on the *Lace and Whiskey* album.

[3] Shocking not for its content—this was 1957, he was from west Texas—but for the fact that nobody—Allison, his mother, the booklet compiler or the record company—read the letter before it went into print! (Spotted by the Sprague brothers.)

1957 The Invention of the Fuzz-Tone Guitar and Other Funny Guitar Noises

Guitarist Paul Burlison was a member of the Memphis-based Burnette Trio along with brothers Johnny and Dorsey Burnette.[1] After several successful appearances on TV's Ted Mack's Amateur Hour, the band got a recording contract. When they got to the recording session, **a tube dislodged on Burlison's amplifier, causing it to take on an ugly, "fuzzy" tone.** "Leave it that way," said bandleader Johnny. The result was a distorted guitar line running through the entirety of "Train Kept a Rollin',"[2] which was then released on Coral Records and sold nary a copy.

This discovery was to be hugely influential, even if Burlison's story was, hmm, fuzzy. Howlin' Wolf's guitarist Willie Johnson had long employed a distorted "fuzz" tone, and Burlison had played with Wolf's band in

Memphis, so he was no stranger to that sound. Whatever the case, when the upcoming crop of British guitarists heard the Burnette Trio's record, it became one of the most copied sounds around.[3]

Jeff Beck, who replaced Eric Clapton in the Yardbirds in early 1965, had heard it. Beck himself pioneered many sounds. Feedback made one of its first appearances in the Yardbirds' "Shapes of Things."[4] And in 1966 Beck introduced the band to "Train Kept A Rollin'," which they recorded during a tour of America.

Meanwhile, Dave Davies created the Kinks' distorted guitar sound himself. Wanting a meaner, fuller and more distorted sound for their recordings, **he slashed the speakers in one of his amps** and out popped the guitar sound for "You Really Got Me," "All Day and All of the Night," "Till the End of the Day" and "I Need You."[5] It is also worth noting that American rock & roll guitarist Link Wray had already done this—well, punched his amp speaker with a pencil—for the massive guitar sound on "Rumble."

In response to rock & roll interest in fuzzy sounds, in early 1965 Gibson Guitars introduced the Maestro Fuzzbox; Vinnie Bell was the first guitarist to employ it on a hit record, the Four Seasons' "Let's Hang On." By May 1965 the fuzzbox was used on several important records, notably the Stones' "(I Can't get No) Satisfaction"[6] (Keith Richards hated it; it was a substitute for horns, which later were used on Otis Redding's version), the Beatles' "Think for Yourself" (played by Paul on bass) and the Monkees' "Valleri."

In the related field of feedback, the intro to the Beatles' "I Feel Fine" in November 1964 was no accident. Bootleg session tapes reveal that feedback was used on every take, **probably inspired by Pete Townshend of the Who, who had opened for the Beatles.** Many people were experimenting with it, back in those days when everyone was experimenting with everything. Townshend, Jeff Beck and Dave Davies were in the forefront, as were Lou Reed and Sterling Morrison of the Velvet Underground.

The next prominent appearance of feedback was in the Who's "Anyway, Anyhow, Anywhere," a record that was sent back by the pressing plant with instructions to remove the "funny squeaking sounds." Hot on the heels of that came the Small Faces' feedback-drenched "Whatcha Gonna Do About It?" (later covered by the Pretenders and the Sex Pistols). *Welshman John Cale took the Who and Faces singles back to America and played them for his band, the Velvet Underground*, and they rushed to use the sound on their album. Unfortunately, the album sat in the can for more than a year, spoiling their advantage.

Things were moving fast back then.

Another prominent record to feature fuzz-tone was Donovan's "Hurdy Gurdy Man" in 1968: Don[7] was backed by Led Zeppelin Minus One (Page, Bonham, Jones). Also, some people (namely, *moi*) like the fuzz-tone intro on the Beau Brummels' "One Too Many Mornings."

In the yet further removed and essentially unnamed field of fuzz-tone/feedback are two records, Marty Robbins' "Don't Worry" and Bob B. Soxx and the Blue Jeans' (Phil Spector's production, Billy Strange on guitar) "Zip-a-Dee-Doo-Dah."

---

[1] The brothers later abandoned their recording career and moved to Los Angeles, where they fell in with Ricky Nelson, Gene Vincent and other rockers. Their songs "Waitin' in School" and "Believe What You Say" were hits for Nelson. Separately, Dorsey hit first with "Tall Oak Tree" and "Hey Little One," then Johnny with "Dreamin'" and "You're Sixteen" (later covered by Ringo Starr). Johnny died in a boating accident on August 1, 1964. Dorsey died of natural causes on August 19, 1979. Both are buried in Forest Lawn Cemetery, Glendale, California.

[2] "Train Kept a Rollin'" was a jump blues hit in the late '40s for bandleader Tiny Bradshaw. The Burnettes took their version from Bradshaw, the Yardbirds later took theirs from the Burnette brothers, and in the 1970s Aerosmith took its version from the Yardbirds.

[3] Of course, they also could have gotten it from the Ventures' "The 2000 Pound Bee," released in October 1962, but that'd spoil this story.

[4] Originally in the solo slot was Beck's approximation of a sitar!

[5] Jimmy Page played on other people's recording sessions all through the British Invasion and has claimed/been credited with playing lead on Kinks singles.

[6] Keith Richards says the "doom-doom, doo-doo-DOO" opening to "Satisfaction" was fashioned around the melody of Martha and the Vandellas' "Nowhere to Run" (and I've read "Dancing in the Street").

[7] Donovan's friends call him Don. But don't you try it.

1960 · Sonny Boy Williamson Gets A New Suit

John Lee "Sonny Boy" Williamson was a blues singer and blues-harp player who made country-blues records, including "Good Morning Little Schoolgirl" and "Sugar Man." Born in Jackson, Tennessee, in 1914, he worked with blues greats Sleepy John Estes and Homesick James before moving to Chicago in 1937. In the early 1940s, Helena, Arkansas, bluesman *Aleck "Rice" Miller impersonated Williamson on a local radio station broadcast and then began appearing as him* at shows around the South when the real Williamson wasn't available. When Sonny Boy died in 1948, Miller filled the vacuum.[1]

Miller/Williamson, known to historians as Sonny Boy Williamson II, played in the 1930s with such immortals (if it were but so!) as Robert Johnson and Elmore James (he played on James' first version of "Dust My Broom"). He was married at one time to Howlin' Wolf's sister. Williamson II's songs have proved even more popular than the original Sonny Boy's, including "Eyesight to the Blind," "Don't Start Me Talkin'" (covered on the second New York Dolls album!) and "All My Love in Vain."

In 1960 a blues revival swept Williamson II overseas, where he performed in England and Europe to enthusiastic crowds. He came back to Helena bragging about his travels, but his country-store buddies simply didn't believe him. So on the second European tour he went to a tailor on Saville Row in London and asked him to make a suit out of a dozen kinds of fabric, reasoning, **"They couldn't make anything like that in America.** That's the kind of suit they could make only in England!"

He wore his "harlequin suit" back to Arkansas, and his friends believed him.

His rock & roll relevance, if any is needed, is that many English blues bands slavishly copied the harmonica style of Sonny Boy II (the sound, not the style; he used small harmonicas, which he sometimes put entirely into his mouth). When asked about playing with the Brits, like the Yardbirds and the Animals, he replied, "Those white boys want to play the blues so bad. And they do."

Muddy Waters

[1] This is one of the two instances in show business history when the understudy has successfully filled the shoes of the master. The other is Sam Butera, who played sax and did the arrangements for Louis Prima from the mid-1950s until Prima's stroke in 1974. Butera now does a letter-perfect Prima show in Las Vegas (often with Prima's one-time singing mate Keely Smith), with the spirit of Louis inhabiting his soul.

1964 Rolling Stones Meet Muddy Waters

The Rolling Stones were little known in America when they did their first U.S. concert tour in the summer of 1964. The shows were sometimes sparsely attended, but it was a great time for the band, who visited American musical landmarks such as the Apollo

Theater in New York and Chess Records studio in Chicago.

The Stones were and still are a blues-based band, and their regard for Chess Records' output was paramount: Chuck Berry, Bo Diddley, Muddy Waters, Howlin' Wolf, Etta James, Jimmy McCracklin, Willie Dixon and so many others recorded at that one studio at 2120 S. Michigan Ave. that the Stones used the address for the title of an instrumental cut on their album *12 x 5*.[1] However, their first encounter with **one of their idols at the studio was different from what they expected**: Keith Richards told an interviewer that Muddy Waters was there in overalls painting the place![2] Which—if true—merits examination.

The Chess brothers, Leonard and Phil, were notorious for perhaps underpaying their acts, but it could have been that Muddy (who's so highly regarded in Chicago that 43rd Street has been renamed Muddy Waters Boulevard) was underearning. Few of those great Chicago blues albums hit the charts or sold millions. **It wasn't until the English guys began recording** their songs that the bluesmen's fortunes soared, both from songwriting royalties and from the spotlight afforded them by their "descendants." In a 1990s documentary, bluesman John Lee Hooker tells how in the early 1980s he and Muddy had a one-upmanship contest over who was buying the most expensive cars: "Got me a Mercedes," Muddy'd say, and Hooker would reply, "I'll come and pick you up in my Rolls."

[1] Thee Midnighters' 1965 hit "Whittier Blvd." is much like this song.

[2] In *Stone Alone*, Bill Wyman's book, he says only that Waters helped carry their instruments in.

1965 Al Kooper Plays Organ on "Like a Rolling Stone"

With a solid music career already behind him,[1] 21-year-old Al Kooper cajoled an invitation from producer Tom Wilson[2] to the June 15, 1965, recording session for the new Bob Dylan song, "Like a Rolling Stone" in hopes of being the guitarist. When scheduled guitarist Mike Bloomfield arrived and let fly with a run that established he was in charge, Kooper decided maybe he was the organist. Dylan, no stranger to serendipity, said yes, this was the person who should play keyboards. Kooper was scared: **he had little keyboard experience,** but wanted to do this session so badly that he stayed riveted to his seat.

Producer Wilson (when Wilson became a staff producer at MGM, it was rumored Dylan would follow him; Dylan didn't. Wilson then went on to produce the first albums for Frank Zappa as well as for the Velvet Underground), a perfectionist, told Dylan the organ playing was weak. *Dylan simply responded, "Turn it up."* The result was an amazing moment of rock history, when a nervy, brash kid "felt his way through the changes like a kid fumbling in the dark for a light switch" and made immortal keyboard sounds on a very important record.

Kooper toured off and on with Dylan from the '60s through the '90s. He also formed the Blues Project in 1965, worked as stage manager at the Monterey Pop Festival, formed Blood, Sweat and Tears, **dated Linda Eastman just before she met Paul McCartney,** played on "You Can't Always Get What You Want" and some cuts on *The Who Sell Out*, made a couple of famous *Super Session* albums with, among others, Steve Stills, Mike Bloomfield and Shuggie Otis, discovered and produced Lynyrd Skynyrd, made several solo albums, wrote one book about his life, *Backstage Passes*, in 1976 and is working on another.

[1] He had already been in the group the Royal Teens, who had the hit "Short Shorts" in 1958 when he was 14. In 1964 Kooper wrote a song (with B. Brass and I. Levine), "This Diamond Ring," for the Drifters, which was recorded instead by Gary Lewis and the Playboys and became a #1 hit.

[2] Columbia staff producer Wilson handled only "Like a Rolling Stone" on the *Highway 61 Revisited* album, which was otherwise produced by Bob Johnston. Wilson was also the guy who added electronic instruments to Simon and Garfunkel's "Sounds of Silence" at Columbia executive Clive Davis' insistence. Paul Simon was in England at the time and became angry when he learned of the addition—at least till the song became a hit. (Davis also ordered the shortening of Big Brother and the Holding Company's "Piece of My Heart" for single release.) This is reminiscent of the Go-Go's complaints in 1980 that veteran producer Richard Gottehrer was ruining their ragged punk sound on the *Beauty and the Beat* album. Or George Tomsco's (of the Fireballs) complaint to producer Norman Petty that the squeaky "bleep" organ sound ruined their otherwise perfect recording of "Sugar Shack." (A lot of people, including Dot Records president Randy Wood, *hated* that sound, created by an organ attachment called a "sweet potato," which still sits in the Petty Studios in Clovis.)

1966 "Gloria" by Them Covered by Chicago Band

In late 1965 the infectious song "Gloria" by the Irish band Them found its way onto the bottom rung of the U.S. charts.

Every kid who heard it loved it, but their parents did not. At the song's end, the words were, "She comes up to my room, and then she makes me feel alright," which was too **suggestive for teenage radio** at the time.

Enter the Shadows of Knight, one of a hundred Chicago-area teen-club bands playing "Gloria" nightly. Dunwich Records in Chicago cannily recorded the Shadows doing the song **without the offending ending,**[1] and grateful deejays across the nation catapulted the "clean" version to #10.

Them's version[2] mustered only #71 after nearly a half year in release.[3]

The Shadows of Knight's subsequent low-charting but highly-regarded records—"Oh Yeah," "I'm Gonna Make You Mine," "Bad Little Woman" and "Shake"— earned them a hallowed standing with '60s-punk aficionados. In the meantime, *Them's lead singer, Van Morrison,* went on to a very successful career of his own.

[1] Chicago always had conservative radio playlists, and for a while bowdlerization beckoned as a Chicago cottage industry. Fortunately, the city's next attempt at lyric sanitization, a local band's "Hold On Don't You Worry" (a de-sexed "Hold On I'm Coming") got only local airplay.

[2] But in Los Angeles, Dallas and many regional markets, the Shadows of Knight's version was unknown and Them's ruled.

[3] Cover versions heretofore had been restricted to white versions of black and country songs. In the 1960s U.K. versions of American hits were often forced on the British record-buying public, but rarely the other way around. But in America during that decade it was fashionable to be English! Just ask the Liverpool Five from Seattle, the Beau Brummels from San Francisco or the Sir Douglas Quintet from San Antonio.

1966 Brian Wilson Quits Touring with Beach Boys, Creates "Good Vibrations" and Goes into Hibernation Like a Bear

As chief songwriter for the Beach Boys,[1] the group he formed in 1962 with his brothers Carl and Dennis, cousin Mike Love and school chum Al Jardine,[2] Brian Wilson was the central plexus of that band: His songs and musical arrangements[3] shaped their sound.[4]

By 1964 they were the biggest band in America, competing head to head with the Beatles.[5] **But touring took its toll on the band's sensitive leader;** on a trip to Australia Brian had a nervous breakdown, and in late 1965 he retired from the road to concentrate on making music in the studio. (Session player Glen Campbell was called to replace him. He was succeeded by surf music maker Bruce Johnston, who still is a Beach

Boy today despite a 6-year suspension in the 1970s for eating meat!) Brian then went in deep for 4 months' work on one opus that *went through many transmogrifications,* from a 10-minute-long piece, to an R&B song with black female singers, to what you finally know as "Good Vibrations."

After that heady triumph, he embarked on another project of sounds he heard in his head, an album to be called *Smile.* Brian devoted his whole being to it: tales about it abound, including the time when, **bare-chested and wearing a firefighter's hat, he set a fire in Gold Star Studios** to get the right *feeling* for the song "Mrs. O'Leary's Cow" (aka "Fire"). *Smile* was never finished,[6] and for the ensuing 20 years, until the release of his solo album in 1988, he contributed fitfully to the Beach Boys, and spent most of his time holed up in his Bel Air home.

[1] Though he had a hand in writing nearly all the band's original material, it was usually with lyricist collaborators. In the mid-1990s Mike Love successfully sued for half writer credit on several Wilson-credited songs.

[2] Jardine dropped out before the group signed with Capitol, and he was replaced by David Marks. When Jardine reconsidered, he was reinstated, to Marks' dismay. (Marks can be seen on the early albums and single picture sleeves.)

[3] But at the time, his thwarted songwriter father, Murry (who proved to be an effective record promoter for the band but a much resented interloper in their music), claimed much of the credit for the group's success. Brian was tormented by his overbearing father; in his book, *Wouldn't It Be Nice*, he said that not only did his father beat him, but he once forced him to defecate on newspaper for a behavioral infraction. Brian fired his father in 1965, and Murry went on to brief success with another Beach Boys-type act, the Sunrays. Murry died in 1973 after selling the Beach Boys' music publishing rights (which the band had ceded to him) to Irving/Almo Music for less than $1 million—a severely undervalued price; true to his Jekyll-and-Hyde nature, he kept the money. His actions removed control of the music from the writers' hands. Brian's 1990s lawsuit against Irving/Almo netted him $10 million. Murry Wilson's legacy is a deep scar on Brian Wilson's soul.

Murry is tied with two others as the worst rock fathers. Lenny Hart, father of Grateful Dead drummer Mickey Hart, absent when Mickey grew up, reentered his life in the late 1960s when the band was big. He offered to handle their finances, then stole it all. At his funeral years later, Mickey spit on his father's casket. And of course, Marvin Gaye's father shot him to death. (See "R&R Shootings," page 198.) Father's Day's two extremes in rock would be Paul Peterson's "My Dad" and the Doors' "The End" (in which Morrison murmurs, "Father, I want to kill you!")

[4] That responsibility of supplying material and inspiration for four other guys (three of whom were family) is often cited as an explanation for his apparent mental problems at the time. Brian wanted to create for himself but had to keep pumping out salable "car" and "fun" songs for the good of the band.

[5] Paul McCartney was quick to acknowledge that *Sgt. Pepper's Lonely Hearts Club Band* was inspired by Brian Wilson's quirky and experimental *Pet Sounds* (which was officially a Beach Boys album, but he created it all in the studio). In 1995 *Pet Sounds* was voted #1 album of all time by writers for the British rock-history magazine *Mojo*.

[6] At least one entire book, *Look, Listen, Vibrate, Smile*, by Domenic Priore (Last Gasp, 1989, available through Rhino Books) documents many facets of the unreleased album. For brilliant speculation on what would have happened if a time traveler had gone back and gotten Wilson to finish *Smile*, read Lewis Shiner's excellent novel *Glimpses* (Morrow, 1993).

Jan Berry Crashes on Dead Man's Curve

Jan & Dean were the prototypical California guys of the early '60s. They sang songs about cars, girls and beaches and were ***blond and handsome and marketable.***

Regular chart toppers before and after the 1964 British Invasion, they were on a chart down-slide on April 19, 1966, when Jan Berry crashed his Corvette into a truck on a section of Whittier Boulevard in Beverly Hills. Head injuries kept him in a coma for months, and he never fully recovered. In the 1970s he was walking and talking again but was not the same fun-

loving "Greek God" who once commanded the air, sea and land.

The legend is that Jan "bought it" on Dead Man's Curve, the site of Jan & Dean's fictional story-song that reached #8 on the national charts in mid-1964. In fact, it happened not far from it. The real Dead Man's Curve was farther west on Sunset, near UCLA, the site of a near-fatal 1961 accident involving Bugs Bunny voice Mel Blanc, but it could be argued that, de facto, Jan's crash site *became* the new official Dead Man's Curve.

1966 Stephen Stills Flunks Monkees Audition

Fresh from the New Christy Minstrels-like folk aggregation the Au Go Go Singers,[1] New Orleansian (born in Dallas, raised partly in Florida, he called New Orleans home) Stephen Stills joined the ranks of then-rare longhairs auditioning for the forthcoming rock & roll comedy series, *The Monkees*. (Reports persist that Charles Manson was an unsuccessful applicant, but that apparently is untrue.)

Stills, in fact, **was a finalist** (there were but two openings; Davy Jones and Micky Dolenz were already locked in), but it's said he **lost points for his thinning hair and crooked teeth.**[2] When he didn't

get the job, he recommended folk-circuit comrade Peter Tork, and then went on to form Buffalo Springfield with some other local musicians, including Canadian transplant[3] Neil Young. That band played plenty in L.A. in late 1966, and their weirdly anthemic song, "For What It's Worth"[4] ("Stop! Hey! What's That Sound") propelled them to fame.

Stills, of course, went on to join David Crosby of the Byrds ("Mr. Tambourine Man," "Turn, Turn, Turn") and Graham Nash of the Hollies ("Bus Stop," "Carrie Anne") in Crosby, Stills & Nash. (On the cover of their premiere album, they are pictured, ironically, from left to right as Nash, Stills & Crosby. When one week later photographer Henry Diltz realized the error, he scheduled a reshoot but found that the house, at 809 Palm in West Hollywood, had been torn down!)

[1] Future Buffalo Springfield mate Richie Furay was also in this group.

[2] Stills did not fret about his denticity, but Queen's Freddie Mercury did. For years he planned to get his crooked teeth fixed.

[3] Springfield bassist Bruce Palmer was also a Canadian, albeit without legal papers, so he frequently had his back to the camera during TV appearances to shield his identity. (Healthy young Canadians in the United States were eligible for service in the U.S. Army.) Palmer eventually was deported and replaced by studio engineer Jim Messina, who later went on to fame with both Poco and Loggins and Messina.

[4] The song is weird not only for its eeriness, but also for how it's been misunderstood by history. Written by Stills, it was inspired by the Sunset Strip riots of December 1966, during which teenyboppers crowding the avenue were dispersed by club-swinging L.A. cops. But its feel of paranoia and fear turned it into a symbol of the Vietnam War for both peace protestors and jungle soldiers. (See "Paranoia Runs Amok," page 201.)

1967 Studio Fracas Forces Change of Venue for First Aretha Franklin Album on Atlantic

Producer Jerry Wexler wanted a special groove for the debut Atlantic album by Aretha Franklin, the brilliant soul singer who'd been languishing at Columbia Records, so he arranged a session at Fame Studios in Muscle Shoals, Alabama, where he had produced Wilson Pickett's 1966 hit, "Land of 1,000 Dances."

Wexler knew that all the studio's regular musicians could produce especially fine soul music. However, fearing the Detroit-born Franklin and her husband, Ted White, **might be uncomfortable** surrounded by whites in the deep South, he asked studio owner Rick Hall to hire black horn men. But Hall instead hired an all-white retinue—not bad of itself, but ultimately calamitous.

The session went well for a day. When Aretha,

whose soul had been squelched for five years at Columbia[1] and was bursting to come out, sat at the piano and began wailing, the players bolted to attention and gave their all. "I Never Loved a Man (The Way I Loved You)" came together after a two-hour session so intense that drummer Roger Hawkins and guitarist Dan Penn and others danced with joy at being *associated* with such a fantasic recording.

But Franklin's husband became involved in a drinking and name-calling game with a white horn player (as Wilson Pickett had a few months earlier) that escalated, in producer Wexler's words, into **"a Wagnerian shitstorm,** things flying to pieces, everyone going nuts." The entire assemblage was tipsy when studio owner Hall went to White's hotel room to try and ameliorate the situation. White loudly lamented bringing Aretha to Alabama and got into a shouting match with Hall that led to (Hall's words now, reported by Wexler[2] in his book *The Rhythm & Blues: A Life in American Music* [Knopf, 1993] "a full-blown fist fight."[3]

The rancor was so strong that even though Wexler had completed one song and a piece of another, "Do Right Woman, Do Right Man," he canceled the rest of the sessions and later resumed them, with most of the same musicians, in New York.

Luckily, the musical magic of Aretha, Wexler, arranger Arif Mardin, engineer Tom Dowd and the Muscle Shoals Sound Rhythm Section continued, and the rest of Aretha's debut Atlantic album was recorded with no loss of feeling.

By late 1967, with "Never Loved a Man" and "Respect" under her belt, Franklin ascended the throne as the queen of soul, a title she apparently will hold for her lifetime.

[1] This was a unique mismatch for Columbia Records' Svengali John Hammond, who seeded the careers of Billie Holiday, Bob Dylan, Bruce Springsteen and others.

[2] Wexler's *reportage* should be trusted—or not, depending on how you feel about journalists—because he was a professional writer for Billboard magazine before becoming a record producer. The list of other writers who went into record producing is slim but noteworthy: Leonard Feather, who continued in both fields, and Jon Landau, who left his typewriter when he became Bruce Springsteen's music producer and handler.

[3] By the time of their divorce in 1969, White had struck Aretha in public and shot one of her production managers.

Late Dead Patriarch Jerry Garcia, 1990

1970 Grateful Dead "Bust" Yields Hit, Anthem

The great San Francisco music scene of 1967 was indisputably fueled by drugs, with marijuana the featured player.[1]

The Grateful Dead was one of The City's psychedelic mainstays, and their fans always nodded favorably to "smoke." After the Dead were busted in 1967 at their Haight-Ashbury house, their reputation (despite charges later being dropped), like a train's smokestack in reverse, preceded them into every town. These were high times; the *air was thick with marijuana* at most rock concerts, and police were overwhelmed.

The Dead's reputation was further solidified after their arrest in New Orleans on January 31, 1970, when LSD and barbiturates were found in their hotel rooms. Subsequently, charges were again dropped. The incident became memorialized in the 1971 single "Truckin'," which became an anthem of sorts for them.

"Just Say No" was a pipe dream at the time. Another record spawned by a drug bust was the Who's hurriedly recorded July 1967 single "Under My Thumb"/"The Last Time," dedicated to Mick Jagger and Keith Richards, who were in jail on drug charges.

Rock & roll dope busts were virtually unknown prior to 1966 because **musician drug use was thought to be uniquely a jazz thing—in a big way.**[2] Subsequently, several pre-"drug era" pop stars would be revealed as heroin addicts, such as Frankie Lymon, who died in 1968 of an overdose, and Dion, who says he was high on smack throughout his teen-idol years.

But after 1966, the busts kept on comin':

1966: Roky Erickson's pot bust was a sad trailblazer (see "Jim Gordon and Other Rock Nuts," page 98).

1966: Lovin' Spoonful: Zal Yanovsky ratted on his dealer, which queered the band with the emerging counter-culture. Underground punishment for the Spoonful was harsh: Dr. Demento (Barry Hansen) remembers a full-page ad in the *LA Free Press* urging a boycott that said, "Don't buy their records. Don't ball them." Ouch. Perhaps coincidentally, who knows, their flow of hits dried up.

(Top) Grateful Dead members jailed in 1967 drug bust in San Francisco, Jimi Hendrix (Left) on his way to face charges of heroin possession in Toronto, 1969, and a typical 1971 yippie protesting laws against pot (Right).

1967, Feb. 12: Rolling Stones Mick Jagger and Keith Richards, and singer Marianne Faithfull (oft rumored to have had a Mars bar up her love canal)[3] nabbed at Jagger's mansion, Redlands; George Harrison, also there, was released by police.

1967, May 10: Brian Jones, London, pot

1967: Grateful Dead, 710 Ashbury, San Francisco, pot, psychedelics (charges dropped)

1968, March: Topanga Canyon bust: Stephen Stills, Eric Clapton, Jim Messina, Neil Young, others. (Little known, seldom-mentioned.)

1968, May: Brian Jones, London, pot

1968, May 24: Jagger, Faithfull, London, pot

1968, Oct. 18: John & Yoko, pot

1969, March 12: George & Patti Harrison, pot

1969: Jimi Hendrix, Toronto Airport, heroin

1973, March 8: Paul McCartney, Scotland, pot

1977: Keith Richards[4] (just after having his blood *replaced*)

1980, Jan. 16: Paul McCartney, Japan, pot; tour canceled

1980: Gregg Allman's testimony convicts roadie/supplier

1980: Mamas and Papas' John Phillips forging doctor's scrip

1986: Boy George, United Kingdom, heroin

1994: David Lee Roth, pot

1994: Steve Earle, heroin

[1] For a wealth of details on the 1965-70 San Francisco music scene, see Joel Selvin's excellent *Summer of Love*, (Dutton, 1994).

[2] Accounts of the county-policed pre-rock Sunset Strip include stories of policemen hitting horn players in the mouth during drug rousts to "teach them a lesson."

[3] An asinine story denied by everyone, including Faithfull, in *Faithfull, An Autobiography* (Little Brown, 1994).

[4] In 1980, when someone told Keith that the Police—meaning the British band—were out in the hall, he flushed his dope down the toilet.

1968 Sly Stone Becomes Famous as Superstar, Then as No-Show[1]

In 1968, Sylvester "Sly" Stone (né Stewart), the one-time San Francisco deejay and Autumn Record house producer (Bobby Freeman's "The Swim" and the Beau Brummels' "Laugh Laugh" and "Just a Little"), shook the rock and soul worlds with his band Sly and the Family Stone's ground-breaking "Dance to the Music." **That insistent, polyrhythmic sound was unlike anything** before, and its impact was sudden and profound. That influence was so decisive that even the mighty Motown machine bowed to him, the Temptations' Sly-style "Cloud Nine" being the best example.

Hits poured from Sly and the Family Stone: "Everyday People," "Stand," "I Want to Take You Higher" and "Hot Fun in the Summertime" all lodged in the nation's consciousness as the multiracial ensemble locked arms with the world.

It lasted nearly four years, through "Family Affair" in late 1971, before **Sly Stone's erratic behavior** brought it all down.

Sly had everything: looks, humor (it helped that he was once a deejay) and that *sound*. But he also had a nose for cocaine and a taste for other drugs, and that is the best explanation for his terrible notoriety as a no-show shortly into his superstardom.[2]

Most notable, in the sense that it got big publicity, was the riot accompanying his July 27, 1970, nonperformance at Chicago's Grant Park bandshell. He and the band were there, ready to play, but soon chose not to because **they sensed a near-riot atmosphere**. Prescient or provocative, their no-show provoked a melee that cemented the public's opinion of his undependability and its consequences. Similar situations followed: Disorder after his failure to appear in a Washington, D.C., show put the kibosh on rock concerts there. Adding insult to insult, in 1974 Stone pulled another no-show in D.C., sparking another near-riot.

Stone failed to show up for about one third of his shows in 1970. His songs took a seemingly biographical turn as he plummeted downward. Instead of the optimistic brotherhood of his previous songs, "Thank You Falettin me Be Mice Elf Agin" let his cynicism show: He *thanks* the world for letting him be who he is. Next, the #1 hit "Family Affair" could be seen **as an attack** on people's interest in his personal problems: Keep out, it's a family affair. And in 1971, he turned his back on brotherhood with the racially militant *There's a Riot Goin' On* album. And his voice dropped, from drugs or stress or both.

He continued to tour and record, but either his music lost its appeal or the audience's interest shifted, and he rode out the '70s in a haze of litigation, drug busts and lack of direction. His 1974 marriage, onstage at Madison Square Garden, to Kathy Silva produced a memorable photo of the newlyweds exchanging tongues but didn't last as long as a hit single. Also memorable was his frank answer to the question of why he missed so many shows: *"Sometimes you don't feel your soul at 7:30."*

If the '70s were a waterfall that trickled to a puddle for Sly Stone, the '80s were an empty well. His occasional albums stirred up no consumer interest, his arrest records outnumbered his phonograph ones, his concert appearances were spotty[3] and guest shots on other people's records[4] didn't put him back in the limelight, but he **doggedly held on, attempting comeback after comeback.** In 1992 he appeared briefly onstage for induction into the Rock & Roll Hall of Fame, timid and soft-spoken and possibly confused. No trace of the heroic young firebrand of 1969 could be seen.

With his inability to get a grip on his life—drug entanglements followed him into the '90s—thus far nobody really knows if his revolutionary talent is still intact. And sadly, because he seems to be most famous for not showing up, he is most remembered as "**the man who wasn't there.**"

[1] He was the first rock musician to become *notorious* for unreliability. His haint brother was heavy-drinking country-music star George Jones, who became so undependable in the late 1970s that he made light of it in the song, "No Show Jones." (And Hank Williams before him was notoriously undependable.)

[2] Sly was one of the people "made" by Woodstock. His electrifying performance at that monumental concert catapulted him to megastardom.

[3] Steve Pond wrote a fascinating account of a late and lame Stone appearance at Los Angeles' Las Palmas Theater in the *Los Angeles Times* on November 13, 1987. What he didn't report was that the next night Sly was arrested outside the theater.

[4] George Clinton's Funkadelic album *Electric Spanking of War Babies*, ex-Time guitarist Jesse Johnson's "Crazay," Martha Davis' cut "Love and Affection" on the *Soul Man* movie soundtrack.

 ## Randy Rhoads Dies in Airplane Prank

Randy Rhoads was a real comer in the early 1980s. As guitarist for the Ozzy Osbourne band, he was making a big, big name for himself, both as a primary songwriter for the revitalized (primarily by Rhoads) Osbourne band and also for his guitar prowess, of which the musical world was taking sharp notice (comparisons to Hendrix were rife).

On March 19, 1982, the band had a break in their tour in Orlando, Florida, and the band's bus driver, Andrew Aycock, who had a pilot's license, decided **it would be fun to buzz their motel compound.** The prank worked to the extent that it frightened the band, but it ended tragically when the airplane hit a telephone pole and crashed—killing Rhoads, Aycock and wardrobe consultant Rachel Youngblood.

Osbourne himself is no stranger to extravagant behavior. He is best known for biting the head off a live dove at a record company marketing meeting. (Probably best remembered is the expression of horror and disgust on the face of Epic publicist Sue Sawyer in photos from that moment.) Osbourne simply strode into Epic's L.A. headquarters on a business day with a photographer, **unsheathed the bird and orally decapitated it.**[1]

Never content to be simply a musician, Osbourne also made his mark by urinating on the Alamo in San Antonio, Texas, in 1982. Whether he lost relatives at the 1836 battle or was just in a mood to do something foul, Osbourne was hauled off to jail.

Also, he employed **a dead bat** in one stage show, which led to Osbourne enduring a painful precautionary series of rabies shots.

[1] Perhaps he'd seen the film *The Hucksters*, in which Clark Gable opens a meeting by spitting on the table and saying, in effect, "You may not like what I just did, but you'll never forget it."

Soul Pioneer Curtis Mayfield Paralyzed in Freak Concert Accident

Chicago's Curtis Mayfield (b. June 3, 1942) weathered stylistic changes in pop music *like a surfer moving up to bigger and bigger waves.*

He started with the Impressions featuring Jerry Butler, whose 1958 hit "For Your Precious Love" was a vocal group classic. Butler left to go solo, but rather than splinter their relationship, Mayfield wrote and cowrote classic songs for Butler such as "He Will Break Your

Heart,"[1] "Need to Belong" and "I Stand Accused." Then the Impressions marched into the 1960s with a staunch new style that reflected the feelings of that era of civil rights hope, including "Keep On Pushing," "We're a Winner," "I'm So Proud" and "People Get Ready." At the same time, Mayfield wrote the hits "Monkey Time" and "Um, Um, Um, Um, Um, Um" for fellow Chicagoan Major Lance, and "Just Be True" and "Nothing Can Stop Me" for another Windy Cityite, Gene Chandler. Also, in 1966 he began making records with a local group, the Five Stairsteps, on his own new Windy C record label, and his tenacity paid off with their big 1970 hit "Ooh Child." In addition he formed the Curtom label in conjunction with Buddah Records. (Buddah president Neil Bogart called Mayfield **"the black Bob Dylan."**)

As a solo artist in the 1970s, Mayfield was at the forefront of the Black Power and exploitation-film movements. His music for the mammoth film *Superfly* in 1972 had a tremendous impact on the pop music world, particularly the black community. Two hits, "Freddie's Dead" and "Superfly" propelled Mayfield into the top ranks of popular artists.

As tastes changed in the '80s, Mayfield's popularity receded somewhat, but in 1990 he was being welcomed back by a new generation of fans. Ice-T, for one, collaborated with him on "The Return of Superfly." **That same year tragedy struck.** At an outdoor concert in Brooklyn on August 14, a wind gust toppled a lighting rig, which fell on Mayfield, leaving him paralyzed from the neck down.[2]

Today the honors continue to flood in. He and the Impressions were inducted into the Rock & Roll Hall of Fame, and two tribute albums, *People Get Ready* and *All Men Are Brothers*, on which he sings one cut, saluted Mayfield's contributions to music and American culture. And in 1996, Rhino Records issued a Mayfield box set,

People Get Ready: The Curtis Mayfield Story (Rhino R272262).

Today, Mayfield moves only with mechanical aids and the assistance of his family. He has, however, signed with Warner Bros. Records for a new album.

[1] When revived in 1975 by Dawn, Tony Orlando changed the song title to the opening refrain, "He Don't Love You (Like I Love You)." It went to #1.

[2] Onstage cripplings are rare; deaths are more common. Frank Zappa was gravely injured by a fan in 1971 (see "Smoke on the Water," page 94). Les Harvey of the British band Stone the Crows was electrocuted by a microphone's short-circuiting in 1973. Jackie Wilson died in 1984 of a stroke he suffered onstage in 1975. Country Dick Montana of the Beat Farmers suffered a fatal heart attack onstage in 1995 at age 42.

Dean Martin Insults Rolling Stones

The Rolling Stones' summer 1964 concert tour of America was premature or developmental, depending on who you ask. Three records had broken onto the U.S. charts, but audiences weren't *straining* to see the group. **In San Bernardino they followed performing seals**; in San Antonio they shared the bill with Bobby Goldsboro, Bobby Vee[1] and George Jones.

Somehow they were booked onto *The Hollywood Palace* TV show hosted by Dean Martin. Martin's persona was a drink-sipping ladies' man, and the show was the standard variety fare of dancing girls, comedy sketches, singers and so forth.[2]

Martin, a singer and character actor, seemed appalled by the rough, unconventional Stones. He introduced them with sarcasm, slurring, *"I've been rolled when I was stoned myself.* I don't know what they're singing about, but here they are at [sic]." After their performance of the Muddy Waters song (that Willie Dixon wrote), "I Just Wanna Make Love to You," Martin applauded with a look of "What the hell was *that*?," and said, "Aren't they great?" to audience laughter.

Hair was the issue. He continued, "They're gonna leave right after the show for London. They're challenging the Beatles to a hair-pulling contest." He then remarked that their hair wasn't really long, "they just have low foreheads and high eyebrows." Later, when an acrobat took a painful fall, he said, "That's the father of one of the Rolling Stones. **He's trying to kill himself."[3]** And before a commercial break, he urged the TV audience to come back afterward, saying, "You wouldn't want to leave me alone with those Rolling Stones, would you?"[4]

There was no press outcry over Martin's rudeness; he was *Dean Martin*,[5] after all, and they were just some English kids with funny haircuts. But one rock & roller reacted. In the liner notes to *Another Side of Bob Dylan*, Dylan wrote, "an dean martin should apologize t the rolling stones. [sic]"

---

[1] Not that there's anything wrong with these acts, per se: After all, Bob Dylan played piano with Vee in Minnesota before becoming Bob Dylan. Not high on the list of rock ironies but good enough to mention is that while Bob Dylan never returned to his Vee-era name of Bob Zimmerman, Vee switched back to Robert Thomas Velline in the early '70s.

[2] Not unlike the revues that Col. Tom Parker insisted Elvis appear in.

[3] In his defense, he was reading from a prompter, so it wasn't Martin saying those things, it was his writers. And the Stones looked pretty weird to 1964 Americans. Brian Jones, playing his harmonica, was so earnest and terrified that he went cross-eyed like Freddy Morgan from the Spike Jones band. Their appearance and their hard blues music probably just confused people.

[4] There is one final unintelligible outburst from Martin regarding the Stones, in which he says, "Fwah, fwah." Some Stones fans have identified this as "Frauds! Frauds!" but it's so garbled nobody knows.

[5] This is a guy, like Sinatra, who revisionists are now embracing as one of the people who laid the foundation for rock & roll. (Yeah, we know Elvis liked Dean Martin. So? Jerry Lee Lewis liked Al Jolson, so was *Jolson* a rock pioneer too?) On the other hand, Steve Allen, another comedian disinterested in rock & roll despite his involvement with it—to this day he cackles while hearing Elvis sing "I Want You I Need You I Love You" on playbacks of his 1956 appearance on Allen's show—is widely reviled by Elvis fans.

1967 Doors Refuse to Alter Lyrics to "Light My Fire," Banished from Ed Sullivan Show

Ed Sullivan, host of the most popular television show of the 1950s and 1960s, had a history of censorship.

He got in the rock & roll game early. On November 20, 1955, he booked "new folk singer" Bo Diddley,[1] but disliking Diddley's song "Bo Diddley," he insisted Bo sing the then-popular "Sixteen Tons." (Diddley did his signature song instead, earning Sullivan's lifelong enmity.) On Elvis Presley's third Sullivan appearance[2] in early 1957, Elvis was telecast from the waist up just in case he slipped into one of *those pelvic-thrust movements* Sullivan had been warned about.

By the mid-1960s Sullivan usually made singers lip-synch,[3] but when the Doors were scheduled to perform "Light My Fire" live, they were instructed to remove the phrase "we couldn't get much higher," because of its drug connotations. Morrison agreed, then left it in anyway.[4]

"You'll never be on this show again," a Sullivan representative told him. **"We already have been,"**

Morrison replied. (Time heals all wounds, and wounds all heels, as Sullivan's heirs will now gladly lease the offensive TV appearance to any takers.)

The Rolling Stones, however, were more career-minded. Earlier that year, Sullivan's people told them to mind their manners and not sing "let's spend the night together," and Mick acceded and sang "Let's spend some time together." He mugged and grimaced when that line came up to show his dissatisfaction, but it was a wan gesture compared to Morrison's outright defiance.[5]

On December 17, 1977, Elvis Costello contributed a widely publicized bit of rebelliousness on *Saturday Night Live*. Booked as a substitute **for the too-unpredictable Sex Pistols** (the Costello band wore T-shirts proclaiming "Thank You Malc" to Pistols manager Malcolm McLaren), he was advised not to perform his current release, "Radio Radio," because its harsh portrayal of formulaic insipid contemporary radio[6] might offend radio programmers and record companies.

The band kicked off with another song, "Less Than Zero," then **Costello shouted "Stop! Stop!"[7]** and performed the proscribed number.[8]

---

[1] Diddley appeared on the show with LaVern Baker, the Five Keys and Willis "Gatortail" Jackson as part of a special "Dr. Jive" rhythm & blues (or, as stumblebum Sullivan, no soul man himself, said, "blues...and rhythm, rhythm...and race") package. This was without a doubt the first appearance of real rock & roll on national television: Jackson's honking-sax performance was as wild, for its time, as Hendrix's style was a dozen years later.

[2] Sullivan's first reaction to Elvis was "I wouldn't touch him with a ten-foot pole." But when his TV rival Steve Allen beat Sullivan in the ratings by adding Elvis, Sullivan changed his tune. He also censored Buddy Holly and the Crickets, forbidding them to do "Oh Boy!" (!!)

[3] Which has made for a pretty lame *Sullivan Shows* CD that has the Lovin' Spoonful's *record* transferred directly from their lip-synched performance.

[4] This was the Doors' first significant TV appearance. Nobody knows whether Morrison bravely stood up to Sullivan or just got drunk and forgot to change the line (which would lessen the impact of Jagger's acquiescence).

[5] Jagger muttered the bowdlerized phrase, while Richards, in the background, sang "night."

[6] Things have improved a lot since then, haven't they?

[7] This is the only known instance of an Elvis Costello moment paralleling an Elvis Presley moment. A few seconds into the slow-paced opening of "Milk Cow Blues" (Sun Records, 1955) Presley stops the song, saying, "Hold it fellas. That don't *move* me! Let's get real, real *gone* for a change," and hillbilly bop ensues.

[8] Replacements fan Kent Wolgamott of the Lincoln (Nebraska) Journal Star insists we mention that on an ABC rock awards show (1989?), the censors removed a reference to pills in the song "Talent Show," so Paul Westerberg added a pill reference to the song's chorus. And speaking of Lincoln, Nebraska, an interesting out-of-print book, *'Til The Cows Come Home: Rock & Roll Nebraska* (Bart Becker, Real Gone Press, Lincoln, 1985), which somewhat parallels (but precedes!) Yours Truly's *L.A. Musical History Tour*, comes to the astonishing conclusion that with the exception of Zager & Evans ("In the Year 2525"), *no* significant national rock act ever emerged from the Cornhusker State—a fact lost on the band Moby Grape, who did a really terrific song called "Omaha." (Thanks , Todd Everett.)

1955 Chuck Berry's Suit Shrinks, and a Duck-Walk Style is Born

For one of his first concert appearances in New York City, Chuck Berry wanted to look extra-sharp, so he had his best suit rush-cleaned in time for the show. Unfortunately, the *hasty cleaner overcooked the garment, and it shrunk.* Faced with performing in his street clothes or in the now-small suit, Berry chose the latter, and a rock & roll walk—perhaps *the* rock & roll walk—was born.

"The darn thing pinched me all over," he recalled, "so that when I walked out onto the stage, I had to crouch over and do a duck-walk to keep the trousers from splitting."

Unlike American singer P.J. Proby, whose Beatles era fame in England ended when he allowed his tight pants to split open during a performance,[1] Berry adjusted to the difficulty and invented an ambulatory performing style—gliding along the floor in a crouched position, sometimes **bobbing his head like a chicken**—that has become as famous a rock & roll stance as Mick

Jagger's strut and Elvis' hip wiggle.

Suits and coats haven't figured much else-where in the history of rock & roll. People wore 'em, but excepting David Byrne's oversized one in the mid-1980s, none have really called attention to themselves.

Wardrobes, however, have. David Bowie's initial assaults on the rock world were haberdasher-driven: on an early 1970s album cover **he wore a dress,** and on his big 1973 tour he was dressed in a spacesuit-type getup that split down the middle when pulled apart by his band members, revealing some fashionable skivvies. And Elton John, of course, reveled in **absurd outfits featuring feather boas, foot-high plat-form shoes**[2] and oversized white glasses when, in 1973, he became the Carmen Miranda of rock.

Going way back, these guys had nothing on early rockers Sonny Burgess and Screamin' Jay Hawkins. Sun Records wildman Burgess[3] had red hair, wore red suits and drove a red Cadillac convertible, while madman Hawkins had zebra- and leopard-skin suits with match-ing shoes and station wagons!

---

[1] And maybe Jim Morrison, whose weenie, maybe, leapt from his pants in

Miami on March 1, 1969, leading to his arrest and persecution. (Reminiscent of Lenny Bruce's fate, legal wrangling took up much of Morrison's final year.) Regardless of whether it did make a public appearance—band members say no, or maybe (there are no photos)—the Doors effectively couldn't get concert bookings (like Lenny Bruce, again) as wary promoters feared the contents of Morrison's trousers would be aired in *their* city and cause them problems. (Whole cities banned the Doors because too many concerts ended up in riots. See "Jim Morrison Caught with Pants Down," page 211.)

[2] Otis Williams poses an interesting "footnote" in the book, *The Temptations*. To this day he regrets that the band—who were "sharp-dressed men" long before ZZ Top—is pictured wearing black shoes with their white suits on the cover of their 1965 album *The Tempting Temptations*. "For all our style and class, we didn't have those damn white shoes when we needed them."

[3] His recordings of "We Wanna Boogie" and "Sadie Brown" are considered the wildest recordings ever made at Sun Records in Memphis.

1960's Bob Dylan Injured at Peak of Career—or Was He?

In mid-1966 Bob Dylan had reached Olympian heights. Every album since he turned to rock & roll— *Bringing It All Back Home*, *Highway 61 Revisited*, and the double lp *Blonde on Blonde*—**deepened his mystique,** every breath he took was of interest to his legion of fans.[1] So when it was announced in August 1966 that he had broken his neck in a motorcycle accident near his manager's rural Woodstock, New York, home (that was three years before Woodstock, the concert, which took some of its luster from Dylan living there), fans mourned the loss of their idol. He was out of the public eye for two years, and when he reappeared with *John Wesley Harding*, an album (including "All Along the Watchtower," quickly amped-up by Jimi Hendrix) that harked back stylistically to his pre-rock, folk-singing days, he was a low-key, unembellished guy decidedly different from the 1000-watt electric imp he'd previously been. (He didn't get back on that organ-led rock & roll track until 1975's *Blood on the Tracks*, and then only briefly.)

Few stars have fallen, short of death, so

precipitously at the height of their careers.

But time goes on, and people talk. They may be lying, but here's what they say.

It was well known that in 1966 Dylan's contract with Columbia Records was up. Record producer Tom Wilson, who had done *Bringing It All Back Home* and, significantly, "Like a Rolling Stone," had left Columbia for MGM Records, where he produced albums for the Mothers of Invention and the Velvet Underground. MGM was holding its own with the Animals and Herman's Hermits and Connie Francis but had no super-stellar act like Dylan. Scuttlebutt at the time had MGM offering a million-dollar advance for Dylan, an unheard-of amount of money, and it was expected that he would take it.

Albert Grossman, Dylan's manager, was a well-known motherfucker. He truly respected his artists and handled their affairs brusquely, if not brutally. (In D.A. Pennebaker's telling documentary *Don't Look Back*, the relationship between the thin wiseguy Dylan and the bearlike brute[2] Grossman is stunningly symbiotic.) At that same time, it's fairly well known that Dylan was high on both success and drugs. (In widely video-disseminated outtakes from Pennebaker's second Dylan documentary, the seldom-seen *Eat the Document*, Dylan, in a limo with John Lennon, slurs his words and thoughts for a half hour before sinking into a torpor of nausea—but it's anybody's guess what intoxicant caused it.) **Grossman, no fool, knew that his big-ticket act was walking around New York City in a drugged haze,** and was afraid that people from MGM Records would see him, or hear about him, and renege on the deal, so he forcibly relocated him to Woodstock for professional detoxification, which lasted a long, long time.[3]

Finally, to fight off MGM's assault on their henhouse, Columbia released Dylan's true sales figures (pioneers rarely make a big sales impact; it's their successors who reap the profits) and that scotched MGM's interest.

If they had signed Dylan, might MGM still be in business today?

If Grossman were alive today, would he validate or deny this story?

If Dylan recalls the true story, will he ever tell it?

[1] Around that time, the off-balance Dylanologist A.J. Weberman began sifting through Dylan's garbage for clues to his essence.

[2] It should be noted that Grossman curried this image, and applied it in support of his truly remarkable stable of talent that included Peter, Paul & Mary (whom he *created*), Janis Joplin, The Band, the Paul Butterfield Blues Band, Joan Baez and others. Grossman's wife is the woman on the cover of Dylan's *Bringing It All Back Home* album.

[3] In the song "Sara" on the 1976 album *Desire*, Dylan sings of "taking the cure" while writing "Sad Eyed Lady." Could mean anything, though.

1992 Sinéad O'Connor, Rock's Impassioned Bumbler, Pisses Off Catholics and Non-Catholics on SNL, Jeopardizes Career

Nobody can deny that Sinéad O'Connor cares. The trouble is, or was, that she cared fervently about nearly everything, so she stumbled through her public life like Godzilla through Tokyo.

O'Connor was the first rock-era Irish Catholic woman singer to have a #1 album (*I Do Not Want What I Haven't Got*, containing her hit version of the Prince song "Nothing Compares 2 U") *in religiously bigoted England.*[1] Her shaved head[2] made a big impression on all who saw her, and her singing was sublime, but her politics were scattershot. Who can forget her refusal to sing at Garden State Arts Center in New Jersey after the American national anthem was played?[3] Who has forgotten—or who knew, it was 1994—her suicide attempt after being rejected by Peter Gabriel?

Besides her music, O'Connor will be forever remembered for her 1992 TV appearance on *Saturday Night Live*. **She sang a song and then, saying that the world's true evil**

must be eradicated, she pulled out a picture of the Pope and slowly tore it to shreds. America, though not as torn by religious strife as the English Isle and its western neighbor (see [1] again), went nuts over this unusual attack. *Wasn't O'Connor herself Catholic?* The Church's intransigence on women's and children's issues spurred O'Connor's anger: A teenage rape victim had been denied an abortion in Ireland by the Catholic church. As a Catholic, O'Connor felt like a daughter who was entitled to criticize her mother, but she went too far: She criticized an entire world body, and the outcry was mammoth. The next week she appeared at a benefit concert featuring Bob Dylan and was forced off the stage by a maelstrom of catcalls (and some cheers).[4]

Radio abandoned her music like it did when Jerry Lee married his cousin, and O'Connor's career fell into ruin.[5] It didn't help that her next album was covers of old rock tunes and standards. And in 1995 she spoiled a "comeback" by dropping out of the Lollapalooza tour because of pregnancy.

---

[1] British books about rock & roll are rife with accusations of American racism, from Otis Redding's death in a plane crash (manipulated by white managers) to Jimi Hendrix's death of drug intoxication (exploited by a white record company) to Sam Cooke's shooting in a motel (probably some white person at fault), so I feel it is my patriotic duty to needle them whenever the opportunity arises.

[2] Never a popular rock & roll style, it was first seen in the Pyramids, the guys who did the surf hit "Penetration." But they must've caught cold and died because the gimmick failed and they were forgotten. (Whoops. At least one Pyramid, sax-player Ron Stender, grew his hair back real long. He roadied for Canned Heat at Woodstock.) Spirit's drummer Ed Cassidy was bald, but he was old, you know, 44 (but he got all the girls, inspiring the Spirit song "Mr. Skin"). Lately baldness is stylin', slightly, with Michael Stipe, Billy Corgan, Bush's guitarist Ed Kowalcyk and Nigel Pulsford from Live. (We also believe one of Spinal Tap's drummers was bald, but that's neither here nor there.—Ed.)

[3] In a letter to a newspaper, Frank Sinatra offered to "kick her ass" for her lack of respect for America. She responded, "If you believe everything you read, I wouldn't be the first woman he's threatened to do that to."

[4] After singing the Bob Marley song "War," which she'd sung on SNL, the only non-Dylan tune at this Dylan tribute, thank you very much. Kris Kristofferson gave her a hearty welcome, hoping to offset what was coming, but it did no good. Thomas Ryan, in his overly personal book, *American Hit Radio* (Prima Entertainment, 1995), recounts being at this show and says O'Connor came out to muted applause and then stood motionless, waiting for, perhaps even encouraging, the crowd to turn on her.

[5] O'Connor's manager, Fachtna O'Kelly, had a knack for finding artists who offended radio. In 1980, he took Bob Geldof, whose Boomtown Rats' English hit, "I Don't Like Mondays," was ready to break in America, to a radio programmers convention, and Geldof said, in effect, "I've heard how you program American radio, and it sounds like shit." The record then disappeared from American airwaves.

1963 "Louie Louie" Banned on Radio Stations, Investigated by Government

To hear "Louie Louie" is to laugh. The monstrous 1963 hit is a big, crashing somersault of fun that sounds like a Ferris wheel collapsing in a wind tunnel.[1]

The words? *What* words? The thing is utterly un-understandable, which is its charm. Originally written (with a debt to Orange County, California Mexican/Filipino band the Rhythm Rockers) and recorded by Richard Berry, a former Los Angeles group member (the Flairs) and session singer (he sings bass lead on the Robins' "Riot in Cell Block #9"), the song's narrator tells Louie the bartender he'll make a boat trip to Jamaica to find his girl. It was not a hit record upon its release and, like most of Berry's solo efforts, disappeared into obscurity.[2]

But someone in the Pacific Northwest discovered the song in the early 1960s. It was recorded in 1962 by the Wailers[3] (who have been subsequently hailed, along with Tacoma's Sonics ["Strychnine"] as the progenitors of all punk-rock) to no avail, but the song continued to be popular with Portland, Oregon, teenagers. In 1963, recognizing the need for a "hometown" version, local work-horses the **Kingsmen paid $37 for a two-hour recording session and cut it**. The rest, as we all know, is history.[4] Ironically, the area's most successful group,[5] Paul Revere & the Raiders,[6] had recorded it, too, but it was the Kingsmen's version that took off like a house afire. When it first hit, the appeal was the sound, not the lyrics, which were indecipherable. But the slurred lyrics created a controversy. Kids made up dirty lyrics to the garbled sounds, and pretty soon parents, the media, and finally the U.S. government declared the record obscene. Obscene! There was actually an investigation by both the Federal Communications Commission (FCC) and the FBI dedicated to ferreting out the "real" lyrics to the song. Of course this was news to The Kingsmen, who had to go to Washington (D.C.) and tell the G-men that they were crazy. (It was resolved when the investigating bodies concluded the song was unintelligible "at any speed.")

The controversy didn't hurt, and "Louie Louie" remains one of the most cherished oldies of all time.

---

[1] Before Phil Spector perfected a big, crowded sound, several records, like "Louie Louie," had BIG sounds, including "Tallahassie Lassie" by Freddy Cannon (Mick Jagger has said "Brown Sugar" was based on this song), "Red River Rock" by Johnny & the Hurricanes, and "Quarter to Three" by Gary U.S. Bonds.

[2] Of course, when he needed money in the late 1950s, Berry sold all of his song rights for a pittance, missing out on millions of dollars in the '60s and '70s. In 1985 he might have gotten his rights back, but the copyright holder renewed them for another 28 years. However, an R&B bounty hunter went to court for him, and in 1992 Berry finally got a taste of the royalties he'd missed over the years.

[3] The name the Wailers resonates through the history of rock & roll, not only from the Seattle band's pioneering garage sounds and, of course, Bob Marley's Wailers from Jamaica, but also from an earlier version of the Seattle Wailers (sounds like a sports team) whose sax-led instrumental "Tall Cool One" charted both in 1959 and 1961.

[4] The studio, Old Northwest Recording, was not miked for rock music, so lead singer Jack Ely had to stand on tiptoes and strain his voice to reach, virtually, the ceiling. And people wonder why the lyrics were slurred! In that history-making session they did another recording, an outtake with altered lyrics, "Love That Louie." It was issued on RCA Records, with the

artist listed as Jack E. Lee. It is as menacing and distorted as the hit, and thrilling because you can tell it was recorded within five minutes of "Louie Louie."

[5] Other early Seattle-area successes were the internationally successful Ventures, who have carried the torch for instrumental rock & roll for more than 30 years; Bonnie Guitar, who had hits in the late 1950s; and the Fleetwoods (from Olympia, Washington, somewhat nearby), whose "Come Softly to Me" and "Mr. Blue" were issued on the Dolton (né Dolphin) label, which Bonnie Guitar owned. Of course, Jimi Hendrix, Nirvana, Pearl Jam, Soundgarden and others came from Seattle later.

[6] Before moving to L.A. and achieving worldwide popularity with "Kicks" and other huge hits in the mid-1960s, Paul Revere & the Raiders enjoyed a national hit in 1960 with "Like Long Hair," a rocked-up version of a classical song in the vein of the current classical adaptations "Nut Rocker" and "Bumble Boogie." (People who listened to and performed classical music were called longhairs then because they were considered either eccentric, like Albert Einstein, who had long hair and didn't wear socks, or out of their time, wearing long, flowing hair like in the 1800s.)

1988 James Brown Imprisoned After Police Chase

James Brown, Soul Brother #1, who went from Georgia poverty to the White House,[1] got himself in a cold sweat on September 24, 1988, when, like people who think they can jump off a roof and fly like Superman, he tried to outrun a police car in his own car. Brown allegedly pulled a shotgun at an insurance seminar in Augusta, Georgia, because someone used his private bathroom. Police were called and a chase ensued. Brown asserted that white police broke his car windows when the chase ended, causing him to resume flight, this time for his life. The high-speed chase from the Augusta area into South Carolina and back *left Brown's pickup truck riddled with police bullets.* When the race was over, to no one's surprise the police won, and Brown was incarcerated on charges of reckless driving and resisting arrest. They checked him for drugs,[2] and he was carrying plenty both in and on his body. That led to his trial and then imprisonment for illegal posession of drugs and firearms, aggravated assault and failure to stop for police.

He was sentenced to six and a half years at the (South Carolina) State Park Correctional Facility. He saw the 1990s from the minimum security site, where he helped prepare meals for elderly inmates, among other things. After his release on February 27, 1991, he was hailed as a rehabilitated hero and resumed making music and counseling people to stay off drugs.

James Brown is a phenomenon. His first record, "Please Please Please," lit up the R&B charts in 1956 but failed to reach mainstream America. No wonder: **Brown's soulful screams of "please" were not like soulmate Little Richard's bouncy romps; they were adult, sexual and a lot more biting than anything America knew** in its popular music. His records continued to chart sporadically in the R&B world throughout the rest of the 1950s; in 1958 he hit again with "Try Me," and in 1960 he returned to the top with "I'll Go Crazy" and "Think." In 1962 his *Live at the Apollo* album[3] crossed over to pop and rock & roll fans. Though purchased mainly by adventurous, nonmainstream record buyers, this album really thrust him into white America's consciousness. In 1963 he had his first pop single hit, "Prisoner of Love," a remake of a Perry Como hit (or the Billy Eckstine version) that more or less opened the floodgates for the hits that followed.

More than a contributor to rock and soul, **he was the engineer, the creator of what became "funk"** music in the 1960s and 1970s. Brown's offbeat, bass-driven sound first appeared in 1964 on "Out of Sight," which made an impressive Top 30 showing, and later on the big hit (#8) "Papa's Got a Brand New Bag." It continued with "Money Won't Change You" and "I Got You" (and regressed, once, with the string-laden ballad "It's a Man's Man's Man's World") and took another sharp turn in 1967 with the even leaner, beat-driven sound[4] of "Cold Sweat," leading down the road to "Say It Loud (I'm Black and I'm Proud)" "Mother Popcorn," and "Get Up (I Feel Like Being a Sex Machine)." He first cracked television on the *Ed Sullivan Show* and made a memorable historical appearance in the epic *T.A.M.I. Show* movie alongside the Rolling Stones, Beach Boys, Jan & Dean, Lesley Gore and others.

In the 1970s he was the Godfather of Soul, Mr. Dynamite and a dozen other sobriquets, the anointed and accepted king. He eased through that decade at the top of the heap, with a little trouble in his personal life (a charge of assault in 1974). In the 1980s, his career in a relative lull, he made a chart comeback with "Living in America," the theme from the movie *Rocky IV* (1986).

---

[1] In his book, James Brown, *The Godfather of Soul* (James Brown/Bruce Tucker, Thunder's Mouth, 1986), Brown tells of the honor he felt over being consulted during Vice President Hubert Humphrey's 1968 presi-

dential campaign. Humphrey told him he'd never forget what he'd done for him, and to call him if he ever needed help. Some years later, Brown says without great bitterness, when he was in income tax trouble, he called Humphrey's office and no one would return his call.

[2] Not an unreasonable idea, since earlier that year Brown had been caught with PCP at a Georgia airport, a week after his wife filed charges against him of attempted murder; she died in 1996 after complications from plastic surgery. (After her death, yet another woman filed charges against Brown for manhandling her.)

[3] The recording was paid for by Brown and released at Brown's insistence despite King Records boss Sid Nathan's objections that it was too raw and crudely recorded.

[4] Described curtly in the *Guinness Encyclopedia of Popular Music* as "a nagging riff over which the singer soared."

1979 Van Halen Cries "No Brown M&M's"

Perhaps intoxicated by their recent rise to more-or-less stardom in 1979, Van Halen's concert "rider," the superstar contract add-on that spells out a band's concert-hall requirements (must have heated dressing room, certain stage size, etc.), required that their meals always included servings of M&M candies—with the brown

Eddie Van Halen

ones removed.

This was true power in the eyes of the band, as the promoter was faced with the task of hand-removing all the offending candies.

While appearing in 1980 at the University of Southern Colorado, the band, doing their best impersonation of hopelessly spoiled rock stars, saw that their proviso was not being met and **decided to trash their facilities—to the tune of $10,000 worth of damage**.[1] The result was nationwide publicity for their tour and helped catapult their current album, *Van Halen II*, into the major-act world.

Formed in L.A. by Dutch-born guitarist extraordinaire Eddie Van Halen and his drummer brother, Alex, bassist Michael Anthony and singer David Lee Roth, the band had a solid following on the L.A. club circuit at the time of their signing to Warner Bros. Records in 1978. (They were brought to the attention of the label by Gene Simmons of Kiss.)

The band's tightness and verve was evident from the outset. Led by Van Halen's guitar playing and Roth's athletic and outrageous performing style,[2] they were an unstoppable force.

After Roth's departure in 1984 to go solo, Van Halen added successful bandleader Sammy Hagar and became even more popular. (See "David Lee Roth Quits Van Halen," page 154.) But now the band has announced Roth is back!

---

[1] In the 1984 press-release book *Van Halen*, allegedly by Gordon Matthews, the band's actions are portrayed as boyish pranks, as in "one bathroom, one dining room, and one dressing room felt the collective mock fury of Van Halen and crew." To make it crystal-clear that these were not just idiotic but humorous and even heroic actions, he writes, "Roll over Jim Morrison, tell Keith Richards the news." Facility bashing wasn't new then; it was just new to them.

[2] Lead singer David Lee Roth's long blond mane, tight pants, raspy voice and penchant for appearing shirtless was, coincidentally, quite reminiscent of Black Oak Arkansas' lead singer Jim Dandy Mangrum, who played the same L.A. club circuit as Van Halen. Memphis record producer

(and Jim Dandy associate) Jim Dickinson has said, "I bet if you woke David Roth out of a deep sleep, he'd admit he took his whole stage act from Jim Dandy."

1977 Fleetwood Mac Soap Opera Yields Multimillion-Selling Album

In 1977 Fleetwood Mac catapulted into superstardom with *Rumours*, the multi-multi-platinum-selling album containing "Dreams," "Go Your Own Way" and "Don't Stop" (that last one revived for the 1992 Clinton presidential campaign).

Their transition from a middling-selling[1] band to 20-million-selling worldbeater was accomplished on this, their eighth album for Warner Bros., in no small part by the contributions of two recently added L.A. musicians. Stevie Nicks and Lindsey Buckingham had made one

poor-selling album for Polydor, *Buckingham Nicks*, and were floundering on the L.A. music scene when *Fleetwood Mac* brought them on board in 1975. At that point Mac was a former blues band committed to contemporary rock. The new blood brought songs of romantic entanglement, *of betrayal, love and hope for tomorrow, which apparently was what the aging[2] rock & roll audience was looking for.*

Success came quickly. Their first album together, ("Mac's" seventh) *Fleetwood Mac,* yielded the song "Rhiannon" and went platinum. Then all hell broke loose when every member of the band broke up with their mates: Mick and his wife, John and Christine McVie, and Lindsay and Stevie.

The result was a bonanza. The fissures running through the band created an artistic explosion that resulted in *Rumours*, which led them all to unimaginable success and fame. (And, in Mick Fleetwood's case, bankruptcy.) In the 1980s the band suffered several personnel changes, and both Buckingham and Nicks embarked on solo careers.

That the band's huge run of success was based on songs of tangled relationships was symbolic of the full history of the band. The group was formed in England in 1967 by blues drummer Mick Fleetwood and guitarists Peter Green and Jeremy Spencer (bassist John McVie, whose surname is the "Mac" in the band's name,[3] actually joined after its formation). Another guitarist, Danny Kirwan, joined shortly afterward. When in 1970 British vocalist Christine Perfect married John McVie and joined as lead singer, **the band took its first shift away from blues toward pop—and the serious weirdness began.**

Guitarist Green was a little eccentric but reliable, at least until the day in 1970 when he walked away from the band, later citing personal and religious qualms about rock & roll, fame, etc. (Green actually failed to tell the band he'd left. They called the police and private detectives, then cancelled a Whiskey gig when the truth was revealed.) Guitarist Jeremy Spencer proved more fanatical and equally unreliable. He sabotaged the band's 1971 U.S. tour when, in Los Angeles, he heeded the words of a religious street group called the Children of God and left the band. Third guitarist Kirwan, also suffering from personal problems, joined the exodus. Guitarist Bob Welch[4] signed on, and their personnel seemed stable for a while.

Then, on the band's late 1973 U.S. tour, Mick Fleetwood fired guitarist/vocalist Bob Weston for having an affair with Fleetwood's wife, Jenny.[5] The band, unable to function, took a six-month hiatus, during which time manager Clifford Davis sent a completely new group of musicians (formerly known as "Stretch") on the road in their place, to the band's intense humiliation (and business loss, since bookers became wary, afraid they'd get a phony group).[6]

But by 1975 they were back on track, on their way to riches and fame.

---

[1] Their only U.S. hit had been the rocker "Oh Well" five years earlier. (Their big 1968 U.K. hit, "Albatross," never charted here.) When *Fleetwood Mac*, contractually their final album for Warner Bros., hit big in 1975, their contract was generously renewed and included a big increase in retroactive and future sales percentages.

[2] The vanguard of baby boomers hit age 30 that year.

[3] The band was actually named after an unreleased instrumental that Fleetwood, Mac and Green did while members of John Mayall's Bluesbreakers.

[4] In 1975 he embarked on a solo career. ("Sentimental Lady" was a 1977-78 hit.)

[5] Shades of Eric Clapton and George Harrison's wife! (See the "Layla" entry, page 68.) Incredibly, Jenny (née Boyd) was the sister of Harrison's wife, Patti Boyd, and the subject of a 1967 Donovan song, "Jennifer Juniper."

[6] This scandal was widely reported in the fledgling rock press.

Eric Clapton's Love for George Harrison's Wife Leads to "Layla"

Everybody knows "Layla" by Eric Clapton; if you missed it as an FM staple in the 1970s[1] and 1980s, you encountered it in the 1990s when he reprised it *au naturel* for "MTV Unplugged."

It's a love song to a married woman, a woman married to his good friend, a woman married to a Beatle.

Clapton and George Harrison were close pals in the late '60s: It's no secret that Eric played lead on a Beatles record, notably George's song "While My Guitar Gently Weeps," and that Harrison and Clapton co-wrote "Badge" for Cream.

But pals they were, and palsy-walsy Eric wanted to be with Patti, George's wife, the former Patti Boyd, the "bird" George met while filming "Hard Day's Night." Eric and Patti's mutual attraction went unfulfilled, they say, and that possibly helped push Eric over the edge (quicker? gave him justification to go?) into full-fledged heroin addiction.

Clapton's "heroin album" was 1970's *Layla*, by his group Derek and the Dominos. His singing sounds all the more ardent when you know that he's hooked on two hopeless things: a married woman and a drug.

Derek and the Dominos was Clapton's fourth or fifth career incarnation. He first emerged with the Yardbirds in 1963. When the Yardbirds seemed to be getting too pop for his blues sensibilities, he left and did a stint with John Mayall's Bluesbreakers. (All English blues-bent musicians, it seems, did time with either Mayall's or Alexis Korner's blues bands.) Then in 1966 he formed Cream

(*the* Cream, at first) with Ginger Baker and Jack Bruce. **When that agglomeration hit big, *big*, BIG he jumped ship in 1969** and went into Blind Faith with Baker, Rick Grech and Stevie Winwood.[2] When that band's stadium tour ended, he joined Blind Faith's opening act, the American band Delaney & Bonnie and Friends, on tour.[3] In 1970 his first solo album, *Eric Clapton*, yielded the hit song "After Midnight," and for once he was center stage. For his next move he formed Derek and the Dominos with Carl Radle, Jim Gordon and Bobby Whitlock and recorded one album, with the everlasting title tune "Layla," a paean to his married *objet d'amour*. Derek and the Dominos petered out after a year, and Clapton went into seclusion.

He cleaned up his heroin habit in 1973.
He married Patti in 1979.
They divorced in 1989.

---

[1] Upon its first release in 1970, deejays didn't know it was Clapton's band and didn't play it. It was a stiff.

[2] Clapton's musical and "moral" flip-flop with Blind Faith may have contributed to—or reflected—his oncoming drug addiction. After all, he had quit the Yardbirds because of its commerciality and went on to huge fame with Cream, which, despite its success, may have satisfied his artistic vision. No such nobility of purpose accompanied Blind Faith, however; it was created to *be* a supergroup (Cream was giant, Winwood was immensely popular in Traffic and the Spencer Davis Group ["Gimme Some Lovin'"] and Grech was in Family, a huge band in England) in an era when people were buying lots of records and slavishly attending rock festivals. Its very name was a thumb in the eye of the record-buying and concert going public, if you interpreted it as "they'll buy this record or go see this band no matter what they sound like."

[3] Once Clapton joined in, others followed—George Harrison, Dave Mason of Traffic (Leon Russell, a sideman, was already in place)—and the troupe became a traveling superstar circus, the blueprint for Joe Cocker's Mad Dogs & Englishmen tour the following year. The Delaney & Bonnie

phenomenon was unique in rock history, a magnet for good musicians[4] who just wanted to play for free. (A TV analogy might be Rod Serling's *Twilight Zone*, which attracted numerous "film" stars eager to be part of an exciting endeavor.) An unexpected result of his touring with them, however, was Clapton's introduction to heroin.

[4] Their album covers attracted stars too. *On Tour* showed a Rolls-Royce with feet sticking out a window: the Rolls was manager Albert Grossman's; the feet were Bob Dylan's. Zealous record collector Peter Holsapple points out that this cover was parodied by the musician Kyle, whose album cover showed a Rolls-Royce in front of an unemployent office.

1993 Another Manson-Related Death... Guns N' Roses Records His Song, Dies

Guns N' Roses was controversial from the git-go.

The L.A.-based hard-rock band fronted by Axl Rose[1] (né Bill Bailey of Lafayette, Indiana) curried the image of a hard-living, on-the-edge lifestyle and to some degree lived it. ***Rose drank, uttered obscenities and beat up neighbors,[2] fans,[3] girlfriends[4]*** and wives (well, only one wife[5]), supposedly, with equal vigor. The band promulgated excess, made clear by their first album's title, *Appetite for Destruction*, its cover (a Robert Williams painting of a recently raped young girl) and the poster "Addiction: Only the Strong Survive."

They started out on top and stayed there for quite a while. *Appetite for Destruction* was a certified smash. Opening shows for Aerosmith[6] and the Rolling Stones cinched their grip on young male America. While all of the band's members contributed to its reputation for wantoness and overt drug use, leader Rose embodied it like from a script, offending at every turn. In GNR's 1988 album *Lies*, the song "One in a Million" lashed out at "immigrants," "faggots" and "niggers."[7]

The final straw, however, was GNR's 1993 album, *The Spaghetti Incident*? Drawing entirely on outside writers and old songs, the band's appetite for self-destruction

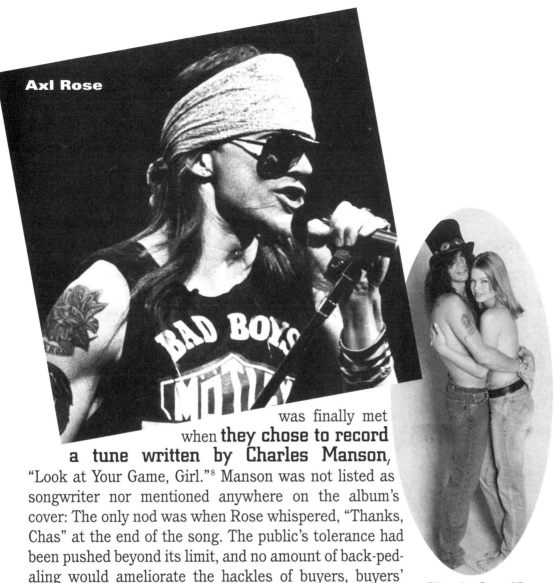

Axl Rose

Slash & wife

was finally met when **they chose to record a tune written by Charles Manson,** "Look at Your Game, Girl."[8] Manson was not listed as songwriter nor mentioned anywhere on the album's cover: The only nod was when Rose whispered, "Thanks, Chas" at the end of the song. The public's tolerance had been pushed beyond its limit, and no amount of back-ped-aling would ameliorate the hackles of buyers, buyers' parents and law enforcement agencies who thought that part of the purchase money was going to Charlie Manson in prison.[9]

GNR didn't formally break up, though individual members had flown off like sparks throughout the band's tenure, but they also didn't release another album (at least not by mid-1996). They have each played various gigs in various combinations, they could reform and Axl could form another band. If politics is any guide, his past notoriety would not inhibit his popularity.

[1] The letters of his name, rearranged, spell Oral Sex. But that could be just a coincidence.

[2] In a 1990 incident, Rose allegedly hit his neighbor with a wine bottle when the neighbor complained about loud music at Rose's house.

[3] In Kansas City in 1991, Rose leaped into the audience to grab a person who seemed to be videotaping him. This and the subsequent riot by some members of the audience led to cancellation of future concerts and, essentially, a dragnet for his arrest. (He turned himself in a year later and was tried and cleared of charges.)

[4] He reportedly struck his girlfriend, model Stephanie Seymour.

[5] Erin Everly, daughter of Phil Everly of the Everly Brothers, married Rose in 1990, then filed charges of battery against him. The marriage was annulled in January 1991.

[6] The cleaned-up Bostonians literally barricaded themselves from the drug-drenched GNR entourage on that tour.

[7] Rose's apology for his word-slinging was less than contrite. In effect, he said: I'm not a fucking racist. Not all black men are niggers, but if someone is acting like a fucking nigger, he is one. Same thing for fucking faggots. If you still want to call me a racist, you can shove it up your ass.

[8] This was not the first Manson song to be recorded by a major rock band. In 1968 Dennis Wilson, who was involved in the Manson family's pre-murder lifestyle (women and drugs), had the Beach Boys record "Never Learn Not to Love," a song bought outright from Manson and then credited to Wilson. The Beach Boys changed the title from the original Mansonesque "Cease to Exist," but the vibe remains in the opening line, "Cease to resist...."

[9] In fact, the band later learned that Manson royalty money would go to Bartek Frykowski, son of Wojiciech Frykowski, one of the people slain by the Manson gang.

Milli Vanilli Unmasked

Not unlike Wham!, Fabrice (Fab) Morvan and Rob Pilatus were *two swell-looking guys* (who based their look on that of Terence Trent D'Arby) whose stylin' appearance on videos helped propel their band, Milli Vanilli, to widespread record sales in 1989 and a Grammy for best new group.

But alas, unlike Wham!, they didn't sing on their records.

Rob and Fab were props for Munich, Germany, producer Frank Farian's studio-created music. When they applied for work at his studio, he had already made a record with anonymous studio singers[1] and needed some-

one to go on the road as the band. Rob and Fab, out-of-work actors and models, jumped at the chance and rode a rocket to stardom.

Unfortunately for them, American singer Charles Shaw stepped forward late in 1989 and announced he was the voice on one Milli Vanilli[2] record. (John Davis and Brad Howe were others.) Rob & Fab owned up to the masquerade, insisting that they, too, had singing talent, but their successive records under their own names failed to impress record buyers. Arista Records disowned the band, claiming they had been hoodwinked,[3] and several consumers' groups, in the most meaningless public display since the controversy over the reformulation of Coca-Cola, actually *sued* the record label for fooling the public[4] and received some symbolic recompense.

Much ado about nothing, someone said, especially when you consider that studio groups and studio doctoring are commonplace in the record industry. Who was Phil Spector? A producer with a musical vision who hired musicians to fulfill his goals, like a conductor hiring an orchestra. Were the Crystals who toured the same group who sang on the record? Nope. Look at the first Village People album cover: there's a bunch of colorful guys lolling around Greenwich Village. None are identified because the group hadn't yet been formed, **but producer Jacques Morali already had the *Village People* record in the can!** Look at the first New Christy Minstrels album cover. The "singers" (right-looking Columbia Records employees and passersby) are backlit on scaffolds because producer Randy Sparks hadn't chosen a group yet, but the record was already being pressed. Ever see the Hondells, whose "Little Honda" was such a big 1963 hit? Not likely, since the band was created by a ring of session musicians led by producer Gary Usher. For that matter, if you go to see the Coasters or the Platters or the Shirelles or the Drifters these days, think you're seeing the real McCoys?[5]

Back and forth, on and on it goes: the 1910 Fruitgum Company, the Cufflinks, the Grass Roots (sometimes), Hollywood Argyles, B. Bumble & The Stingers, the Archies and many many other bands existed on record alone, while fill-in performers were hired to go on the road.

---

[1] Farian's previous creations included '70s European hitmakers Boney M, which was a more or less identical setup of different touring and recording bands. But since they had no U.S. hits, there was no uproar, because Europeans don't give a damn about such trivialities.

[2] In 1990 session singer Yvette Marine sued singer Paula Abdul, claiming Marine's background, or "scratch" (used for another singer to sing with), vocals were too prominent on Abdul's records.

[3] And I've got a bridge in Brooklyn to sell them.

[4] Why didn't they sue MTV for running the videos?

[5] However, if you see the McCoys ("Hang On Sloopy"), they're probably real. (Not like the Strangeloves, the band that discovered them. The production team of Goldstein, Feldman & Gottehrer really *were* the Strangeloves, really *did* record "I Want Candy" and really *were* pictured on their album cover but were not Australian sheepherders named Miles, Niles and Giles,[6] as their publicity claimed.)

[6] You see, musicians were *desperate* to be English in 1965. Australian was the same to them.

Monkees Announce They're "Plastic"

In 1967, in a move foreshadowing Milli Vanilli's admissions 22 years later, the Monkees held a press conference[1] to confirm the long-bandied rumors that they didn't play, or sometimes sing,[2] on their own records. Their choice of words was typically '60s, when they said they were, indeed, 'plastic.' (What does that really mean? Records were plastic then. It means bendable, versatile—no bad things those.)

The Monkees were chosen through auditions by producers Bob Rafelson and Bert Schneider. They all were musicians, but the Monkees TV show took precedence over making records, so the instrumental beds were done by hired musicians. Nothing was new about that in Los Angeles, where "live" recordings were routinely done (or altered) in recording studios (*Johnny Rivers Live at the Whisky*, *The Beach Boys Party*) and good bands were replaced on recordings (the Byrds' "Mr. Tambourine Man," the Beach Boys from 1965 on, Paul Revere & the Raiders) by seasoned studio musicians.

The Monkees made brilliant singles at a time when the market was splitting into a "them" and "us" mentality, and they were labeled "them" by the newborn rock press. *But the Monkees were not unhip!* The Beatles put Mike Nesmith in their vid-clip for "A Day in the Life," serious peer-group approval. And the renowned Plaster Casters of Chicago (game gals who immortalized musicians' sex organs; see "Some Sexual Landmarks," page 214) first plied their trade on them. Stephen Stills, a Monkees wanna-be (see "Stephen Stills Flunks Monkees Audition," page 34), recommended Peter Tork. The Monkees session players included Elvis guitarist James Burton, Billy Preston and most of Phil Spector's famed "Wrecking Crew."[3] The producers of

Easy Rider, the film that defined a generation, earlier produced the Monkees film *Head*, which now *also* stands tall
in the ranks of '60s rock movies.

The band also furthered the careers of some important musicians. Right after Jimi Hendrix wowed the
world at Monterey (see "Hendrix Sets Fire to Guitar,"
page 180), the Monkees signed him as an opening act on
their July tour, fully aware that his hard, sexual rock
would be lost on their teenybopper audience, and delighted to give him the benefit of their fame. (That ended after
nine days. See "Hendrix Booted from Monkees Tour,"
page 209.) The final episode of their TV show featured
Frank Zappa (as Mike Nesmith) and singer-songwriter
Tim Buckley, whom the Monkees thought deserved a
shot.

Micky Dolenz, who sang lead on many Monkees
songs, had a fine pop-rock voice especially suited to the
times, like Mark Lindsay of Paul Revere & the Raiders.
Mike Nesmith's brand of country-rock, which showed up
as early as the first album, was pioneering; it's a stretch,
but not an impossible one, to cite Nesmith's sound as
leading to the Byrds, Poco and the Eagles. (Nesmith continued writing—while a Monkee he wrote "Different
Drum," a hit for Linda Ronstadt's Stone Poneys—and
performing country-rock semisuccessfully[4] after the
band's breakup.)

The Monkees were selling millions of records to
teenagers, but they couldn't get respect from their peers.
In 1967, the year of Hendrix and Joplin at Monterey,

word of mouth battered them. (Dolenz and Tork attended Monterey, but Tork appearing onstage did little to further the band's, or Tork's, acceptance among the *avant-garde*.) The talk that they didn't play on their records eventually got to them, so they felt compelled to tell the truth. They gladly mocked themselves in *Head*, singing "Hey, hey, we're the Monkees, on that we'd all agree, a manufactured image with no philosophy." **Zappa, for his part, maintained that Monkees records were better than any record out of the San Francisco scene.**

It did little good. They became more involved in their recordings, but after two years, despite their playing on *Headquarters* and subsequent recordings, Peter Tork deserted, followed by Mike Nesmith, leaving the band to carry on like that knight in *Monty Python & the Holy Grail* trying to fight after his limbs are cut off. By 1968 the heat of the show's first two seasons had dissipated, and they soon found themselves self-produced and out of work.

In 1986 MTV began airing the old TV shows to an eager new audience, and Dolenz, Jones and Tork returned to touring. Like setting a place for Elijah at the Passover table, though he never shows up (at least as of this book's writing), a place was held in the heart of every Monkees fan that Nesmith would show up, but he surfaced only twice—in 1986 for a two song encore at the Greek Theater in Los Angeles and for half a set at the Universal Amphitheater in 1989.

Their old recordings were acquired by Rhino and became hot sellers, and a new album sold well, too. In 1995 Rhino issued a box set of all their TV shows with a list price slightly over $300. It sold out immediately. And the Monkees reached their goal of a wholly self-produced album in the fall of 1996, all four recording for Rhino Records.

[1] Perhaps setting a precedent for New Kids on the Block's announcement in 1991 that *they* were not plastic. They appeared unaccompanied on the "Arsenio Hall Show," but failed to truly endear or distinguish themselves.

[2] The Monkees record "A Little Bit Me, A Little Bit You" featured Jones alone, its recording not known to the others.

[3] Collectively known as the L.A. Wrecking Crew, these musicians played on a billion dollars' worth of hits: Hal Blaine, Ray Pohlman, Larry Knechtel, Leon Russell, Tommy Tedesco, Jim Gordon, Carol Kaye.

[4] He alone among the Monkees "retired" to a successful postband career, recording several medium-selling albums for RCA Records in a country-rock vein and establishing Pacific Arts Video, a booking and multimedia agency in northern California. Of course, it helps that his mother was a multimillionaire from inventing Liquid Paper correction fluid. The Nesmith family also produced the films *Repo Man* and *Tapeheads*.

1972 Big Safety Flap Over Alice Cooper's Panties

The outrageous Alice Cooper band was formed in Arizona in 1966 by Vincent Furnier (whose birthdate meanders from 1944 to 1948, depending on the source) as rock's equivalent to Grand Guignol theater. Wearing a tattered dress, his eyes blackened, swinging a dead (or rubber) chicken and getting himself mock-decapitated by a guillotine,[1] he was a shocking presence on a rock playing field strewn with flowers and love.[2] They were first signed to Frank Zappa's aptly named Bizarre label, but it wasn't until their first releases on Warner Bros., *Love It to Death* and *Killer* (1971), that they catapulted to national prominence. **Then came the panty episode.**

In keeping with their leering sexual image, Cooper and Warner Bros. decided to wrap each copy of his 1972 album, *School's Out*, in disposable panties. But those panties were not, strictly speaking, up to code—meaning non-flammable—and a great row broke out,[3] leading to a bonanza of publicity for the group and the album. Whether they were extras or just made up for the concert isn't known, but at Cooper's Hollywood Bowl concert in

1972, thousands of panties were dumped from a heli-
copter onto the audience.

[1] One wants to remember the name of the critic who in 1970 said "It is
nothing new for a man to grow his hair long, blacken his eyes and swing
a dead chicken while wearing a dress. What's new is that there is an audience for such a person."

[2] Longtime Cooper manager Shep Gordon supposedly signed them after
seeing an audience flee—like from a fire—from their set, reasoning "any
band this bad must have some merit."

[3] When the Federal Trade Commission charged that the panties were
unsafe, the Cooper camp responded that surgical masks were made from
identical material and offered to promise that the panties would be worn
only on people's faces.

Zappa with
Johnny Winter,
New Orleans,
1974

Frank Zappa/Lou Reed Feud Begins in 1966, Ends at Rock & Roll Hall of Fame

Bad blood existed between Frank Zappa and Lou Reed from their early days as labelmates on Verve Records.

Both bands were produced by Tom Wilson, who'd produced Dylan's *Bringing It All Back Home*, around the same time in 1966. In retrospect, neither Zappa's Mothers of Invention's *Freak Out!* album nor Reed's group the Velvet Underground's album was, strictly speaking, ultracommercial (with the edge given to the relative tunefulness of the latter). But Reed felt that *Freak Out!*, which was released in the summer of 1966 while his languished in the can for 6 months, got the majority of the airplay and attention, leading the fretful Reed to conclude that the record company was doing more for Frank's group than for his.

Also contributing to Reed's fears[1] was the fact that when the Velvets made their West Coast debut at the Trip[2] in 1966, the Mothers of Invention were their opening act, and Zappa made a point of calling the Velvets the worst act in the world.[3] **The bad badinage went back and forth over the next few decades, most of it emanating from Reed**, whose career dipped and turned while Zappa's continued apace.

The final irony, and it wasn't too funny to people close to Frank, was that after Zappa was elected posthumously to the Rock & Roll Hall of Fame in 1994, the elders of that organization selected Reed to do the induction speech, apparently unaware of their bitter past relationship. It then was safe for Reed to say, "I admired Frank and he admired me," for who was around to say otherwise?

[1] Some would use the word *paranoia*, but Reed's fears were grounded.

[2] A fundamental L.A. club on the Sunset Strip formerly called the Crescendo, which featured jazz greats (*Mel Torme Live at the Crescendo* from 1954 is still a worldwide seller). Changed to the Trip in 1965. Donovan switched from folk singer to electric guru during a 1966 residence here, leading to the song "The Trip" on his *Sunshine Superman* album. The building has been torn down.

[3] Did he consider them art-rock poseurs? New York lowlifes? Drug-besotten idiots? Frank never said exactly what bothered him about them—but then, he wasn't a hard one to rankle.

1991 Freddie Mercury of Queen—First Rock-Superstar AIDS-related Death

Freddie Mercury was a comet in the rock & roll sky. From the outset of Queen in 1971, *his glam, theatrical and sexually ambiguous presence* led that band to the superstratospheric heights of "Bohemian Rhapsody" to its swan-song album, *Innuendo*, in early 1991, the year of his death from AIDS. (A final album, *Made in Heaven*, was released in 1996.)

Mercury never dealt publicly with his gayness. You

didn't pick up the *Advocate* and see his picture as "one of us"; somehow he made his mark without a noticeable gay following. One of his mid-'70s stage presentations included such hints as donning a ballet tutu and singing "Hey Big Spender," a show tune (!) sung by a hooker in the Broadway show *Sweet Charity*. But **this was the '70s and everybody, it seemed, from the trashily heterosexual New York Dolls to ex-Byrd Gene Clark, was sporting make-up,** and girls were squealing and squirming at the sight of Tim Curry in a bra and bondage pants in *The Rocky Horror Show*…so who was to know what was what? Even the Village People didn't significantly alarm America: They could've just been a regular bunch of guys in funny getups.

Ironically, Queen lost its U.S. footing by spoofing[1] sexual roles. In 1984 they made a video for the single "I Want to Break Free" in drag: Freddie as a miniskirted housewife, Brian as a woman in curlers, John as an old lady and Roger a little too convincing as a tartish schoolgirl. (In an interview, when asked how he convinced the other—straight—band members to dress up for the video, Freddie said, "I didn't have to push them at all. They all rushed to get into their frocks!") This was too dead-on for Queen's American fans, who'd suffered through the group's '70s disco-oriented output (such as "Under Pressure," done with David Bowie) in hopes they'd **return to opera-based Sturm und Drang**.

What they'd suspected about Freddie now appeared to apply to the whole band,[2] and their American record sales plummeted.

Though immensely popular outside the United States[3] Queen still experienced a "renewal" at Live Aid in the summer of 1986. Their performance, an unprecedented display of "unplugged"-ness, close together on a makeshift stage without props and effects, was a startling triumph, and the tightly packed stadium audience showed its approval with a swaying sea of hands. Some unusual tours followed of hitherto unattempted rock venues such as far-off Budapest and Rio de Janeiro,[4] but as the '80s waned, Freddie's personal appearances became rarer, and rumors began to fly that he had AIDS. An interview with Brian May in the *Los Angeles Times* in February 1991 did little to stop them: **When asked whether Freddie was ill with AIDS, May replied evasively, "I've heard those rumors,** and I know where they start. The British press." A $200,000 party was held that spring for the *Innuendo* album's release, in the "old" '70s fashion[5]: The *Queen Mary* was rented, sword swallowers, fan dancers and fortune tellers were provided and tons of gourmet victuals were provided to celebrate

the band's signing to Hollywood Records. But Freddie wasn't there, which added fuel to the burning rumors. Then, on one Sunday in November came the terse announcement that he was dead.

Hollywood Records was caught flat-footed by Freddie's death. The band had been signed for a large advance, but unlike adding a new employee to a company, nobody gave the artists a physical checkup. There was brief panic when the execs realized they'd signed a "dead" band; fortunately for them, sales of Queen's catalog climbed upon Mercury's death. And *"Bohemian Rhapsody's" inclusion in the 1992 hit film Wayne's World catapulted their old albums,* and their new ones, into multiplatinum all over again.[6]

[1] It is hard for Queen nonfans—or certainly, Queen antagonists—to imagine Queen as a band with a sense of humor, but it was there for all to see. They named their two big albums *Night at the Opera* and *Day at the Races* after Marx Brothers films, and in interviews *urged* people to go see them. The hundred nude girls on bicycles on the *Jazz* inner sleeve was not the work of sourpusses. And Queen's enormous smoke-bomb, stage-lifting, laser-beam-filled stage shows trod a delicate line between bombast and hilarity that greatly appealed to its audience and infuriated the band's detractors.

[2] In an interview, Brian May said the band members all kept their sexuality ambiguous to contribute to their theatricality and mystique.

[3] Queen did not tour America after 1980. However, they continued to be one of the two most popular bands in the world—the Rolling Stones being the other.

[4] The Rio promoter was notorious for not paying foreign acts. Queen had their own airplane land next to the stadium, and after the show they loaded their gear into it and flew away. The next morning the promoter said he was not going to pay the established price and was going to hold their gear as ransom. "Guess again," Queen's people said. They got paid.

[5] Queen's '70s parties were notorious: at the *Jazz* album release party in New Orleans, hookers were reportedly available to partygoers *on the spot*.

[6] It's rare when hit singles, other than seasonal ones, hit twice. The only other one to re-hit #1 intact was "The Twist" in 1960 and 1961.

1980 Car Crashes Into Blondie Recording Session; "Suzy and Jeffrey" Results

In 1980, Blondie was recording at Western Recorders (now Ocean Way) on Sunset Boulevard in Hollywood when a car came crashing through the studio wall. A guy named Jeff was having an argument with his girlfriend Sue, and he lost control of the car and rammed it through the wall.

Nobody was hurt, according to KROQ deejay and longtime scene person Rodney Bingenheimer,[1] but the incident prompted Blondie to write a song, "Suzy and Jeffrey," which was the non-LP flip side of "The Tide Is High" (from the 1980 album *Autoamerican*).

[1] Bingenheimer's presence on the L.A. music scene spans the past 30 years, starting when he moved to L.A. from Mountain View, near San Francisco, and befriended Sonny Bono. (He hung tight with the Bonos during the Sunset Strip riots of late 1966, and Sal Mineo, an important scenemaker, dubbed him "the mayor of Sunset Strip.") He hung out with Brian Wilson, attended the "River Deep Mountain High" sessions for Ike & Tina Turner, was Davy Jones' TV stand-in on *The Monkees*, showed newcomer David Bowie around L.A. when he was promotion man for

Mercury Records ("We went over to Hollywood High to look at girls, but none of them would talk to David because he was wearing a dress"), ran the E Club, *aka* Rodney's English Disco, in the early 1970s, which attracted the glam crowd of its day (along with visitors as notable as…but then, who could BE as notable as?…Elvis Presley) and has continued his frankly *inevitable* grip on the pulse of the L.A. and international scene with records, TV appearances and a weekly radio show on KROQ.

1976 The Band's Swan Song Is Filmed; "The Last Waltz" Is a Hit Movie

On November 25, 1976, The Band, the Canadian quintet (well, one American from Arkansas) who moved from modest fame backing early rocker Ronnie Hawkins, to rock fame backing Bob Dylan, and then to world fame on their own as The Band,[1] closed the book on their career with a performance at San Francisco's Winterland Ballroom. On hand to help them mark this passage were musical friends Neil Young,[2] Neil Diamond,[3] Eric Clapton, Joni Mitchell, Bob Dylan, Stephen Stills, Dr. John, Muddy Waters,[4] Ringo Starr, Emmylou Harris, Van Morrison, Ronnie Hawkins, and "See You Later Alligator" writer Bobby Charles.

Filmmaker Martin Scorsese,[5] heretofore known as a doo-wop and vocal group fan ("Mean Streets" and "Taxi Driver" reverberated with those early New York sounds) came in and lensed the whole proceedings, and the result, *The Last Waltz*, became a surprise box-office success,[6] as did the soundtrack triple album.

[1] Their first Capitol single, "The Weight," listed all the band members' names because a name hadn't yet been chosen. And a name never really was.

[2] Rumor persists to this day that a lot of money had to be spent to darken, frame by frame, the cocaine residue that appeared in Young's nostrils when he was shot from below.

[3] Diamond, while a fine musician, is odd man out in this aggregation, like Kim Carnes was in "We Are the World." In both cases it's business connections: Band principal Robbie Robertson had just produced Neil Diamond's *Beautiful Noise* album, and Carnes' manager organized WATW. It's a good bet that if Robertson had just produced the Village People, they would've been up there, too.

[4] Drummer-vocalist Levon Helm wrote bitterly in his book, *This Wheel's on Fire* (Morrow, 1993), that Robertson was hedging about including Waters on the already crowded show until Helm threatened to boycott if he wasn't.

[5] Scorsese's role as interviewer was lampooned by Rob Reiner as director Marty (!) DiBergi in the film *This Is Spinal Tap*, which was a sendup of *The Last Waltz*.

[6] Rock & roll concert movies, with the exception of *Woodstock*, which was a *phenomenon*, generally didn't make box-office waves. Incidentally, Scorsese was a supervising editor of *Woodstock* and worked on *The Medicine Ball Caravan!* Scorcese's druggy days are described in *The Warhol Diaries*.

1974 Al Green Scalded by Grits, Joins Ministry (the Vocation, Not the Band)

In 1974 soul vocalist Al Green was on top of the world after a spectacular string of pop and R&B hits that started in mid-1971 with "Tired of Being Alone" and "Let's Stay Together," and continued through "Sha La La (Make Me Happy)." On October 25 it all came crashing down.

A girlfriend, Mary Woodson, burst in on Green in his Memphis home while he was showering and scalded his body with hot grits[1] from the stove, then shot herself dead with his revolver.[2] Green, who, like **Little Richard before him, had been troubled about the conflicts between stardom and God,** turned fully away from secular music that day, bought a church in Memphis and became its pastor. He continued recording, however, and his self-produced[3] 1977 hit "Belle" mixed the secular with the spiritual in a soul-satisfying blend. However, after escaping serious injury in a fall at a Cincinnati concert in 1979, he discontinued touring and concentrated on recording exclusively gospel material.[4]

Green returned to popular performing in 1988, singing "Put a Little Love in Your Heart" with the Eurythmics' Annie Lennox for the film *Scrooged*. This was Green's only brush with new-release chart success; though he was welcomed on the concert trail, the record market had changed decisively in his absence.

[1] Sometimes the word *grits* draws chuckles from non-Southern people because it sounds down-home and rural (but not *black*: Everyone in the South eats grits). Grits are coarsely ground hominy, resembling watery, textured mashed potatoes. So if you imagine boiling lava clinging to your skin, it's less funny.

[2] In a book-prospectus interview with author Davin Seay, Green said he had been involved with Woodson but distanced himself from her as he gradually learned she had omitted bits of her past from him, including her stint in a mental hospital and the husband and four children she abandoned to pursue Al.

[3] His long string of hits up to that point had been produced by Hi Records producer Willie Mitchell.

[4] Again, like Little Richard, who turned to the ministry in 1957 after a personal crisis. (Richard was flying to Australia for a rock & roll show when an engine caught fire; he swore he'd enter the ministry if the plane would only land safely. It did, and then he did.)

Beatles Smoke Dope at Buckingham Palace? Turtles Follow Suit at the White House?

Smoking marijuana at historic national shrines

seems to have been a favorite pastime of privileged rock stars in the 1960s—or was it?

On October 26, 1965, the Beatles went to Buckingham Palace to receive **MBE (Member of the British Empire) medals[1] from Queen Elizabeth, the country's highest honor and a rarity for pop musicians.**

If you believe what you hear, in the heady days of the 1960s few musicians traveled without their stash of marijuana, and the Beatles, reportedly, were no exception. Nervous about meeting Her Nibs, a Beatle or two supposedly stole away to the loo and had a few hits off a joint to calm their nerves. The English music press reported this speculation (one Brit-press-photo cutline read, "MBEs: Marijuana Brings Enlightenment") and it has passed into history as neither fact nor fable. In the late 1995 official Beatles TV documentary, the remaining Beatles dismissed this as balderdash and say they only repaired to the W.C. for cigarettes. True enough, one can't picture a Beatle or anyone else greeting a royal with a fag in hand ("fag" is slang for cigarette in the U.K., but it still sounds funny—Ed.), so their denial holds some weight, but the American broadcast of **their documentary skipped over a lot and revealed, shockingly, conflicting memories about certain events, so who the heck knows?**

Supposedly, the Beatles first encountered "smoke" during the filming of *Help!* early in 1965 (though one wonders how they managed to slip through the drug-besotten Reeperbahn in Germany without a toke or two[2]), which might lend credence to the idea that they were smoking doobies in the royal bathroom. And Macca (Brit-press for McCartney) apparently remains a marijuana advocate and has been busted several times in several countries (Sweden, Japan, Scotland) for possession. Of course, the rascally mop-tops seem to be the type of fellows who would do such a thing for a giggle.

On the American front, the California hit-making Turtles were invited to the White House by First Daughter Tricia Nixon[3] in 1969 and made a much-heralded "breakthrough" in smoking dope in the waiting room there, and reportedly in snorting cocaine off a table that Abraham Lincoln once used. However, times being what they are and time being what it is, some remaining Turtles are less forthcoming about their derring-do. Turtle Howard Kaylan says, "Listen, maybe we didn't do those things, you know? I'm not so sure now. That was years ago."

[1] Many older English MBE bearers returned their medals in disgust, feeling the award was dishonored by its issuance to the Beatles. On November 25, 1969, John Lennon returned *his* medal in protest against the Vietnam War, the Nigerian/Biafran problem and "Cold Turkey" slipping down the charts. (The chart position mention was a gag.)

[2] Remember, *Hard Day's Night* has an unmistakable dope joke in it, when Lennon puts a bottle of "Coke" up to his nostril and sniffs.

[3] Being a Nixon who was the same age as the new rock stars was a thorny crown for Miss Trish. She liked rock & roll as much as the next person but couldn't invite, say, the Doors to her dad's house; the seemingly benign Turtles were Tricia's favorite rock group anyway. Still, she got *near* some trouble when she invited Finch College alumni to the White House, including fellow Finch gal Grace Slick. When Slick's date Abbie Hoffman showed up at the White House gate wearing an American flag shirt, they were firmly turned away. Then Trish had to put up with being the subject of a war protest song by Jay and the Americans, "Tricia, Tell Your Daddy."

1975 Springsteen's Face Graces *Time* and *Newsweek*; Climbs the Wall at Graceland to See Elvis

You think Bruce Springsteen has always been a megastar?

Nope. It happened on October 27, 1975. Through unprecedented publicity machinations and a genuine surge of fan interest, new hitmaker Bruce appeared on *the covers of both Time and Newsweek,* hailed as the new savior of rock & roll. His song "Born

to Run" was moving up the charts, and everyone, it seemed, wanted a piece of him. Previously, Springsteen's efforts had been noticed only by **hipsters who dug his old-time energy**—this was the era of Emerson, Lake and Palmer and Yes, don'cha know—and his close connection to the roots of rock & roll on his low-selling albums *Greetings from Asbury Park*, and *The Wild, The Innocent and the E-Street Shuffle*.

"Born to Run" was a hit single with a difference: It soared emotionally and hit peak after peak with clanging Spector chimes and galloping glockenspiels and reckless hopeful imagery of one last motorcycle ride to greatness. *Bam!* In 1978, at the height of the hype (it was real, but it was hype; the single stalled at #23, though the album went to #3), he made two media-frenzied appearances at L.A.'s Roxy Theater that were met with second-coming-of-Elvis-like acclaim.

And speaking of Elvis...

On April 29, 1976, Bruce did a concert in Memphis

and after the show he asked a taxi driver to take him to Graceland, where he climbed over the fence and walked up the driveway. A voice behind a tree said, "Hey, come here a minute," and Bruce sheepishly asked if Elvis was home. Told that the King was in Lake Tahoe, Bruce responded that he was a rock star who had been on the cover of *Time* and *Newsweek* and that he had to get a messsage to Elvis! The guard[1] said, "Yeah, sure," and calmly escorted him off the property.[2]

[1] If this had happened 14 years earlier, the guard would have been Billy Swan, writer of "Lover Please" and hitmaker of 1974's "I Can Help," who was a Graceland guard in 1962.

[2] It is said that these days Springsteen regrets his youthful derring-do for its karma: Kids now scale his fence, and he hates it.

Why Did I Open My Big Mouth? Some Famous Misspeakings

People know now that in 1966, when John Lennon said the Beatles "are more popular than Jesus right now," he meant it as a sad observation. Based on zeal the Beatles had seen around the world, their fans' adoration equaled religious fervor. *He also added, injudiciously, "Christianity will go. It will vanish and shrink."*

But when word got to America via *Datebook* magazine (the paper "of record" of its day?), America went nuts. Ex-fans burned Beatles albums, preachers railed against them, and Jay North, TV's former Dennis the Menace, wrote to *Time* magazine that the Beatles' time was over, but God's time was eternal (or something like that). The brouhaha grew and grew. Lennon made an intelligent denial and clarification, but it wasn't enough to stanch the bonfires of fundamentalist America. Anti-Beatles fever was a rallying point for religionists, **so a kind of Beatlemania in reverse**

swept the countryside, not unlike the witch burnings—likewise imported from England—that crisscrossed America in the 1600s.

After some time the flap died down and went away, but by then it was 1967 and the world was about to be turned upside down once again by the Beatles, courtesy of their album *Sgt. Pepper's Lonely Hearts Club Band*.

Another English guy had a problem 13 years after Lennon. This time it was the new singing-song-writing sensation Elvis Costello. Hailed for his incisive lyrics on 1977's *My Aim Is True* and 1978's *This Year's Model*, in 1979 he found his foot jammed squarely in his mouth when, at a bar in Columbus, Ohio, with Stephen Stills and Bonnie Bramlett, he uttered the sarcastic—and doubtlessly insincere—**opinion that Ray Charles was "a blind, ignorant nigger."**[1] Bramlett, who has loudly proclaimed herself a battered woman (by her former husband, Delaney Bramlett), *slugged the skinny Costello for his remark* (she was once a white Ikette, and probably exceptionally sensitive to racist remarks). The repercussions of it (the remark, not the punch) dogged Costello for the better part of a year, as he struggled to make it seem what it probably was, a provocative statement designed to piss someone off. (Aren't you glad the things *you* say in a bar aren't printed in newspapers the next day?)

Third in the misspoken category is Brian Wilson, for revealing that he put sand around his piano so he could feel "the beach" under his feet when he composed songs. When the feeble-minded press seized this, they dished him for "playing in a sandbox," which absolutely was not the case.

---

[1] The somewhat bitter Costello was a symbol of a new order, the New Wave punk what-have-you movement. He said that in Ohio he was uncomfortable around people he considered to be holdovers from Woodstock, and his desire to upset them prompted his ill-chosen remark.

1971 Deep Purple Watches Club Burn During Zappa Concert in Switzerland; "Smoke on the Water" Results

On the night of December 3, 1971, the English rock band Deep Purple was recording at a chateau in Montreux, Switzerland, when they noticed a fire at the nearby Montreux Casino concert hall across Lake Geneva. Frank Zappa was performing there. He, his band and the patrons fled, leaving all the tour equipment behind to be destroyed.

That was the bad news. The good news was that Purple songwriter Ian Gillan seized the moment and wrote his impression of that eerie night in what became the band's signature song, "Smoke on the Water" ("Frank Zappa and the Mothers were at the best place in town, but some stupid with a flare gun burned the place to the ground").

It wasn't Zappa's only onstage problem that year. A week later, on December 10, during a concert at London's Rainbow Theater, a jealous fan named Trevor Howell decided Zappa was making eyes at his girlfriend. **Howell climbed onto the stage and hurled Zappa into the orchestra pit.** Frank sustained a broken leg and skull fracture and spent much of the next year in a wheelchair. (His voice grew deeper after this incident, too.)

1966 Beatles "Butcher Cover" Banned; and Some Other Notable Covers

Perhaps chafing at being called the lovable mop-tops, in June 1966 the cover of the Beatles' eighth[1] Capitol album, *Yesterday and Today*[2] featured a photo of them in butcher's smocks holding *dismembered*

baby dolls and bloody slabs of meat. It so out-raged news media and retailers that Capitol Records called back the few hundred advance releases and re-covered them with a bad-looking photo of the Beatles gathered around a steamer trunk: All look vaguely resentful, with Paul red-nosed and sleepy.

According to *Rock & Roll Confidential* author Penny Stallings, Capitol lost $200,000 over this cock-up—but I'll bet the album sold 200,000 copies and that Capitol made at least a dollar on each one. To save money Capitol simply slapped the new cover over the already printed one, thereby putting a few hundred thousand "butcher covers" into circulation; industrious Beatles fans and money-minded resellers peeled back the overlaid cover to reveal, like the Mona Lisa under a Red Skelton painting, the naughty grins of the Beatles.[3]

Today, a peeled mono butcher cover fetches a couple hundred dollars, and a peeled stereo more. Actual slicks and unrecalled copies[4] get quite a bit more, up to and exceeding a thousand dollars.

Several other shocking album covers made news over the years:

• One example was the 1977 Lynyrd Skynyrd album *Street Survivors*, which showed the band surrounded by flames. Subsequently, several members died in a fiery plane crash, causing the cover to be redesigned.

• If you looked closely at the cover of the 1974 album by Mom's Apple Pies, featuring a woman holding a pie with a missing slice, you'd see a "pink hole" with almond-shaped folds and a central slit. It was soon removed from distribution.

• Earlier, there was Jimi Henrdrix's celebratory *Electric Ladyland* UK cover—special female nudity edition (see "Some Sexual Landmarks," page 214).

• Recent offerings include Tori Amos' *Boys for Pele* album, featuring an image of her breast feeding a little pig, which says something about men, apparently, and certainly something about herself.

[1] That is, if you don't count *The Beatles' Story* and *Help!*, with its George Martin instrumental filler tracks (it was released as a solid 14-song Beatles album in England) as Beatles albums.

[2] A non-album in England, for it contained tracks removed by Capitol Records from American versions of their U.K. albums, which at the time contained 14 tracks. U.S. releases contained only 12 cuts, later 10, in a well-known American record label practice, known in other businesses as "watering the ketchup" or "short-changing." It has been said that the Beatles, indeed, chose the butcher motif as a protest against the way Capitol was "butchering" their original albums for American release. (In American record companies' defense—the only time you'll see *that* phrase in this book—British music publishers were paid a percentage of a fixed price per album, so they got a one-fourteenth share on a 14-cut album and one-twentieth on a 20-cut album, while American publishers received a fixed per-song rate which ate into the royalties when the number of songs rose.)

[3] Whoops. In an interview in the March 9, 1996, *Billboard*, George Harrison said it was the idea of the photographer, Bob Whitaker, and was meant to be avant-garde, not about albums being butchered.

[4] Many people simply steamed them off. I peeled maybe 20 of them in 1966-71, and I'm not sure if it works now, after the glue has hardened for 30 years, but here was my technique:

1. Inch by inch, press Scotch tape down hard and pull back, ripping off the glossy surface.

2. With warm water, rub gently on the white ragged paper, until first the paper rubs away, then the glue beneath it.

3. Move carefully to the next spot. DON'T OVERRUB; you could break through the "good cover," which has already been weakened by dampness.

And remember, you can see the old cover underneath: The triangle of Ringo's black turtleneck peeks through the white paper beneath the word *Today*.

If you want to see a grown man cry, ask L.A. deejay Rodney Bingenheimer about the box of butcher-cover albums he was given by Capitol—mint ones—that he distributed free to people on the Sunset Strip.

1965 Sonny Bono's Ejection Spurs Hit of Rejection, "Laugh at Me"

Sonny Bono was a validated man in 1965. After many, many years on the edge of the record industry as a promotion man, percussionist, A&R man, songwriter, go-fer, and unsuccessful recording artist,[1] at age 30 he was now a certified rock & roll star as his duet with his wife, Cher, "I Got You Babe," climbed to the top of the charts.

So it was especially painful the day that Sonny and Cher triumphantly strolled into Martoni's restaurant, a prestigious Hollywood record industry watering hole and the scene of many of his years of struggle, and were ulti-mately kicked out.

According to Sonny's book, *And the Beat Goes On* (Simon & Schuster, 1991) he and Cher entered dressed in their avant-mod bell-bottoms,[2] long hair,[3] loud flower-patterned shirts, and perhaps a fur vest, and were greet-ed not with embraces as the nation's newest hitmakers, but with remarks like **"Hey, faggot, who's the hooker? I never would've guessed you like girls."**[4] Tension grew to such a point that the tormentors *and* the Bonos were thrown out. "You guys are always getting into trouble," said the manager, Sonny's instant ex-friend.

Sonny worked it out in the studio. Within 24 hours he wrote and recorded "Laugh at Me," a plea for tolerance and understanding of people who are "different." Released just by "Sonny," the song made a respectable #10 on the national charts in September 1965 and was covered by Mott the Hoople on their first album.[5]

---

[1] It's easy to understand why, in 1964, he sang with the stronger-voiced Cher: Sonny's whiny, nasal delivery (Sonny, incidentally, was a meat delivery man the day he was hired in 1957 as A&R man for Specialty Records) was not unlike the style of Bob Dylan, whose success opened the gates for legions of bad singers. It's harder to imagine what he was thinking prior to 1964,

when he made solo singles without the comforting model of Dylan.

[2] Like so many facets of "the '60s," bell-bottomed pants didn't become common in the general populace until the '70s.

[3] Younger readers may not realize that for long-haired men in 1965, the rest of the world seemed composed of crew-cut Marine sergeants who would verbally, or worse, physically attack you at will. Long hair for men did not become "normal" until the '70s. (Look at the hairstyles in the movie *Woodstock*; "freak" hair was still attention-getting in 1969.)

(See "Hair, a Song Subject," page 196.)

[4] Though Martoni's record industry customers were up to their eyeballs in a rock & roll-dominated business, they were personally more attuned to Sinatra and Sammy Davis Jr. (both of whom patronized the restaurant). Unlike today's record execs, who were raised on rock from the '50s, '60s and '70s and *secretly* hate today's music,[5] these guys didn't disguise their feelings.

[5] And the beat goes on.

An excellent Sonny Bono tribute album is the seldom-found *Bonograph: Sonny Gets His Share* (1991, Bogus Records, Box 42385, Pittsburgh, PA 15203), compiled by Ben Vaughn, featuring Sonny songs performed by musical admirers including Flat Duo Jets and Peter Holsapple. Not included on it, however, is the cover of "Laugh at Me" by the Skeletons (descendants of 1980 roots-rock favorites the Morells), in which the narrator complains of being spurned not for having long hair, but for having *no* hair. It's available on the Skeletons' until-recently unavailable *In the Flesh* album (Next Big Thing Records, Scotland), which is now on CD (East Side Digital ES80552).

"Layla" Co-Writer Jim Gordon Murders His Mother: Other Rock Nuts

Jim Gordon was one of the most active rock & roll session drummers in the business in the 1970s, playing on records by John Lennon, Jackson Browne, Leon Russell, Derek and the Dominos, Traffic, Frank Zappa, Delaney & Bonnie, Steely Dan and many others. And though he was a drummer, he played the distinctive piano riffs at the end of "Layla" by Derek and the Dominos. But as the '80s dawned, his workload fell as reports of his increasingly strange behavior spread throughout the music industry; he seemed to be carrying on a dialogue in his head that took precedence over the world around him.

On June 3, 1983, he'd heard "the voices" long enough and felt it was time to act: he beat his mother's head in with a hammer, then stabbed her with a knife.

Gordon, 38, was living with her at the time. Since his trial and conviction (he was diagnosed as an acute paranoid schizophrenic, but this did not deter a prison sentence), Gordon has been serving a 25-year stretch at the California Men's Colony[1] in San Luis Obispo, California, while quietly collecting royalties from "Layla," which he co-wrote, and other songs recorded by Traffic and George Harrison.

Rock & roll, like any field, has had its share of mental breakdowns. The most notable, though, were drug casualties:

• Pink Floyd founder Syd Barrett, whose songs led the band to its first popularity in England, overindulged in LSD. His behavior had become so erratic (once he supposedly emptied Nembutal capsules, mixed them with milk and poured them on his head before a show; other times he stood stone-still through gigs, watching his own private parade) ***that the group hired guitarist David Gilmour to sub for him*** onstage so Barrett could concentrate on songwriting (shades of Bruce Johnston replacing Brian Wilson on tour!). However, in 1968 he left the band, and after recording two solo albums he entered a mental hospital and never returned to active music making. ("Shine On You Crazy Diamond," on the 1975 Pink Floyd album *Wish You Were Here*, is dedicated to Barrett.)

• In Austin, Texas, 13th Floor Elevators founder Roky Erickson has had off and on (mostly on) mental difficulties since the band's 1966 semi-hit "You're Gonna Miss Me." (Drugs were involved, but it's hard to pinpoint the problem. Arrested with pot twice, in 1966 and 1968, he faced either a long jail term or a mental hospital and chose the latter, where, it is said, they medicated him into oblivion.) **Erickson's first book was a reissue in 1995 by Henry Rollins' 2.13.61 publishing company.** And in 1992 Warner Bros. exec and fellow

Texan Bill Bentley gathered together artists including R.E.M., ZZ Top, Jesus & Mary Chain and Julian Cope on a Roky Erickson/13th Floor Elevators tribute album, *Where the Pyramid Meets the Eye.*

• Skip Spence, a founder of Moby Grape,[2] has had mental problems stemming back 30 years. He's a diagnosed schizophrenic whose troubles probably were accelerated by drug use.

Any suggestion that these people unite in a supergroup called the Drooling Wilburys is cruel and unnecessary.

No discussion of rock & roll and mental illness is complete without mentioning the Cramps' June 16, 1978, concert at the chronic ward of Napa State Mental Hospital. How they booked it is a mystery, but the hard-core inmates responded off and on (with one man hugging Lux as he writhed on the floor screaming "Love me!"), and much of it was captured on a black-&-white video distributed by Target Video. That song, "Love Me," was originally done by the Phantom in 1957 on Dot Records. The Phantom, a bit of an oddball, too, drove his car off a cliff to see what would happen—and suffered paralysis as a result.

---

[1] The low-security facility from which Timothy Leary walked off in 1970, and which housed Ike Turner for a couple of years in the early 1990s.

[2] On the cover of their first album, that isn't Spence giving the finger to the camera. But maybe it was his idea to make one of the cuts on their second album, *Wow*, playable only at 78 rpm[3].

[3] For younger music fans, RPMs (revolutions per minute) measured the speed which "records," flat vinyl discs which, in conjunction with an electrified needle and amplification equipment, turned on a "turntable" to produce music much like today's. (Only better.)

Live Aid Unites Two Countries, and the World; Phil Collins Plays Same Show on Two Continents; "We Are the World" Precedes It

Live Aid, the transcontinental (London/Philadelphia) rock concert held on July 13, 1985, to aid the starving people of Ethiopia, was the biggest rock TV event of the '80s, linking people worldwide in an 18-hour concert featuring, in London, the Who, David Bowie, Queen, Paul McCartney, U2, Elvis Costello, Dire Straits, Elton John, Wham! and others, and, in Philadelphia, **Madonna,**[1] Prince, Tom Petty, Neil Young, the Cars, Rod Stewart, the Temptations, the

Beach Boys, the Pretenders, Bob Dylan, Lionel Richie, Mick Jagger, Tina Turner, Hall & Oates and more.[2] (Bob Dylan's comments about farmers at Live Aid prompted the founding of Farm Aid.)

Bob Geldof

Of special note, geographically speaking, was Phil Collins' presence at both shows. He played early in London, hopped a supersonic Concorde jet and played later in Philadelphia.

Organized by former Boomtown Rats leader Bob Geldof *(who later received an honorary knighthood for his efforts)*, the mammoth concert came a half year after Geldof's first rock-charity event for Ethiopia, **a 1984 all-star recording session of "Do They Know It's Christmas"** featuring the voices of Geldof, Sting, Duran Duran, Culture Club, the Eurythmics, Wham!, David Bowie, Paul McCartney, Phil Collins and more. That record, credited to Band-Aid, became the largest-selling record in English history and also sold a million and a half copies in the U.S. (with all proceeds going to Ethiopian relief). That inspired American promoter and manager Ken Kragen[3] to organize a similar event in Los Angeles. The recording of "We Are the World" took place on January 28th, 1985, and the song raised money for the newly formed USA for Africa fund. Featured artists included **Dan Aykroyd**, Lindsay Buckingham, Kim Carnes, *Ray Charles,* Bob Dylan, Sheila E, **Daryl Hall and John Oates**, James Ingram, the Jacksons, Al Jarreau, Waylon Jennings, Billy Joel, Cyndi Lauper, Huey Lewis & the News, Kenny Loggins, Bette Midler, Willie Nelson, Jeffrey Osborne, Steve Perry, the *Pointer Sisters,* Lionel Richie, Smokey Robinson, Kenny Rogers, Diana Ross, **Paul Simon**, Bruce Springsteen, Tina Turner, Dionne Warwick and **Stevie Wonder.**[4]

---

[1] In *Bill Graham Presents*, Graham says that Jimmy Page, Robert Plant and Eric Clapton were standing backstage at Philadelphia when Madonna's entourage soberly pushed through the crowd intoning, "Move, please, move, please." When one touched Clapton's arm and said, "Look out, Madonna's coming," Slowhand said, "You *must* be joking."

[2] Cat "It's OK by me if you kill Salman Rushdie" Stevens was on hand for this charity event but his performance was cut at the last minute because of time.

[3] His clients Lionel Richie and, especially, Kim Carnes were prominently featured in the lineup: client Kenny Rogers was more in the background.

[4] Singers John Denver and Harry Chapin, who had worked tirelessly for the cause of world hunger for many years, were ironically absent from this big-name hoo-ha: Chapin was dead, and Denver was not considered hip enough.

1979 Eleven Die at Who Concert

December 3, 1979, was probably the worst night in the history of rock & roll. Eleven young Who fans were trampled to death in a rush for the front of the stage when doors opened at River Front Coliseum in Cincinnati. Blame was placed on inadequate crowd control and insufficient access doors. *In addition, the concept of "festival seating" was brought into question.*

Festival seating was **pioneered by promoter Bill Graham in 1973.** It was a useful tool for promoters to shove 800 people into a venue that seated 500. In a business that constantly invents new ways to put their vacuum cleaner nozzle in fans' pockets, this title surely is the most cynical, for "festival seating" is what you get when you remove all the seats. (Another name for it, "jam in the suckers," was reportedly rejected.)

Surprisingly few people complained when this "idea" was first introduced. Kids wanted to see their rock & roll heroes, and they would **put up with whatever inconvenience promoters threw at them: ticket surcharges, increased parking fees, higher concession prices, exorbitantly priced T-shirts and programs.**

Though he wasn't the first to do it and probably didn't invent it, Bill Graham goes down in history for laying claim to this ugly and miserly concept. But to say it was responsible for the kids' deaths in Cincinnati would be unfair...

Another tragic death, although dissimilar, occurred in England in 1974, when a 14-year-old David Cassidy fan became overexcited and died of a heart attack at his concert at London's White City Stadium.

Dangerous Liaisons, Odd Couples, and "Mixed Marriages"

TOMMY LEE of Mötley Crüe married Pamela Anderson of TV's *Baywatch* in 1995. Previously he'd been married to Heather Locklear, now of *Melrose Place*, who is now married to RICHIE SAMBORA of Bon Jovi, who used to date CHER.

EDDIE VAN HALEN married Valerie Bertinelli of *One Day at a Time*.

MICHAEL JACKSON married Lisa Marie Presley, of inherited fame.

CHER married GREGG ALLMAN.

SONNY married CHER.

PATTI SMITH married FRED "SONIC" SMITH of the MC5 (and didn't have to change her last name!).

TINA WEYMOUTH of the Talking Heads married CHRIS FRANTZ of the Talking Heads.

MADONNA married Sean Penn.

LYLE LOVETT married Julia Roberts.

BRUCE SPRINGSTEEN married subsequently wealthy actress Julianne Phillips.

BELINDA CARLISLE married actor James Mason's son Morgan.

PETER WOLF of the J. Geils Band married Faye Dunaway.

NEIL YOUNG and actress Carrie Snodgress

JACK NITZSCHE and BUFFY SAINTE MARIE

LINDA RONSTADT and Albert Brooks

LINDA RONSTADT and director George Lucas

LINDA RONSTADT and former California Governor Jerry Brown

JACKSON BROWNE and Daryl Hannah

MICK JAGGER and Margaret Trudeau

RON WOOD and Margaret Trudeau

JONI MITCHELL and GRAHAM NASH (Joni's nickname for him, "Willie," is a Britishism for what Americans call a diminutive of Richard)

JONI MITCHELL and (fill in the blank with your own rock person from the '70s)

MAMA CASS ELLIOT and GRAHAM NASH, DAVE MASON

SLY STONE and DORIS DAY? (Just a rumor, but a delicious one)

WHITNEY HOUSTON and Jodie Foster? (Stop that! They've never met!)

If CHER married STEVE CROPPER she'd be CHER CROPPER.

ANDY WILLIAMS and CLAUDINE LONGET (Eek! A Spider!)

PAUL SIMON and Carrie Fisher

PAUL SIMON and EDIE BRICKELL

1982 US Festival, the '80s Woodstock, is Mixed Blessing

It's many a rock & roll fan's dream: If they had a million dollars, they'd throw a big party and hire their idols to play.

Steve Wozniak had such a dream, and he had the money. The co-founder of Apple Computers wasn't as much idol-driven as he was party-driven. He wanted a

good-vibe event that mixed the **world of rock & roll with** the forthcoming **world of computers,** so he secured a large tract of land 60 miles east of Los Angeles and threw a no-frills-barred rock festival that, rather than being a remake of Woodstock '69 turned out to be the blueprint for Woodstock '94. The result, the US Festival, was held on Labor Day weekend, 1982.

Wozniak poured money from his personal fortune (estimated to be in the hundreds of millions[1]) into first-class amenities and *first-class acts: Tom Petty and the Heartbreakers, the Kinks, the Cars, the Grateful Dead, Santana, Dave Edmunds, the English Beat,* Eddie Money, Jimmy Buffett, Oingo Boingo, Fleetwood Mac, Talking Heads, Jackson Browne, Jerry Jeff Walker, the Ramones, Gang of Four, Pat Benatar, Charlie Daniels, the B-52s and the Police. There was an elaborate stage setup, a huge video screen (broadcasting, besides the fest itself, a live performance by a band in Russia!), air-conditioned computer-display tents, security and parking. Everything was thought of and done right. So why, then, isn't it a landmark in rock history?

It was the '80s, man.

The thing that probably got the most attention was the acts jockeying for more and more money. When a guy with a pot of gold announces that he's sharing it, people sniff it like bankers at a corporate merger and try to grab all they can. And when the gold-dispensing involves Hollywood agents, well…have *you* ever heard of a favored-nations clause? **Big acts have them in their contracts for their egos**, to ensure that they're the *biggest* act in the world, the *most* admired entertainer on the planet and the *best*-loved person in the universe. They demand that they get paid the most possible to reassure them of their wonderfulness—it's a gesture, a salute, *not*, you know, money-lust. So as the date grew closer and Wozniak, whom everybody knew had unlimited resources, yearned for this act or that and paid top dollar for them, the other top acts thrust out their hands like bellhops and said, "Me too."

Other than some behind-the-scenes stuff, the festival went well. The worst factor was the weather. It was a pressure-cooker-hot day with dust to boot, which kept people crowded in computer-rep tents just for the air-conditioning, and which kept attendance a little under what was expected (**on a hot day in LA, local people don't head out toward the desert**). On the whole, though, it was a party many will never forget. Wozniak estimated that he lost $10 million on it, but he felt fine: It was his party, and his son—how did he arrange this?—was born there!

So, having done it once, he leaped into US Festival 2 for May 28, 29 and 30 1983. Bad idea. It wasn't quite Altamont, but it was **Wozniak's Altamont.** Once again it was heavy with stars, including David Bowie, Van Halen, Stevie Nicks, Johnny Cougar, the Pretenders, the Clash, the Stray Cats, Men at Work, the Divinyls, INXS, Wall of Voodoo, Flock of Seagulls, Oingo Boingo, the English Beat, Scorpions, Triumph, Judas Priest, Ozzy Osbourne, Joe Walsh and Mötley Crüe, and was followed by a country day a week later with Willie Nelson, Alabama, Waylon Jennings, Emmylou Harris, Hank Williams Jr., Ricky Skaggs and Riders in the Sky. *Nearly every one of them* held out for more money and got it. (Van Halen benefited nicely from David Bowie's half-nelson on the promoter. Bowie, who had to start his 1983 American tour somewhere, made them feel like he was greatly pained to do it *there*. He demanded, and got, $1.5 million, which automatically kicked Van Halen's fee up a half million to match.) The weather was again steaming *(New York's* Newsday *called it "Smogstock")*, the

amenities were again top-notch, but the vibes fell dramatically. For some reason **this US Festival generated 145 arrests, 120 major injuries and two deaths** (one OD, one beating), permanently retiring the earnest millionaire from rock-festival promoting.

[1] Asked about losing between $10 million and $15 million on the first US show, he said, "If I do this for another 55 years I'm in trouble!" Anyway, Apple stock rose $18 million that day, so the loss was offset.

Woodstock 1969[1] A Whole Lotta Mud

What really happened August 15-17, 1969, on Max Yasgur's farm near Bethel, New York, 60 miles from Woodstock, the fest's originally designated site? We've

Santana at the original scene of Woodstock, 1969.

seen the movie and heard the lore, but what was the significance of it?

The Woodstock rock festival was billed by the promoters as a **"gathering of the tribes"** at a time when the youth of America were at their most tribal. Love and peace and flower power were at their height, and rock festivals were in vogue, so these feelings and the tendency for these people to gather together were already firmly in place. Though the people who survived it talked about it (and talked about it and talked about it[2]) like it was the Harmonic Convergence, it was a big, messy[3] rock festival like a whole bunch of others that summer, this one featuring Jimi Hendrix, Jefferson Airplane, The Band, Sly and the Family Stone, Creedence

Clearwater Revival, the Who, the Grateful Dead, Janis Joplin, Santana, Joe Cocker, Alvin Lee, Canned Heat, Crosby, Stills & Nash, Country Joe & the Fish and others. (One might say that the biggest attraction was Bob Dylan, who was neither booked nor present. His living in the actual city of Woodstock lent an air of anticipation that he'd appear at the festival, a tangible factor in ticket sales.)

It was a biggie, no question, but prior to it, *that same summer*, there'd already been rock fests nearly as big in L.A., Denver, Atlanta, Seattle and Atlantic City, featuring various combinations of most of the groups that played Woodstock.[4]

So what was so special, then, about this particular gathering? **Why is it remembered over all the others? Four reasons:**

1. **It got overcrowded.**
2. **It was near New York City.**
3. **Someone made a movie about it.**
4. **Crosby Stills & Nash got a hit song out of it.**

First, the ads, the acts and the proximity to half the nation's population (or whatever it is the northeast quadrant possesses) drew an unanticipatedly large crowd estimated at 400,000 people. Ticket taking was stopped almost immediately, roads were clogged for 50 miles, food ran out, toilets were abandoned, babies were born, people OD'd and it rained a bunch. Some people took this to mean they were founding a "new nation." Except for the music, it wasn't much different than an avalanche or a train wreck or any other natural disaster where the Red Cross and the National Guard had to be called.

Second, its proximity to New York City, the nation's communications hub, meant that it—unlike, say, Newport '69 in Los Angeles in June (featuring Jimi Hendrix, Jethro Tull, Janis Joplin, Creedence, etc.) or the Atlanta Pop Festival on July 4 (with Joplin, Led Zeppelin,

Creedence, Delaney & Bonnie, Spirit, etc.)—was meaningful because the New York media caught on.[5]

Third, other festivals were filmed, but they weren't *overrun* by people, so their naked bathers didn't get immortalized to their lifelong humiliation.

Fourth, "Woodstock," the song written by Joni Mitchell (she wasn't there) was debuted the next night on the Dick Cavett show, to the delighted ears of David Crosby and Stephen Stills, who recorded it with Graham Nash, whom Mitchell was dating.

Suddenly, the press found it OK to talk about rock & roll and the youth culture with something like acceptance. So you could say the true effect of Woodstock was that it woke up the media to something that had already been going on for a long, long time.[6]

[1] It wasn't called "Woodstock 1969" any more than Hank Williams called himself Hank Williams Sr., as nobody knew at the time that a sequel would ensue. But does anyone remember Woodstock '70, featuring Procol Harum and others?

[2] It's no surprise that little humor emerged from this mock-profound event, unless you count the Who throwing Abbie Hoffman off the stage when he tried to politicize the moment. (Every performer who took a drink backstage was involuntarily dosed with LSD, prompting John Sebastian's famous "far out" monologue and Townshend's vicious fury in dispatching Hoffman.) However, "Woodstock," on the hard-to-find comedy album *Are You on Something?* (you'll recognize its cover take-off on *Bringing It All Back Home*) by Ray D'Ariano on Kama Sutra Records (KSBS 2072), neatly satirizes and summarizes the silliness of the event and the time. Also, many *Saturday Night Live* future stars made the Broadway show and album, *Lemmings*, about the same subject.

[3] Not everyone "dug" the mud and dung and chaos. Robbie Robertson of The Band remembers "a ripped army of mud people. We felt like a bunch of preacher boys looking into purgatory." Pete Townshend felt it was "a disgusting, despicable, hypocritical event." John Fogerty's eyes scanned the horizon for someone not dozing in mud and, finding one guy who was awake, played the whole set to him.

[4] But Melanie and Sha Na Na debuted there.

[5] CBS's 1994 look back at the original event showed tape of a 23-year-old Connie Chung covering Woodstock for CBS News. Though mod-dressed, she was just as stiff and remote as an older newscaster, so maybe TV news zombies are born, not made.

[6] But in their rush to enshrine their vision, they dubbed the age group the "Woodstock Generation," to most of that group's utter dismay.

WOODSTOCK (GREEDSTOCK) '94: WHOLE LOTTA MUD AGAIN

The 1994 staging of the 25th anniversary celebration at Winston Farm, **near Saugerties, New York (only 10 miles from the original Woodstock)**, was a success on many levels, including:

- 400,000 or so people showed up.
- Green Day and Nine Inch Nails became stars.
- The bathrooms worked for a while.
- OD came to mean "overdraft," as in the acres of credit-card booths and cash machines.[1]

Nobody chanted, no babies were born, but incense and tie-dyed T-shirt sales were plentiful as **the affluent but equally misguided[2] sons and daughters of the first Woodstock Festival attendees shook and shimmied** in the summer heat, egged on by a near-equal number of MTV cameras. (Friday, giant water hoses were employed to make mud; Saturday rain came on the natch.)

Musicians spanned the breach between 1969 and 1994: Bob Dylan, **Joe Cocker**, Crosby, Stills & Nash, the Allman Brothers, Melissa Etheridge, The Band (w/Bob Weir, Roger McGuinn and Hot Tuna), Mavis Staples, Ce Ce Peniston, Thelma Houston, *the Neville Brothers,* Jimmy Cliff, **Peter Gabriel,** Blind Melon, Salt-N-Pepa, Collective Soul, the Orb, Spin Doctors, Sheryl Crow, Aerosmith, Violent Femmes, Metallica, Cypress Hill, Porno for Pyros, Green Day, Jackyl, *Red Hot Chili Peppers* and Nine Inch Nails.

"Nuremstock" was another appellation for this funfest, which formally banned drugs, alcohol, *food, cameras and children*. Despite its up-front artificiality—trying to relive an actual moment in history—many people enjoyed the communality of the gathering. Musician

Marshall Crenshaw, who did not play but wandered down from his home in the real Woodstock, said he was surprised at the vibes and the fun of it.

[1] The '69 fete cost $18, but hardly anyone paid. This one cost $135, and about half paid (the 250,000 prepaid tickets were never collected). Special "Woodstock '94" scrip was issued in lieu of cash, probably in hopes people would take it home as a souvenir. (This same "scrip" trick is employed at Disneyland.) It is understandable, I guess, that the on-site capitalists grabbed at visitors' dollars so eagerly; they couldn't expect any future coin from *Woodstock '94: The Movie.* (In fact, such a film was planned, then shelved when Polygram stopped funding. Maybe in 2019 they'll release it for the 25th anniversary.) On this same tacky note, the Hard Rock Cafe in Las Vegas puts rock star faces on their poker chips and profits handsomely. When a casino visitor takes home a $25 Jimi Hendrix chip as a souvenir, the Hard Rock makes $24.50.

[2] Like the first congregation, this bunch celebrated *itself*, and, lacking the false notion that it meant something, reveled solely in their youth and affluence.

1986 Ozzy Osbourne Indicted for Causing a Suicide; Judas Priest Likewise

In 1986 hard-rock favorite Ozzy Osbourne was sued in California by the parents of 19-year-old John McCollum, who committed suicide on October 25, 1984, while listening to the song **"Suicide Solution"** on Osbourne's *Blizzard of Ozz* album. The boy's parents sued Osbourne and Epic Records for permitting suicide-friendly music to be made. Osbourne, who faced a legal hearing in U.S. courts (which rejected the validity of the charge), was extremely dismayed at the 180-degree-wrong interpretation of the song. **He says it was written in bitter irony about Bon Scott, lead singer of AC/DC,** who "drank himself to a slow, painful death" in 1980.[1]

That same year, 1986, English metal band Judas Priest was sued in Reno, Nevada, by the parents of two teenagers who attempted suicide while listening to "Better by You" (a cover of a Spooky Tooth tune!), a cut on Priest's *Stained Class* album. The parents claimed the song contained subliminal messages which, played backward, caused their sons to shoot themselves. After a month-long trial, the band was exonerated—vocalist Rob Halford called it "a very sobering experience"—but the trial's publicity gave momentary credence to a whole stratum of bent people who listened to records backward and found garbled revelations from the Devil,[2] and worse.

[1] Hmm. Scott died choking on vomit while in an intoxicated stupor, à la Jimi Hendrix and John Bonham.

[2] Typical of news coverage at the time, the *Newsline New York* show interviewed "expert" Wilson Bryan Key, who testified that messages in heavy-metal music led to violence. Key previously claimed to have found satanic or sexual messages on $5 bills, Howard Johnsons' place mats and Ritz crackers. Sometimes the Devil is listening, though. Richard Ramirez, the so-called Night Stalker, credited his inspiration to AC/DC songs.

 The Day the Music Died: Buddy, Ritchie And The Big Bopper Die in Frozen Iowa Cornfield

Ellis Amburn, in his book *Buddy Holly, A Biography* (St. Martin's, 1995), says that the 1959 deaths of Buddy Holly, Ritchie Valens and the Big Bopper (J.P. Richardson) in an **Iowa plane crash[1] were the most shocking deaths in the rock world until John Lennon's.**

Obviously, Amburn is no fan of Elvis, but the comparison is dead-on. What people felt on December 8, 1980, was the same thing others felt on February 3, 1959.[2] For you see, this was the first big rock & roll tragedy. Buddy Holly was a 22-year-old Texan who'd seen his song[3] "That'll Be The Day"[4] become a #1 record for his band, the Crickets. Several more hits, both by the Crickets and by Buddy solo, followed on the charts.[5] Ritchie Valens was a 17-year-old kid from a Chicano section of L.A. who was on the launching pad of a fabulous and versatile career, judging from the two singles, "Come on Let's Go" and **the double-sided hit "Donna"/"La Bamba," and the album, Ritchie Valens,** which were released before his death. His brush with fame had lasted less than a year. The Big Bopper had the novelty record "Chantilly Lace" riding the charts at the time of his death. The former Texas deejay had also just written and sung background on "Running Bear," which became a big hit for Johnny Preston in 1960, and wrote "White Lightning" for country singer George Jones.

All were tired and cold from a punishing midwinter Midwestern tour, and opted for a quick plane flight to the next town so as not to endure another night on their unheated bus. That plane took off in a white haze and nosed down moments later in a cornfield, scattering bodies like baby dolls. The crash was attributed to pilot error.

One big difference between 1959 and 1980 was that one of the dead guys was just 17—a teenager like his fans! Young Don McLean, 14, felt it, and kept his feelings pent up until 1970, when he wrote and recorded "American Pie," in which he laments "the day the music died."

At the time, rock & roll fans were too young to "get it together." **There were no candlelight vigils or**

televised weepings because the news media cared litttle about them. They were kid stars at best, fomenters of juvenile delinquency at worst. The death of three members of the *Howdy Doody* children's TV show[6] would have excited more interest because those people were in "real" show business. Rock & roll was marginal, noisy, foolish music to most people in America, a kid's fad that was expected to go away any minute.[7]

So kids internalized their grief, and faced life a little more soberly, gearing up, it turned out, for the next trauma, the death of another young rock star a year later. (See "Eddie Cochran Dies," page 117.)

[1] For many years, *everyone* on that winter tour seemed to claim that he was destined to fly on that death plane, but gave up his seat at the last minute. Today we know that country guitarist Tommy Allsup and neophyte Waylon Jennings (both were Crickets recruited for this tour) were the ones whose seats were usurped by Valens and Richardson on the fatal flight, which was initiated by Holly.

[2] Though many rock fans' lives spanned both traumas, few cared equally about both: If you were around for the first, you didn't care much about the second. And vice versa.

[3] The song was recorded twice, in 1956 by Holly on Decca, and a year later by the Crickets, with Holly singing lead, on Brunswick. All of Holly's first hits (the Nashville Decca recording flopped) were done under the aegis of Clovis, New Mexico, record producer Norman Petty, whose studio produced many hits ("Party Doll" by Buddy Knox and "Sugar Shack" by Jimmy Gilmer & the Fireballs among the notables). When "That'll Be the Day" was initially released, Holly was sole songwriter; when it was cut again, Petty's name was added. Because of this, and the fact that Holly was forced onto the fatal winter concert tour because his money was tied up in a dispute with Petty, Petty's legacy in rockdom is forever cloudy.

[4] The title was taken from John Wayne's repeated utterance in the film *The Searchers*. Just think of the impact on English music if Holly'd named his band the Searchers: the Beatles would be what?—the Scouting Party? the Investi-Gators? The Shoes? And those English guys who did "Needles & Pins" would have no name. The Hollies would still be the Hollies, though.

[5] It should be noted that Holly, a quick-thinking, entrepreneurial-minded young man, was preening himself for success at the time of his death. He had left his original backing band, the Crickets, and was off on a solo career led by the string-laden pop hit "It Doesn't Matter Anymore," written for him by Paul Anka. His loss was to the mainstream pop world; he had already left rock & roll.

[6] In a way, this had already happened. Elvis Presley's costar in the 1957 movie *Jailhouse Rock*, Judy Tyler, died in a car crash right after filming ended. Just a couple of years earlier, she had played Princess Summerfallwinterspring on the *Howdy Doody* show, and her death was reported with more weight than the rock stars'.

7 In fact, it wasn't going away, but it was in the throes of being coopted for the first time by television (MTV's arrival would be the second) by Dick Clark's *American Bandstand*. His hand at the helm ushered in a new generation of harmless, well-merchandised young entertainers who removed the stain of roughness, and the heartbeat of life, from rock & roll.

1960 Eddie Cochran Dies in London Taxi Crash

The death of Eddie Cochran on April 17, 1960, seemed to signal the death of rock & roll.

Cochran, like Buddy Holly before him,[1] was just past his teens and carrying the torch for rock & roll. That he, too, should meet a violent and untimely death was almost too much to bear for many rock & roll fans whose very *souls* hung in the balance.[2] It was as if a larger plot were afoot to squash them.[3] That death would take another genuine rocker instead of the Philadelphia hit squad or, say, Ferrante & Teicher, made it nearly unbearable.

Eddie Cochran's rock dominance began in 1958 with a record that is as good a definition of rock & roll as you could want: **"Summertime Blues."**[4] From the opening guitar/drum interplay, everyone recognized that this was an anthem for the young people of the world, as much a clarion call as "Rock Around the Clock." He followed it with "C'mon Everybody," the best second hit anyone with a great first hit ever had, and followed that with the brilliant, insidious "Something Else."[5]

In London in April 1960, his career and life literally skidded to a halt when the taxi carrying him, his girlfriend, songwriter Sharon Sheeley,[6] and his good friend and concert mate, Gene Vincent, skidded in the rain and crashed, killing Cochran and seriously injuring the other two.[7] The troupe was en route to Gatwick Airport outside London after a triumphant gladiatorlike concert tour of the United Kingdom—**where they were hailed,**

rightly, as American heroes, the last defenders of rock & roll—to catch a flight back home to Los Angeles.[8]

[1] One of Cochran's last recordings was "The Three Stars," a tribute to fallen comrades Holly, Valens and Richardson.

[2] For many youngsters at the crossroads of teenhood, rock & roll was the emotional glue that kept them together.

[3] A lot has been written and said about the upheavals of 1957-60. On one hand, rock & roll was being watered down naturally through the mechanics of the marketplace, with blandness attracting larger audiences. On the other hand, it seemed like a *plot* was afoot to silence the originators. In 1957 Elvis was drafted into the Army, and Little Richard quit rock & roll to join the ministry. In 1958 Jerry Lee Lewis was hounded from the airwaves for marrying his 13-year-old cousin. In 1959 Chuck Berry was arrested for Mann Act violations (and jailed from 1960 to 1962). Add Holly, Valens, Richardson and Cochran, and who does that leave? The leftovers, of course. If Oliver Stone wants to investigate a conspiracy…

[4] A song covered repeatedly in the years to come, including famous versions by Blue Cheer (1968) and the Who (on *Live at Leeds*, 1970), and a country hit for Alan Jackson.

[5] Of course, that his fourth hit was the string-laden "Hallelujah I Love Her So" belies this rock-solid theory. If he had lived he might've gone the route of Bobby Darin, turning to nightclub work, or moved toward fluffy teen hits like Johnny Burnette. But we can't know that, can we?

[6] She co-wrote "Poor Little Fool" for Ricky Nelson, "Dum Dum" for Brenda Lee and "Somethin' Else" for Cochran.

[7] Before the crash, Vincent wore a metal brace on his left leg, which was nearly crushed in a motorcycle accident in 1956. The London taxi crash exacerbated that leg problem to the point where he had to take drugs and alcohol to ward off the constant pain. (Although doctors suggested amputation more than once, Vincent declined.) So it could be said that his death, too, from a ruptured stomach ulcer in 1971, was a delayed result of the crash.

[8] Cochran is buried in Forest Lawn Cemetery in Cypress, south of Los Angeles. Non-rocker Karen Carpenter is interred in a nearby crypt.

1967 Keith Moon's Stage Explosion Prank Partly Deafens Pete Townshend: Antics Persist Until His Death

The Who were veteran stage performers and hit-makers in their native England and were trying like mad to transfer that excitement to the U.S. when they made their second American tour in the summer of 1967.

Champions of a mod movement that found little truck with the flower power that was sweeping the country, their wild performing style—which ***included mandatory amp and guitar destruction at every performance***—helped supply an alternative for kids who weren't buying the love generation thing. In June 1967 they made an impressive showing at Monterey (see "Hendrix Sets Fire to Guitar," page 180), and in July were booked on the antiestablishment *Smothers Brothers Comedy Hour*, taped in L.A.

Tommy Smothers had seen the band at Monterey and invited them to make their American TV debut on the brothers' TV show. They were to lip-synch their imminent American hit, "I Can See for Miles," and mime to a live recording they made of "My Generation," after which drummer Keith Moon was to detonate a small packet of explosives in his drum kit. At rehearsals, the band played **at excessive volume,** which bothered the technical people, and their planned explosion set temperatures rising with their insurance carrier. But Smothers pushed it through.

Moon, however, thought it would be fun to increase the explosive load without telling anyone, so he tricked several technicians into adding gunpowder to the pack—without telling any of them someone else had already done it.

The band lip-synched their first song without a hitch. Smothers, resetting Moon's fallen cymbal, said "Here's the sloppy drummer over here." Moon's tart response about "sloppy stage hands" sounded a little harsh, befitting the seeming culture gap between the wild rockers and the two clean-cut guys, but that was part of the deal: The brash newcomers would act up, and the clean-cut hosts would act upset.[1] After the band mimed "My Generation," Moon stepped gingerly away and set off the blast.

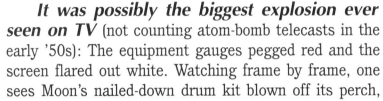

It was possibly the biggest explosion ever seen on TV (not counting atom-bomb telecasts in the early '50s): The equipment gauges pegged red and the screen flared out white. Watching frame by frame, one sees Moon's nailed-down drum kit blown off its perch, and Moon himself rocketed back off the drum riser. Poor Pete Townshend, doing his guitar-smash finale, takes the full force of the explosion. **The blast burned and flattened his hair against his head**. Years later, he credited the near-deafness in his right ear to this blast.

Keith Moon was a loon who lived life at a pace that almost compelled him to die young. In fact, when he "excessed himself" to death in 1978 (overimbibing an anti-alcoholism drug), he left behind a legacy of wreckage and disturbance:

• In Jackson, Mississippi, he put cherry bombs in the toilet at a hotel, causing commode destruction. The whole band had to leave town.

• Checking out of another hotel, the road manager was presented with a bill for a $600 phone call. He went to Moon's room, where he found him asleep with a phone in his hand still connected to London.

• In New York he threw cherry bombs out his hotel window, **causing the SWAT team to burst his door down** and seize him. (However, the cops recognized him and **let him go after he signed autographs.**)

• On August 23, 1967, the Who's party in the Holiday Inn ballroom in Flint, Michigan, got so out of hand the cops came (when party-goers had already, among other things, ruined the ballroom's carpet with marzipan cake, trashed a piano to kindling and turned fire-extinguishers upon the cars in the parking lot). Moon hid in an open Lincoln Continental. Crouching on the floor, he let the emergency brake go, and the car rolled slowly but surely into the swimming pool. Returning to the party, he saw a sheriff and tried to run away but slipped on a piece of cake and broke his front tooth. (Hotel damages during that stay exceeded $75,000, and the **Who were banned from all Holiday Inns for life.)**

• Moving to Malibu, California, he frequently paraded around the beach in a Nazi uniform.

• In 1976 he accidentally killed his chauffeur by backing his car over him while fleeing fans.

[1] Looks can be deceiving. In the late 1960s revolution was in the air, and the *Smothers Brothers'* show was the most radical on national television. They joked about dope and aired criticism of the Vietnam War and many other taboo subjects. And the Beatles chose them to debut their "video" of "Hey Jude," as Donovan did with "Atlantis." The Smothers Brothers were finally hounded off the airwaves in 1969 by their network, CBS, who had grown tired of defending them. It is high irony that when they decided to make a comeback performance at L.A.'s Troubadour club in 1974, five years after their noble TV effort failed, John Lennon and Harry Nilsson, drunk as lords, hooted them and disrupted their show. (See "Lennon Ejected from Troubadour—Twice," page 216.)

1995 R.E.M.'s "Surgery Tour"

R.E.M.'s 1995 concert tour was plagued by medical breakdowns: Three of its four members (Peter Buck escaped) suffered health crises during the tour, all of which led to surgery.

First, on March 1, onstage in Lausanne, Switzerland, drummer Bill Berry[1] got such a severe headache that he had to leave in the middle of the show. The opening act's drummer took his place.[2] Berry got no better as the night progressed and was rushed to a hospital, where he underwent brain surgery to fix not one, but two ruptured blood vessels.

This type of surgery often leads to death or mental impairment, but fortunately for Berry, he had his aneurysms near one of the most advanced brain surgery centers in the world.

Within six weeks he was better, and the band's tour resumed, opening May 15 at the Shoreline Amphitheater in Mountain View, California. A few weeks later they were in Cologne, Germany, trying to salvage some of their European tour, when bassist Mike Mills became gravely ill and had to be operated on for an adhesion in his abdominal tract caused by scar tissue from a 1994 appendectomy, which had caused a portion of his intestine to grow onto the wall of his stomach. Several more dates were canceled.

Once the Europe tour resumed, lead singer Michael Stipe was felled by a hernia, which necessitated his flying back to Atlanta for surgery. No concert dates were missed, but some songs with high notes were scrapped, as Stipe couldn't hit them without pain.

Guitarist Peter Buck commented he was definitely looking both ways every time he crossed the street.

[1] Perhaps Berry should not tour. In Munich, at the start of the band's 1989-90 *Green* tour, he developed Rocky Mountain spotted fever (not *Alpine* spotted fever?).

[2] He was good, but not as good as teenager Scott Halpin's shot as the Who's drummer during the band's 1973 San Francisco appearance. Halpin was pulled

out of the audience because Keith Moon was unable to finish the set (due to ingestion of booze and elephant tranquilizer), and the kid drummed excellently on the remaining four songs in the set (including an unreleased song, "Naked Eye," yet!).

1976 Jerry Lee Lewis Waves Gun Outside Graceland Demanding Elvis Come Out: Trouble Follows "the Killer"

Jerry Lee Lewis has embodied the spirit of rock & roll ever since his first national appearance on July 12, 1957, on Steve Allen's Sunday night variety show. During that H-bomb appearance, the young cat from Ferriday, Louisiana, **rocked America with the most fervent, hyped up, piano-pounding, mike-strangling performance ever seen on TV, before or since**. (Little Richard's shows were equal but never televised.) His subsequent behavior through marriages, divorces, drugs, deaths and headlines, have **marked him as the man, the big one, the rock & roller by which all others are measured.**

That might've been what *he* was thinking the night of November 23, 1976, when he drove to the home of fellow Memphian[1] Elvis Presley and demanded Elvis come out and see him, waving a Derringer pistol at the guard to back up his request. Elvis did not come out, and Lewis went home.

He had a lot to think about. The previous September 29 he had been shooting holes in his office door when bass player Norman Owens wandered into range and was shot in the chest. Owens recovered, then sued Lewis. And the night before the Graceland incident, Lewis drove his Rolls-Royce into a ditch while driving drunk. And over a 10-year period, several of his wives died.

[1] Actually Lewis' home was across the state line, in Mississippi, south of Graceland.

"Savage Young Beatles" Kick Out Drummer; and Some Other Defections

To this day, nobody's talking about the Beatles' decision on August 16, 1962, to remove drummer Pete Best and replace him with Ringo Starr.

The explanation given is simple: When they were first signed to Parlophone[1] Records, their producer George Martin said their drummer was inadequate and insisted they use a professional drummer for recordings. So it's obvious the "villain" was George Martin, who forced the young lads to abandon their longtime pal.[2]

But everyone knows the haste with which the Beatles acted. "You don't like our drummer? We'll sack him" was apparently the first thing out of their mouths. Perhaps more forces were at work than simply drums.

The Beatles with Motown boss Berry Gordy—and the mop-topped beatnik Ringo at bottom.

To look at those early pics, one cannot help but notice their looks: **The baby-faced Paul, triangle-faced George and long-faced John are nice-looking enough but lean toward "interesting."** Best, with his dark hair slicked back, looks better. And it's been said—by Pete— that Pete got all the girls, and that's why the Beatles fired him.[3]

Now look at who replaced him. Was it a Mel Gibson look-alike? A Fabian kinda fella? No, it was a big-nosed beatnik, Ringo Starr.

Best was bereft. Abandoned by his friends (?), he formed a few bands, releasing, among other things, a version of "Boys" that sounded quite like Ringo doing the Beatles version. For years—and we mean years, say, thirty—Best stewed in bitterness in Liverpool. At one point he released an album of early band tapes entitled *The Savage Young Beatles*.[4] His fortunes never improved markedly **until the 1995 release of the *Beatles Anthology*,** which contained many early Beatle recordings that he played on, including "the Decca sessions"[5] and the original version of "Love Me Do" (which had prompted producer Martin to request another drummer[6]; session man Alan White played on the released version). The multi-million-selling performance of that anthology yielded Best an astonishing $18 million in 1996.

Best left the band not at its height, but as the glimmer of success was on the horizon. Other musicians have voluntarily left successful bands to succeed as solo artists, and many have failed, including Tony Williams of the Platters, Peter Tork of the Monkees, David Lee Roth of Van Halen (ultimately) and, if you get right down to it, Mick Jagger of the Rolling Stones.

[1] Parlophone was EMI's spoken-word and comedy label; hence "Parlo," as in parlance, "to speak." An unpredictable result was that producer George Martin got on famously with the boys: They enjoyed the "Goon Shows" and other albums he'd produced, and he enjoyed their humor.

[2] The early '60s were times of political activism, and angry Best fans were no exception. They picketed record stores and Beatles concerts to protest the canning of their man.

[3] Though the source of the "I'm so sexy" explanation is Pete (and in 1995 rock fans finally got to evaluate Best's drumming on "Love Me Do" on the *Beatles Anthology*, and most found it wanting), this is not at all out of line among big British rock bands of the time. The "sixth Rolling Stone," stout, homely Ian Stewart, played piano on most of their records but was relegated to background work because he was physically unappealing.

[4] So well known among record collectors that early Rhino band Mogen David & the Winos patterned their debut album cover after it and appropriated the title on their *Savage Young Winos* album.

[5] The Beatles auditioned for Decca (not connected to Decca of America; its U.S. label was London Records) on January 1, 1962, and were turned down by A&R man Dick Rowe. Though his name is as infamous as Wrong-Way Corrigan's is in aviation history, it should be noted that he subsequently signed the Rolling Stones.

[6] All right, so maybe he was a bad drummer and was dragging the band. They didn't pick Ringo Starr for his proboscis, but because he was the best drummer in Liverpool, playing with Rory Storm & the Hurricanes, previously Liverpool's most successful band.

1969 "Paul is Dead" Hoax Sweeps the World

Word that Paul McCartney was dead spread like wildfire in the fall of 1969. Clues that led fans to believe he had expired in 1966 and had been replaced by a look-alike suddenly began cropping up everywhere, and many fans around the world began to mourn his passing.

In late 1969 he held a press conference to say he was indeed alive. When some skeptics still demurred, *he simply fled to his Scotland home and watched with astonishment as the world continued to debate his existence.*

The phenomenon got its first print exposure in the *Michigan Daily*, the newspaper of the University of Michigan, in the fall of 1969. Student Fred LaBour, an aspiring journalist, had the plum assignment of reviewing the new Beatles album, *Abbey Road*. The night before writing it he tuned in to Detroit disc jockey Russ Gibb's[1] show and listened to a caller tell of some strange things he had heard on the Beatles' previous releases.

"This guy was saying that if you played part of 'Revolution #9' backward, they were saying, 'Turn me on, dead man,' and that in 'I Am the Walrus' (or was it in 'Strawberry Fields Forever'?) you could hear **'I buried Paul,'** and that it all meant that Paul was dead,"[2] says LaBour. "I was astonished at the craziness of this, so the next day I led off the review with those and a bunch of other observations I made up. It was a satire on seeing things that aren't there,[3] but people took it seriously."

Seriously indeed. Detroit papers picked up his "report," and it quickly spread to Chicago, then to New York. Soon LaBour was besieged with interviews ("I prefaced them all with things like 'Sure it's all true, I made it up myself,' but they weren't always listening") and finding clues to Paul's alleged death replaced Scrabble as the world's parlor game.

Many of the clues[4] came from LaBour, such as:

• On the Sgt. Pepper album cover, the band is standing on a grave...Paul's (?); flowers outline a left-handed Hofner bass, Paul's instrument; on the inside cover, the letters on the patch he wears, O.P.D., stand for Officially Pronounced Dead (actually, the patch was a souvenir from Canada, from the Ontario Police Department).

• In "Glass Onion" on *The Beatles*, (aka the *White Album*) John sings, "Here's another clue for you all, the walrus is Paul," so LaBour said that walrus was Greek for "corpse." (A clue in itself, as it is easily checkable nonsense.)

• On the *Abbey Road* cover, Paul is barefoot (the way people are buried) and is out of step with the others; George then must be the grave digger, Lennon the priest and Ringo the undertaker. Right?

- On the *Magical Mystery Tour* cover, three Beatles wear red carnations, symbolizing life, while Paul wears a black one, indicating death.

LaBour stopped doing interviews after a while because things were getting too crazy. "People were calling me up crying," he recalls. "You've got to be careful what you write because people are liable to believe you."

The controversy died down when the band itself died a few months later, on the Apple Records rooftop in London.

LaBour went on to write songs in Nashville, ultimately landing where he is today, known as Too Slim in the band Riders in the Sky.

---

[1] "Uncle Russ" Gibb was a popular Detroit deejay on WKNR-FM who co-owned the Grande Ballroom, Detroit's most popular late '60s venue, and was a big muckety-muck promoter à la Bill Graham for a time. The day after the call, Russ opened the phone lines to push the "story," adding fuel to the fire.

[2] So LaBour wasn't the originator of the hoax; it was actually the unidentified paranoiac who called the radio station. LaBour, then, was the popularizer, or as they say in psychobabble, the enabler.

[3] These were pretty crazy times, and not like in the Gene Vincent song of the same name. Around that same time, an asteroid or lightning bolt or big scary monster was supposed to strike the world, and the only safe haven was reported to be a hilltop outside of Boulder, Colorado, which consequently became overrun with pilgrims. Although this kind of Apocalypse Tomorrow thinking was not new—similar waves swept the U.S. in the 1840s, when the idea of "ascension robes" (proper attire for ascending to heaven) entered the lexicon—but it was the first example of a mass delusion spurred *by electronic media*, unless you count the previous

year's presidential election.

[4] For a list of 25 signs that Paul is dead, see Dave Marsh's *Book of Rock Lists*.

Fuck and Other Four-Letter Words[1]

Listed below are some of the controversial appearances—and mirages—of the word "fuck" in rock history. (We're omitting punk rock and rap songs because, you know, we only have so much space.)

• "Woman Love" was the flip side of "Be Bop a Lula," the big Gene Vincent & the Blue Caps hit of 1956. Extremely echoey and sung extremely hiccupy, the phrase **"huggin' and a kissin'"** could be construed as **"fuckin' and a kissin"** if you wanted it to be, and many kids did. The record was banned widely. (In the late 1960s, Vincent told rockabilly producer Rockin' Ronny Weiser, "I said it, I said 'fuckin'' on that record," but there is no reason to believe him. As Nick Lowe said on the *Party of One* album, "All men are liars.")

• "Louie Louie's" "real" lyrics, which is to say the false ones, include the passage, "Every night at ten, I lay her again, I fuck a girl all kinds of ways."

• Jefferson Airplane's *Volunteers* album contained a much-played revolutionary song, "We Can Be Together," which contained the line "up against the wall, motherfuckers." When the band performed the song on the Dick Cavett Show, they left in that line, slurring it slightly.

• In the late 1960s, every show by the "revolutionary" **Detroit band the MC5 included the cry "Kick out the jams, motherfuckers."** *Kick Out the Jams* was in fact the title of their first Elektra album in 1970, and although singles were pressed with "brothers & sisters" substituted for you-know-what (the publisher says there's a limit on the number of times we can say fuck in this book), albums included the offending compound-word, at least until parents complained and it was excised.

• Doug Fieger of the Knack says that one night his father, lawyer Bernie Fieger, was asked by the managers of Detroit's Grande Ballroom to distract a police lieutenant, who was present to arrest the MC5 when they said "fuck" during their set. Supposedly the band itself had called the police, in order to be arrested, *but the ballroom's owners feared their hall would be shut down.*[2]

• Country Joe & The Fish,[3] the Berkeley-based '60s band, recorded "The Fish Cheer" on their first album, in which the band, and presumably the audience, spelled out F-I-S-H. Substitute three other letters for I-S-H, and you've got what they chanted at concerts (most famously at Woodstock).

• Jim Morrison, in "The End," can clearly be heard screaming, "fuck fuck fuck kill kill kill" to Admiral Morrison and the missus.

• John Lennon in "Working Class Hero" says, "'til you're so fucking crazy you can't follow their rules."

• **In the Who's "Who Are You," they ask specifically, "who the fuck are you?"**

• In 1972 the Grateful Dead insisted their live album be called *Skullfuck*. When Warner Bros. objected that no large retail chain would stock that title, the band said, "Sell 'em somewhere else." Ultimately, the band relented, and the album went out as *Live Dead*.

▪ **In rare copies of one Village People song, they sing, "You can fuck your buddy at the YMCA..."**[4]

• The late '70s British band King Brilliant's name was a shortening of the common Brit expression "fucking brilliant."

• The Knack's "Baby Talks Dirty" says, "no fucka, no fucka me today."

[1] A little rock-literary joke, if ever the two can be connected: Critic Richard Goldstein wrote an early rock & roll book called *Rock and Other Four-Letter Words*.

[2] Fieger's brother, lawyer Geoff Fieger, represents Dr. Jack Kevorkian and Mitch Ryder.

[3] Leader Joe McDonald was a Navy veteran who grew up in El Monte, California. The Fish was not his group, but his partner Barry "Fish" Melton, now a San Francisco attorney. Some other rockers-turned-lawyers are Elliot Cahn from Sha Na Na, now practicing in San Francisco; Jackie Fuchs, once Jackie Fox of the Runaways, now specializing in intellectual property in Los Angeles; lawyering in Houston, Al Staehely, once of Spirit, and Manny Caiti, ex-bassist for the Del-Lords and Joan Jett.

[4] I worked at Casablanca and heard the line through a partition wall. Maybe it was recorded but not issued on a record…

Teenage Randy Wolfe Plays with Hendrix, Forms Spirit

L.A. teenager Randy Wolfe was trying out a guitar in a Greenwich Village music store in 1966 when a black musician, Jimmy James, asked him to join his band. Wolfe said yes, and he played with Jimmy James & the Blue Flames for several months until James decided to go to England. The underage Wolfe, now called Randy California (there were two Randys in the band; the other was Randy Texas), was too young to go with him. Returning to L.A. in the summer of 1967, he formed the band Spirit with John Locke, Jay Ferguson, Mark Andes and Ed Cassidy, his bald, 44-year-old drummer stepfather.[1]

One day at the band's house in L.A.'s Topanga Canyon, resident Barry Hansen, not yet but soon to become **Dr. Demento, showed Wolfe the debut Jimi Hendrix album from England.** Randy cried out, "I know this guy! I played with him in New York!"

Spirit went on to become a top-selling act, first in Los Angeles and then worldwide[2] with the memorable songs "I Got a Line on You" and "Fresh Garbage." They still continue with original members California and Cassidy.[3]

[1] Cassidy is a rock rarity who entered the field when he was already "old." Raised in Bakersfield, California, Cassidy drummed first with big bands and country-western outfits, and in the '50s with jazz greats Thelonious Monk, Art Pepper, Cannonball Adderley and Gerry Mulligan before hooking up with Spirit. Just before joining Spirit he was in a combo with keyboardist Ray Manzarek. Mrs. Wolfe and Cassidy have since divorced.

[2] Lost to history is the fact that L.A. sported four big acts in 1967-70: Steppenwolf, Spirit, Love, and the Doors. Alas, only the latter is, you know, worshiped. I think it was the trousers.

[3] Original members Ferguson (singer) and Andes (bass) went off to form Jo Jo Gunne in 1972 and had a hit, "Run Run Run." In 1976 Andes joined Firefall, which had several hits, including "You Are the Woman" (#9, August 1976), and in 1980 joined Heart. Ferguson had a solo hit, "Thunder Island," in 1977 and now works in television as a music producer. All the original members have been known to participate in Spirit reunion shows.

Led Zeppelin Summarized

Since it is daunting to select one Led Zep story from the lot of them (we have omitted the famous fish-in-the-girl story for reasons of taste[1]), let us just reproduce the index listings for John (Bonzo) Bonham from Richard Cole's book *Stairway to Heaven* (HarperCollins, 1992):

- **alcohol and drug use by**
  —*blackouts and disorientation*
  —*heroin*
- **automobile accident**
- **background of**
- **cars, and**
- **death of**
- **as drummer**
- **financial matters**
- **fishing at Edgewater Inn (Seattle)**
- **formation of Led Zeppelin**
- **funeral for**
- **girls, and**

—at Copenhagen sex club
—handcuffing episode
- **mischief and pranks**
  —Alvin Lee, incident involving
  —bugging of technicians' bedrooms
  —Chuck Berry, incident involving
  —Copenhagen art gallery incident
  —demolishing his hotel suite
  —Edgewater Inn (Seattle) incident, 1970
  —George Harrison incident
  —Grant's son, incident involving
  —gun-pointing incident
  —Jeff Beck, incident involving
  —kicking dents into Rolls-Royce
  —motorcycle incident in Auckland
  —pissing in his pants
  —restaurant incident involving Dublin
  —shitting incidents
  —shitting-in-shoe incidents
  —staged "séance"
  —throwing hotel refrigerator into the ocean
  —throwing television sets out of hotel window
  —urinating on a disc jockey in Tokyo
  —Volkswagen incident in Iceland

To fill in the blanks, get Cole's book; he was their tour manager for 12 years.

---

[1] For the record, according to Cole it was the girl's idea. Frank Zappa—crediting it to Vanilla Fudge, some of whose members, in fact, were there —immortalized it in the song "Mudshark."

1960 Elvis Comes Through for Roy "Good Rockin'" Brown

It was 1960, and Roy "Good Rockin'" Brown's glory

days were over.

The writer of "Good Rockin' Tonight" (he recorded it first, then Wynonie Harris had the bigger hit), Roy was one of the greatest stars in R&B from about 1947 to 1952. He toured America in a fleet of Cadillacs, playing sold-out clubs and theaters till the bottom fell out of his market; younger cats came up with doo-wop and vocal group sounds that rendered his church-derived wailing[1] out of date. By 1957 he was struggling to get by, **wasting his talent on "black covers" of rockabilly** (his version of Buddy Knox's "Party Doll" was OK, but a waste of his soulful voice: It was like having Rembrandt paint your barn). By 1960 his past caught up with him in the form of the IRS, who told him if he didn't come up with a large amount of money, he was going to prison.

"I was in Memphis, and I heard that Elvis Presley was having a party," said Brown, who died in 1981. "Elvis used to come see my shows when I played there in the early '50s, one of those white kids who snuck in to see what we were doing. Well, they let me into the party, and I told him my story. You know, I never made any real money from 'Good Rockin' Tonight'—it didn't sell that many copies in the '40s, and afterward I sold all the rights—*so Elvis said, 'I'll help you, Roy Brown,'* and he wrote out a check for $1,500 on a paper bag. That check was good as gold. **When you took a paper bag signed by Elvis Presley to a bank in Memphis, they cashed it!**"

Sadly, it wasn't enough to rescue Roy from the jaws of the IRS, and he served a little jail time. He floundered during the 1960s and 1970s, finding work where he could (he sold door-to-door and always made the sale when women recognized him from his salad days) and recording sporadically. In the late '70s he was rediscovered by U.S. and European enthusiasts and was back performing in top voice until he died of a heart attack on May 25, 1981.[2]

[1] If you want to know where Jackie Wilson got his singing style, check out the Rhino CD compilation, *Roy Brown*, *Good Rockin' Tonight*.

[2] Lubbock/Austin, Texas, country-rocker Joe Ely, who had seen Brown for the first time and planned to play a show with him, was devastated by his death and wrote a song, "Let's Rock It One Time for Roy, Boys" about him.

Mellow Yellow: Rock Fans Go Bananas

Don't feel too envious if you missed the 1960s; they were often incredibly stupid.

When Donovan, the Scottish troubadour-turned-flower-power-guru, made his second psychedelic album, *Mellow Yellow*, the title cut spurred a fad almost too ridiculous to retell.

Because the song said, "Electrical banana, gonna be a sudden craze, electrical banana, gonna be the very next phase," someone at the *Berkeley Barb* (an underground newspaper) wrote (sarcastically? probably) that banana skins contained a powerful hallucinogen. The story was reprinted in the *L.A. Free Press* and was scattered around the world.

The summer of 1967, otherwise remembered as the Summer of Love might be better remembered as the

Summer of Banana Smoking. People all over the world dried out the linings of banana skins and smoked them. Though the psychedelic content was nil, some people still insisted they were getting high (though maybe only in high-altitude climates, where breathing deeply makes you dizzy).

By that fall, banana sales returned to normal, and hash pipes were filled again with hash. **Somebody asked Donovan what "electrical banana" meant, and he replied it was a vibrator—imagine if that** had been the very next craze. (The group Steely Dan might've formed earlier: Their name is taken from a steam-powered dildo in William Burroughs' book *Naked Lunch*.)

The five-year ban on banana mentions was broken in 1972 with Paul McCartney cryptically singing, "Gonna do ya gonna do ya sweet banana" on "Hi, Hi, Hi."

1984 Money Doesn't Swear, It Talks: Michael Jackson's Lacquered Hair Catches Fire and Other Advertising Fables

In 1984 Michael Jackson's features were in a state of flux, but his skin color stayed cocoa brown and his hair shiny black.

The reason for his hair's sheen was the generous application of Jheri Curl gel that created a very popular look among show business people.

At a taping of a TV commercial for Pepsi at the Shrine Auditorium in L.A., an advertising agency stylist added flammable hair spray to Jackson's cosmetic goo pile and nearly prompted the first rock-star immolation. Somehow, no one really quite knows how, the hair spray ignited, and his hair burned like a candlewick soaked in gasoline. Aides doused the fire within a minute, but not before his scalp and neck sustained second-degree burns.[1]

What's noteworthy lately is **Corporate America's rush to embrace music heroes**. Jackson, a little odd if you believe the tabloids (talking to monkeys, staring into newborn babies' eyes), was paid **$5 million to grasp[2] a can of Pepsi** whenever he made a promotional appearance. (At that same time Pepsi paid Lionel Richie the same amount for a series of endorsements, but his career fell steeply right afterward and the ads never materialized.) By the late '80s, new groups and singers were lining up to endorse virtually anything, *as TV replaced music (thank you, MTV)* as musicians' main source of communication: If you didn't have a video, you were stone cold dead in the market. (Madonna, in 1989, became the first Pepsi rep to be dropped after one showing: Her Pepsi ad, done in conjunction with her steamy sexual/religious "Like a Prayer" video, ruffled the feathers of Pepsi execs, who feared losing Catholic consumers. Madonna bagged the $5 million and went home.)

But if one is to slag, say, En Vogue for racing to endorse Coke or Hertz or Hartz Mountain Birdseed, one must remember the first spurt of rock & roll endorsements back in 1966, when bands rushed to fill their pockets with advertising dollars. (Prior to then there were no, say, Bobby Vee product endorsements, the exceptions being Elvis' 1956 print ads for RCA,[3] Chubby Checker's Thom McAn ads for "twist shoes," Bobby Darin's Atco 45 for "Tanfastic" and Little Richard's oft-bootlegged radio testimonial for Royal Crown Hair Dressing.)[4] Coke had fickle Ray Charles (who switched to Pepsi in the '90s), the Supremes, Jay & the Americans, Jan & Dean and others,[5] but the *shocking* ad was the supposedly revolution-spouting Jefferson Airplane's one for white Levi's.[6] And let us not forget Tina Turner's ads for Pearl Drops tooth polish, and the Who's[7] and the Yardbirds' radio ads for Great Shakes!

The 1972 *National Lampoon Radio Dinner* album (Banana/Blue Thumb BTS-38) contained the cut "Those Fabulous Sixties," which was a mock ad for a "'60s greatest hits" package with "Bob Dylan" drawling, "Remember the '60s? These tunes can be yours." The humor (it sounded preposterous then but eerily real today) was that it was unimaginable, absolutely beyond the realm of possibility, that Bob Dylan would do an ad or let one of his songs be used in one. **Of course, ultimately Dylan loaned "The Times They Are a-Changin'" to a brokerage house.** Furthermore, Janis Joplin's caustic "Oh Lord, Won't You Buy Me a Mercedes-Benz," a barb at wealthy people, was used for a Mercedes-Benz ad, and Michael Jackson—he opened this entry—licensed the Beatles' "Revolution" to Nike shoes.

Maybe the times aren't a-changin' after all.

---

[1] Compare this hair-blast with Keith Moon overloading stage explosives (see "Keith Moon Stage Explosion Prank," page 118) on the Smothers Brothers TV show.

[2] That's 5 mil for *grasping*: As a Jehovah's Witness, he could not drink it!

[3] Also memorable, in the sense that it makes you cringe, is Elvis' intro to the 1956 RCA promotional EP "Perfect for Parties," where he sounds like there's a gun to his head when he says, "Here's a really swinging collection of college songs."

[4] The BBC in England bans product mentions in songs (but if they banned plugs in movies, they'd never show one made after 1970), so the Kinks had to replace the words "Coca-Cola" with "cherry cola" in the 1970 hit "Lola," George Hamilton IV had to change his 1957 song "Rose and a Baby Ruth" to "Rose and a Candy Bar," and Paul Simon's 1973 "Kodachrome" was simply unairable.

[5] Including Roy Orbison, Nancy Sinatra, Sandy Posey, the Troggs, Lulu, the Left Banke, Lesley Gore, the Everly Brothers, Vanilla Fudge, Freddy Cannon, the Bee Gees, Los Bravos, Gary Lewis, Neil Diamond, Tom Jones, Petula Clark and Moody Blues.

[6] The Fugs, the Greenwich Village sort-of equivalent to the Mothers of Invention,

would send up the band in their shows, posing the vexing question "Do they *come* in their white Levi's?"

[7] The Who parodied advertising on *The Who Sell Out*; the album cover featured Roger Daltrey in a tub of baked beans. (Ann-Margret got the bath o' beans treatment in *Tommy*, the movie.) Their advertising cynicism was mild compared to the Pet Shop Boys; in *Magic Christian* spirit, they sold advertising space on one of their albums.

Rumor Mill: You Heard 'Em Here Last

- In the '60s, Little Richard married James Brown.
- Rod Stewart had to have his stomach pumped after a romantic encounter with members of a sports club.

- The lead singer of a popular late '70s English-American band was "Rumoured" in the 1980s to have hired a companion to travel with her for **the sole function of blowing cocaine up her ass.**

- The girl screaming on the Ohio Players' "Love Rollercoaster" is actually being murdered.

- Brenda Lee (when she was age 11 in 1956) was actually a 35-year-old midget. (U.K. rumor. She sued the writer and won.)

- The hand claps on "Instant Karma" are John Lennon slapping Yoko Ono's tits.

- The finale to "All I Want to Do" on the Beach Boys' *20/20* album contains the sounds of Dennis Wilson fucking a hooker. (Supposedly true.)

- *The scream at the end of the Doors' "The End" is Morrison's sexual climax.*

- The reason the Transamerica pyramid is on the cover of the Doobie Brothers *Livin' on the Fault Line* album is that they bought the building.

- Lionel Richie sorta dropped out of sight in the mid-1980s after his wife beat him up.

Lynyrd Skynyrd Blasts Neil Young's "Southern Man" in "Sweet Home Alabama"; and Some Other Answer Songs

There's a long, rich history of "answer songs" in rock & roll, but the second song usually mentioned the first in the title:

hit: "Will You Still Love Me Tomorrow"
answer: "Yes, I Will Love You Tomorrow"
hit: "(Who Wants to Buy) This Diamond Ring?"
answer: "(Gary Please Don't Sell) My Diamond Ring"
And on and on.

But the Lynyrd Skynyrd/Neil Young thing is a whole 'nother matter. Young recorded two slaps at Dixie, "Alabama" and "Southern Man" which were out of date when they were released. In an era when the Vietnam War towered over everything, jabs at the South's supposedly unique racism rang a little naive; by then, most liberals knew that **racism lurked throughout the land, not just down South.** (Young, of course, was a chronic Northerner: You don't get much more north than Canada, whence he hailed, and he's lived the past quarter century in Northern California, don't ya know.) But it was a liberal era in music, and the preceding decade of Dylan and peace marching and integration was still being felt, but not by everyone, especially the guys in L y n y r d Skynyrd, who were so provoked by Young's South-baiting that they recorded "Sweet Home Alabama" specifically in response: the line "Well I hope Neil Young will remember/ Southern man don't need him around anyhow."

Ultimately, this turned out to be a Jack Benny-Fred Allen-type feud, because after "Sweet Home Alabama," lead singer Ronnie Van Zant wore a Neil Young T-shirt onstage, and Young submitted songs to Skynyrd.

It's unusual for one band or singer to name another. More often, it's a singer mentioning himself, like the Killer singing, "If you don't like Jerry Lee's peaches, don't mess around on his tree," or Bo Diddley inserting his name into every song he wrote. (Actually, he's inserting Bo Diddley's name, a mythical character; his real name is Ellas McDaniel né Bates.) Randy Newman recounts a meeting (imaginary?) with Bruce Springsteen in the song "My Life Is Good" on his *Trouble in Paradise* album, and Hugo & Luigi name everyone *but* rockabilly singers (Tab and Tommy, Pearl Bailey) on their rare and worthless 1957 single "Rockabilly Party."

In 1963 there was a cross-country rivalry between, if you can believe it, two groups with falsetto singers, the Four Seasons and the Beach Boys. A refrain at the end of "Surfers Rule," on the Beach Boys' *Surfer Girl* album, chants, "Four Seasons better believe it" over and over. That the Valli boys later recorded "No Surfin' Today," about a dead surfer, on their *Born to Wander* album could just be coincidence.

A far less-known artist-bashing record was the Guess Who's 1973 single "Glamour Boy." The Canadian band, led by Burton Cummings, were **somewhat miffed at being on the same label with David Bowie, whose ambi-sexual image** was a mirror image—a funhouse mirror, I mean—of their down-to-earth style. To strike back, they cut "Glamour Boy," about a guy who'd do anything to make an impression. The ballad asserted sweetly, "You're on top for a while, with your million-dollar smile" but ended, just as nicely, "You've had your fill, now it's all downhill." In the middle they introduced the glam band Ricky and the Balloons and chanted, "For $29,000 you can dress like your sister tonight" (each verse escalating the price) and then warned record buyers, "You gotta take care, 'cause there's not many there, who want to take time and sing and play an honest song for the people tonight."

It made no dent, either on the charts or on Bowie, but the trade-paper ad that showed their portly manager bare-chested in tights was actually better than the record—and that's saying something.

We could comment here on the Beatles bashing each other, but that's, you know, family stuff.

1969 The Band's First Show: Delayed by Stage Fright?

The Band's drummer and vocalist Levon Helm's excellent book, *This Wheel's on Fire*, is a **delightful, informative and sometimes acidic**[1] **history** of both his group and American rock & roll.

The five musicians, Arkansan Helm and Canadians Garth Hudson, Richard Manuel, Rick Danko and Robbie Robertson, cut their musical teeth backing up Arkansas rocker Ronnie Hawkins in the late '50s and early '60s. Helm's provides an invaluable firsthand view of that music and the scene that surrounded it, documenting not only the crazy highs but also the lows when, in 1960, the world seemed to turn its back on real rock & roll.[2] Eventually they departed from Hawkins to become Levon & the Hawks, the Crackers and, briefly, the incredibly uncatchy Canadian Squires. They were playing in Greenwich Village in 1965 when Bob Dylan, whom they had never heard of, asked Robertson and Helm to join his touring band. They toured with him through 1966 (at least until Levon quit, tired of being booed every night[3]) (see "Dylan Booed at Newport," page 170). In 1966 Dylan, recuperating from a motorcycle accident (see "Dylan Injured in Motorcycle Accident," page 53), asked the whole band to join him in Woodstock, New York. Their musical collaboration yielded first the widely bootlegged (officially released in 1975) *Basement Tapes* and, in 1968,

The Band's debut album, Music from Big Pink, which turned the music world on its ear with "This Wheel's on Fire," "I Shall Be Released," "Tears of Rage" (Dylan collaborations from the basement sessions), and "The Weight," the latter of which was credited solely to Robbie Robertson.[4] Following this auspicious debut, they scheduled their world debut performance for April 17, 18 and 19, 1969, at Winterland in San Francisco.

The pressure was on for that show, Helm says. The Band's music was heralded as not just good but mythic, important, earth-shaking. They enjoyed this praise, but after more than 10 years of playing together they were perplexed by its magnitude. So much, according to Helm, that Robbie Robertson was felled by what some called a psychosomatic fever: In other words, **he was scared to death to face the world's expectations.**[5]

That night, Robertson, ill with a high fever, was so immobilized he could not move from his hotel room. The Winterland audience endured extended sets by the Ace of Cups and the Sons of Champlin and an hour and a half wait through silence before The Band took the stage. Through the encouragement of his bandmates, an itinerant hypnotist and their truculent manager Albert Grossman, Robertson arose from his sickbed and managed a 35-minute set, which, "nostalgically" for Robertson and Helm, ended in boos for its brevity. Their next set, two nights later, was fine, and likewise their subsequent career—it was just a shaky start.

Their second album, *The Band*, was already in the can, but their third one was titled *Stage Fright*.[6]

---

[1] Helm's bitter attacks on Robbie Robertson make fascinating reading. He is furious that Robertson gets sole credit for many songs The Band co-wrote in the studio and is apoplectic about Robertson's grandiose 1976 announcement that his retirement meant the end of The Band; the other members weren't asked. He also gleefully points out that Robertson's mike was off for several songs in *The Last Waltz*—because Helm thought Robertson was a horrible singer and had it discon-

nected! (Helm has been known to disavow his more rancorous statements, but in 1994 he refused to appear at the Band's induction in the Rock & Roll Hall of Fame because he did not want to share the stage with Robertson.) A similar songwriting rift has long divided the Animals. "House of the Rising Sun," their first hit, was a public-domain song credited as "arranged by" keyboardist Alan Price, resulting in his getting the royalty money. The other four Animals still bristle with anger that the money wasn't shared with them. "The manager told us they couldn't put all our names on it, so we should credit it to Alan alone and he'd split it," says lead singer Eric Burdon, "Like hell he did."

[2] This theory correlates with your author's view that rock & roll died in 1959. Others pin it at 1967. Many believe it was dead by 1981, its last breaths stomped and sold by MTV.

[3] A similar situation happened to Steve Jones of the Sex Pistols, who was thrust into a fractious sociopolitical situation when he really just wanted to make music and have fun. But then again, if you're going to play punk rock, knowing that the audience will spit on you somehow *should* be considered part of the fun.

[4] Helm points out in his book that this song's numerous cryptic references were just, you know, words. The idea of "going down to Nazareth," which was widely interpreted to have biblical weight, was about Nazareth, Pennsylvania, home of the Martin Guitar factory, and the names in the song were just actual and made-up names of people they knew.

[5] This did not inspire the song "Chest Fever;" it was already recorded.

[6] In his book, Helm refers to this album as The Band's recorded apogee, and says its follow-up, *Cahoots*, was far inferior. This was news to *Cahoots* fans.

Bon Jovi's Career Begins with Strippers; Same for Other Rockers

In *Rock Lives* (Henry Holt, 1990), writer Timothy White reports that Jon Bon Jovi's band unwound in a Vancouver striptease joint during the recording of *Slippery When Wet*. The young musicians loved this type of entertainment (Tico and Alec of the original band had played in strip bars) and, if stories are to be believed, **frequently went home with the performers.**

Striptease clubs figure here and there in rock history:

• Carlos Santana began his musical career playing in striptease clubs in Tijuana. "We played for one hour and the prostitutes undressed for an hour. We got an education from them."

• The true-life subject of Jan and Arnie's first big hit, "Jennie Lee," was a stripper in downtown Los Angeles. An ad for her performance is included in the Jan & Dean

Anthology Album issued in 1971 on United Artists Records. (On *The Little Old Lady from Pasadena* album cover, Dean Torrence wears a sweatshirt saying "Eat at the Blue Fox," one of Tijuana's most notorious strip joints.)

• Little Richard's best woman-friend and sometimes sexual helpmate (See "Little Richard Forms a Sex Train," page 176) Angel was a professional ecdysiast (look it up).

• The Coasters had a big hit with the Leiber & Stoller song "Little Egypt," about a stripper. Elvis recorded it too. **Reportedly, Elvis was deeply interested in one stripper:** In her biography, stripper Tempest Storm said he climbed a wall to get into her hotel room and make love to her.

• The party to commemorate Van Halen's first gold record was held at the Body Shoppe, a Sunset Strip striptease club. (Their then-manager Marshal Berle got his Uncle Miltie to get up and toss off a few one-liners, including custom-tailored record industry jokes.)

• Sources report that the Beatles worked with strippers in Liverpool.

• Jim Morrison used to hang out a lot at the Phone Booth, a striptease club at La Cienega and Santa Monica in West Hollywood.[1]

• Wendy O. Williams of the Plasmatics was a stripper.

• The Red Hot Chili Peppers debuted their "socks-on-cocks" fashion statement at the Kit Kat Club, a Hollywood strip place, to compete with the strippers. (Mötley Crüe got their gold record here in 1984.)

• Momentary country **heartthrob Billy Ray Cyrus may have been a male stripper in a former life.**

• L.A.'s prestigious Roxy Theater is a former striptease club, the Largo. The Ivar theater in Hollywood, where Lord Buckley concertized and the

Grateful Dead played February 25, 1966, became a strip club later.

•Supposedly, Courtney Love was a stripper pre-Kurt, pre-Hole.

[1] For much more detailed information about L.A. rock & roll sites, read my book *The L.A. Musical History Tour* (Faber & Faber, 1991).

1984 Cyndi Lauper's "She Bop" Is First Out-and-Out Masturbation Hit

When Cyndi Lauper, who burst on the music scene in late 1983, sang "Girls Just Want to Have Fun," she didn't say *how*.

That didn't happen until her third hit in mid-1984, "She Bop." Asked if the song **referred to female masturbation, she allowed it did**, but times being what they were, it didn't cause a *serious* outcry (though it got on the nerves of the Parents' Music Resource Center and some religious groups) and didn't have a detrimental effect on her career. Her subsequent records slipped a bit, but in 1986 she returned to the top of the charts with "True Colors" and "Change of Heart."

Around 10 years ago, masturbatory artists seemed to crop up everywhere. Madonna, Prince (in "Darling Nikki," masturbating with a magazine), Michael Jackson ("Beat It") and many others—the Divinyls "I Touch Myself," virtually the anthem of the movement, and the Vapors' 1980 hit, "Turning Japanese," is known to be onanistic. But we can't examine *all* toss-off tunes because they're too numerous.

Songs about sex in any era were not unusual; songs not about sex, or romance, were rarer. Two by Frank Sinatra, for example, mentioned sexual functions not too subtly: *a spent male's lament, "Softly As I Leave You,"* and a resigned view of female sexual apparatus, "The Tender Trap." Fats Waller made it clear what he was after when he sang, *"I want some seafood, mama," in the song "Hold Tight"(!)* but the message was less clear (or perhaps more, this was World War II, and few men were around) when it was successfully covered by the Andrews Sisters.

In the rock era, songs touched on male genitalia ("The Happy Organ"), female equipment ("The Honeydripper"[1]) and both when Joe Turner[2] sang in "Shake, Rattle & Roll," "I'm like a one-eyed cat peeping in a seafood store!"

Cyndi Lauper

And on Pablo Cruise's 1978 hit "Love Will Find a Way," the chorus "It's all right once you get past the pain" was a variation on an old saying about a sexual act—name your own—"it's all right once you get past the smell."

Masturbation, per se, was never confronted in rock of the 1950s, unless you count Johnny Otis' "Willie and the

Hand Jive" or Gene Vincent's **"Who Slapped John?"** in which everyone pairs off except John, who's left "holding his own." The Who's "Pictures of Lily" in 1967 was the first to address it directly: There was no double meaning, those pictures got the boy aroused so he could…you know. The Who also did **"Mary Anne with the Shaky Hands,"** but I'm not sure if using someone else's hand still qualifies as masturbation. Ref? (While I tried admirably to stay out of this fray, Webster's secondary definition does include "stimulation, by manual or other means exclusive of coitus, of *another's* genitals."—Ed.)

The next year, in the song "A Simple Desultory Phillipic," on the Simon & Garfunkel *Parsley, Sage, Rosemary & Thyme* album, Paul Simon asides, "Well, that's the hand you use, oh, never mind." (We now know Simon is left-handed, at least in regard to *that*.)

Joel Selvin of the *San Francisco Chronicle* likes to point to "Rattle Snake Shake" by Fleetwood Mac as the *ne plus ultra* of wanking[3] songs. And Cub Koda of Brownsville Station insists we mention his band's "Self Abuse."

Aretha Franklin (who, you'll remember, sang ardently about riding on "the freeway of love, in a pink Cadillac…") got in on "the act," or so it seems, in the 1980s when she sang with Annie Lennox about sisters "doing it for themselves," with some emphasis on "ringing their own bell."

---

[1] There are rock historians so pie-eyed they think this compound noun, used first by Joe Liggins & His Honeydrippers on their hit of the same name, then usurped by Robert Plant's 1984 jump band, referred to male genitalia. This cannot be, for the simple reason that no male in the history of sexual bragging has boasted that his organ *drips*.

[2] Bill Haley's version, the bigger pop hit, omitted the Turner version's references to "one-eyed cats," "seafood stores," "you wear those dresses the sun comes shining through" and, after summarizing his woman's attributes, "I can't believe my eyes, all this mess belongs to you."

[3] British for masturbating.

George Michael Sues His Record Company, Stops Making Records for Years

In a move not meant to endear him to his or any other record company, George Michael sued Sony Corporation in London in 1992 to be released from his eight-album contract, **contending that the company was unsympathetic to musicians in general,** and to George Michael in particular.[1]

Michael had signed originally to Columbia Records, a division of CBS Inc., but the company sold its record division to Sony in 1987. In his suit, Michael maintained that the new owners had hired new administrators, in both America and England, who danced to a different tune. He felt he was treated more like an electronic component than an artist.

A 1995 *New York Times* article[2] reported his breaking point was in October 1991, when Sony Entertainment

president Tommy Mottola and Columbia Records president Don Ienner left Michael's performance in Toronto, Ontario, before its conclusion. (Some people with less than $5 million in the bank might view this as petty, but then we're not privy to pressures at the top.)

In 1994 Michael's petition for separation was denied by the high court in London. No Sony albums by Michael were issued in the 1990s. In 1995 he signed with the new Dreamworks SKG label for a reported $12 million, with Dreamworks forking over $40 million to Sony for his contract.[3]

Disaffected artists have tried to break contracts before. In 1990 Don Henley tried to get released from Geffen Records when, after a long hiatus from recording, he felt he no longer knew anyone there and felt no sympathy from the new employees. In the mid-1970s, John Fogerty sacrificed his Creedence Clearwater song publishing rights to secure a release from Fantasy Records. (See "John Fogerty Sued," page 189.) And English rocker Graham Parker had bad words about *his* former label, Mercury Records, when he switched to Arista and released a record called "Mercury Poisoning." And, as often happens with him, **things were different for Neil Young: His record label, Geffen, sued him,** saying that the records he delivered didn't satisfy their contract because "they weren't Neil Young records!"[4]

Finally, probably the most eloquent statement of dissatisfaction with a record company was Inger Lorre's in the early 1990s. Unhappy that her band, the Nymphs, had not been allowed to play live for two years and that a record producer was pulled off their album to mix a Guns N' Roses album, *she stood atop a Geffen Records executive's desk, hiked her skirt up and urinated,* invoking each band member's name as she tossed flower petals into the stream. She concluded with, "Don't ever piss on my fucking band again." (Which explains why the Geffen Nymphs album is hard to find.)

[1] Record companies the world over trembled with fear that their indentured servants might be permitted to leave if their careers or lives were being mishandled.

[2] Richard W. Stevenson, "Long Detour in Search of Respect," *New York Times*, December 24, 1995.

[3] The times are a-changin': This time an American firm paid a fortune to purchase talent from a Japanese-owned firm.

[4] Specifically, they complained that on *Everybody's Rockin'*, *Old Ways*, *Landing on Water* and *Life* he didn't sound like himself. The first, a collection of rockabilly tunes, sure didn't. In concerts during that album's release, he would do a set of Neil Young songs, then come back out as the '50s band Neil and the Shocking Pinks to do songs off the new album. Audience members with less than 20/20 eyesight would scream "Bring back Neil Young," thinking another band had invaded the show.

Vince Neil Car Crash Kills Hanoi Rocks: Band Dies with Drummer Razzle

In 1984 the Finnish band Hanoi Rocks was poised to conquer America. **Their combination of glam-rock and punk**—hailed by many for expanding the genre pioneered by New York Dolls—had stormed Europe, and their debut American tour promised to be equally monumental.

Unfortunately, it came to a sudden halt when Hanoi Rocks drummer Razzle was killed in the crash of a car driven by Mötley Crüe's flamboyant, and at the time drunk, lead singer Vince Neil.[1] It happened in Hermosa Beach, California. After successful East Coast shows, the band flew out to L.A. ahead of their scheduled dates to relax, meet record company people and prepare for their premiere West Coast concert, a concert that never took place.

Hanoi Rocks could not recover. They were **knocked off their toboggan just as it was picking up speed,** and never got back on. They tried a substitute drummer for a while, but, heartsick, they eventually broke up. Sadly, this confirmed their oneness as a band: When one member was lost, the whole band was lost.

Car crashes[2] have claimed many rock musicians, but few have had so permanent and disastrous an effect on a band as this one.[3]

Probably the best known career-damaging car crash in rock & roll was Carl Perkins' in 1956. Perkins was the man Sun Records owner Sam Phillips dumped Elvis Presley to promote; Phillips felt his song "Blue Suede Shoes" would make him the world's next big rock star, and in fact **upon its release the song rocketed up the charts past Elvis' "Heartbreak Hotel"!** But in March, 1956, Perkins and his band were en route to New York for his first big TV appearance, on the *Perry Como Show,* when their car hit a truck: The driver was killed, and Perkins and his brother Jay were injured. *Supposedly* that night, instead of singing "Blue Suede Shoes" on network TV, Perkins lay in a hospital bed and saw Elvis Presley sing it on the *Milton Berle Show*, sealing his fate.

Though disturbing enough, the truth wasn't quite that dramatic. Perkins knew that ex-Sun stablemate Presley had recorded his song for RCA Records several months earlier. And Presley had already sung it twice before on national TV, on the Dorsey Brothers' variety show. And Perkins' crash was a week before Elvis' TV appearance.

The skinny, balding, *earnest Perkins never had a chance of unseating Elvis anyway,* as he's quick to tell you.

---

[1] Neil was convicted of vehicular manslaughter and served 20 days in jail. When pressed for $2.6 million in damages, he coughed it up and did 200 hours of community service.

[2] Car-crash songs soared in the late '50s and early '60s and constitute one of the few genres not (yet) compiled by Rhino Records. At the lead are "Tell Laura I Love

Her" by Ray Peterson and "Teen Angel" by Mark Dinning.

[3] Which is not to minimize, say, the crash that disabled singer Teddy Pendergrass in 1982. We're talking about a band breaking up because of the death of one member in a car wreck. Metallica lost member Cliff Burton in a tour-bus crash in 1986, but the band carried on; Duane Allman's death in 1971 did not break up the Allman Brothers Band; even the loss of two members of For Squirrels did not end the band.

1985 David Lee Roth Quits Van Halen, Band's Popularity Soars; Other Groups Who Got More Popular When Lead Singer Left

In 1985 David Lee Roth's departure from Van Halen sent shock waves through the hard-rock community and the record industry (Van Halen's label, anyway). After all, wasn't **Roth their frontman? The guy who sang all the songs?** The focus of the band?

All true, but everything worked out. In a move paralleled only once in rock history, an existing popular band drafted an independently popular singer to front them[1]— in Van Halen's case, Sammy Hagar, whose career, first with Montrose and then with his own Sammy Hagar Band (his signature hit, "I Can't Drive 55," was just the previous year), was solid and on a steady climb.

Van Halen with Sammy Hagar

As a result of their pairing, Hagar and Van Halen's popularity soared. And now, it appears David Lee is back. Go figure.

It's normal, when a frontman leaves a band, that the frontman gets a hit or a career, and the rest of the band fades into obscurity. There are so many it would be pointless to name just a few. But sometimes, just sometimes, it works the other way around:

the frontman leaves a popular band,[2] and the band gets bigger:

• Jay Traynor sang lead on "She Cried," by Jay and the Americans in 1962. Traynor left to make solo records and was replaced by Jay Black, with whom they had more and larger hits.

• Blood, Sweat & Tears founder Al Kooper departed after their first album, and the band became enormous with Canadian singer David Clayton Thomas.

• Peter Gabriel left Genesis in 1975, embarking on a successful solo career. Lead-singing responsibilities **fell to the drummer, Phil Collins,** whose voice led the group to massive popularity and unimagined success.

• When David Ruffin left the Temptations in 1968, they were momentarily thrown into disarray—in some quarters, given up for dead, so fundamental was Ruffin's voice to the group's sound—but shortly afterward Eddie Kendricks, Dennis Edwards and others led them to wider popularity with the more modern-styled (Sly Stone-styled, actually) sounds of "Cloud Nine," "Papa Was a Rollin' Stone," "Don't Let the Joneses (Get You Down)" and "Ball of Confusion."[3]

• Jefferson Airplane really took off after their singer, Signe Anderson, left, *and Grace Slick came in.*

• Pink Floyd became popular after Syd Barrett retired due to mental problems.

• The Moody Blues hit big after Denny "Go Now" Laine departed.

• Fairport Convention got bigger when singer Judy Dyble left and Sandy Denny replaced her.

• Slightly differently, The Drifters got bigger after the entire band was fired and replaced by the 5 Crowns, featuring Benjamin (Ben E.) King.

• And, gulp, the Beach Boys scored their first #1 hit since 1966, "Kokomo," in 1988, without founder Brian Wilson.

• (The Hollies got their biggest U.S. hit when

Graham Nash left, but he wasn't lead singer.)

And finally, what do the bands Van Halen, Manfred Mann, the J. Geils Band, the Spencer Davis Group and the Dave Clark Five have in common? (Answer: The lead singers aren't the person the band is named after.)

Rod Stewart (in feather boa) and Small Faces

[1] The other was Rod Stewart joining the Small Faces in 1970. After he replaced the departing Steve Marriott, they gained the worldwide fame that had eluded them.

[2] Many unknown bands succeed when they get a new singer, but that's not what we're talking about here.

[3] As ominous and foreboding a song as you could ask for: With David Ruffin gone, the group's beautiful and stirring harmony was replaced by what sounded like newspaper headlines shouted over chaos. Not so much a complaint as an observation; the new sound accurately reflected the bleak, frightening timbre of the time.

1969 Altamont Becomes the Anti-Woodstock: Stones Concert Features Death, Confusion

The Rolling Stones decided to give a free concert at the end of their 1969 cross-country tour to "give a little something back" to their fans.[1] The locale was to be San Francisco, a burg still **reverberating with hippie-nirvana vibes.** What they got was a free rock festival whose salient features—brutality, disorganization and death—marked the literal and symbolic end of the '60s.

At the start of their tour, the Stones announced their intention to do a free show December 6, 1969, in San Francisco's Golden Gate Park, local solons hit the roof. The Grateful Dead organization (yeah, I know, an oxymoron back then) took the reins and found the Sears Point Raceway 50 miles northeast of San Francisco. However, Filmways Corporation owned the site and demanded it be let in on any filming done on the premises. Jagger & Co. had already hired their own film company so the deal, including three weeks' construction at Sears Point, disintegrated two days before the show. A replacement site was secured in Altamont, 50 miles south of San Francisco. *Stages set up 100 miles to the north at Sear's Point were ripped apart, helicoptered down* and reset up the day before the concert.

The day's acts were to include the Jefferson Airplane, Santana, the Flying Burrito Brothers, the Grateful Dead[2] and the Stones. While the Airplane was

Jefferson Airplane

performing, the **Hell's Angels, who were hired to maintain security, began pummeling people in the audience.** Airplane lead singer **Marty Balin was so incensed** at what he viewed at stage front (and onstage: Motorcycle toughs were chasing people across the stage while the show was on) that he first yelled at them, then dove in to aid a man being beaten. The Angels beat Balin unconscious. By the time the Stones arrived, it was like a prison free-for-all, with the Hell's Angels beating people willy-nilly. The Stones took the stage and tried to complete a set, but the security forces were so brutal that Jagger had to stop several times to try and calm the situation. It didn't work.

Then came the incident the festival is famous for. An 18-year-old guy, Meredith Hunter, ran toward the stage brandishing a gun, or what seems to be a gun in slow-motion playback (the place was crawling with movie cameras[3]). Supposedly his last words were something about not wanting to hurt anyone, just wanting to show the Rolling Stones his gun…He was stabbed and beaten to death by the Angels.

The **nightmarish movie *Gimme Shelter* documents the pre-show wrangling, showtime horror and post-show bewilderment.** It's bleak, bleak, bleak and frustrating: You know what's coming and you want to stop it, then you see it unfold and you're sick over your inability to do anything, and then you see the outcome and you wonder why it happened and what it was all about.

To say Altamont reflected the times would be true.

The Vietnam War was raging, drugs were turning people grim and more ugliness was just around the corner. In fact, it was the beginning of the end. The corridor between the nightmare at Altamont and the killings at Kent State and Jackson State[4] (1970) *marked the*

Group of hippies settling in for a weekend festival of music in St. Helens, Oregon in 1969. Altamont, Kent State and other events turned an ideological page and made this peaceful scene nearly obsolete.

end of the hippie/youth/whatever-you-call-it culture.
It was kicked, stabbed and shot to death.

[1] In a way, this whole disaster put the lie to the idea that the rock press has never accomplished anything. Rock writers 'round the land lambasted the Rolling Stones for making too much money on their 1969 tour—remember "the music belongs to the people"?—and that pressured them to give this ill-planned and ultimately tragic concert.

[2] Though this was a Dead-led concert, the band did not appear there after word of the disastrous doings reached them.

[3] The Maysles Brothers film company shot the show from many vantage points. Filmmaker George Lucas, a cameraman on this shoot, said that there was a pall in the air, that from the start it felt like something terrible was going to happen....

[4] On both of these college campuses, students were killed during war protests. The incidents spurred Crosby, Stills, Nash & Young to write the bitter song "Ohio," which was recorded and released within a week of the Kent State massacre.

M-M-M-M-M-M... Music Mistakes and Memorable Music Moments in Movies

This subject is highly subjective: People like and notice different things.

The most frequent mistake mentioned is wrong record labels in films. They're wrong so often that wrongness seems to be the norm (art directors and continuity people are never, alas, record collectors), so I'm loath to mention two for omitting a thousand.

Another area is time-period inconsistencies, like

when a movie set in 1967 includes a song from 1970. I have become tolerant of such things after music-supervising a TV show. I discovered that some time shifts were acceptable; for example, "Woolly Bully," 1965, would have fit nicely in *Animal House*, set in 1962, because **it felt like a 1962 song**. What's wrong is *inappropriateness:* Jimi Hendrix music in 1965; Punk-rock in 1973; Disco anytime.

Mistakes, I Know I've made a few:
- In the 1981 movie *The Postman Always Rings Twice*, set in 1948, someone plays a 78 record, which is right, but the phonograph arm has a 45/78 flip switch not even invented in 1948.
- In the American film version of *Breathless*, starring Richard Gere, the central character is obsessed with the Jerry Lee Lewis song of that name and plays it over and over. However, the tune played is a Mercury/Smash rerecording. **Imagine how crazed he would have been if he'd heard the Sun recording!** (Director Jim McBride continued his obsession with the Killer with the 1989 fantasy/bio pic *Great Balls of Fire*. A good way to start an argument in a room full of rock fans is to say you liked this film, which was great.)
- In *Animal House*, the dean's wife has a picture of Elvis on her night stand. Irrespective of the logic of an educator's wife having such a thing in 1962, the picture is from Elvis' comeback period in 1969.
- In *The Buddy Holly Story*, Gary Busey inverts the lyrics to several songs, as when he reverses the first and second lines of "Maybe Baby." Rock-book author[1] *Marshall Crenshaw says he went crazy watching Busey play a 1974 Fender Telecaster throughout the movie* and switch to a '70s Stratocaster at the end.[2] Holly was the popularizer of the quite pre-1974 Stratocaster. Fellow sufferer (and Crenshaw friend)

Peter Holsapple likewise shuddered seeing '70s silver-face Music Man amps altered to resemble early '60s (!!) models.

Great music moments on screen:
• The Yardbirds smash instruments during the song "Stroll On" in the 1966 film *Blow Up*; director Michelangelo Antonioni originally wanted the Who.
He happened to catch the Yardbirds at a point when both Jeff Beck and Jimmy Page were in the band.

• For some reason, in a late scene in *Who's Afraid of Virginia Woolf*, behind the bar is the album *Another Side of Bob Dylan*.

• Near the end of *Annie Hall*, Woody Allen sits with Diane Keaton at the Source, an outdoor restaurant on L.A.'s Sunset Strip. Behind Allen's head is a huge billboard for Kiss. (Through about 1980, Sunset Strip was lined with music billboards.[3])

• Albert Finney is a detective obsessed with Dion in *Gumshoe*.

• Phil Collins is a kid screaming for the Beatles in *A Hard Day's Night*.

• Courtney Love plays a role in *Sid & Nancy*.

• Frank Zappa did the music for the never-seen *The World's Greatest Sinner*, made by actor Tim Carey in 1963.

•In John Landis' *Into the Night*, Carl Perkins and David Bowie fight to the death.

• *High School Confidential* opens with Jerry Lee Lewis and his band performing the title tune from the back of a moving flatbed truck. Pretty hot. (Oddly, this version of the song has never been released.)

• In the 1977 Wim Wenders film *The American Friend*, a troubled character silently sweeps his workshop while the Kinks' "There's Too Much on My Mind" spells out his thoughts...

• The greatest use of rock & roll I ever saw on TV

was the episode of *Moonlighting* when the two characters "do it." After slapping and fighting each other, the action stops, the first beats of "Be My Baby" come in, and they lunge for each other.

• And the greatest use of rock & roll in a movie is at the opening of the preternaturally fantastic *The Girl Can't Help It*.[4] Tom Ewell, in a tux, gives a stuffy talk about classical music, surrounded by violins and other "square" props. As the black and white turns to color and the edges of the screen are pushed aside into Cinemascope, the sound is gradually overtaken by the title song, and the scene **cuts to Little Richard in an electric-green suit hollering like God on high. Movie audiences stood up and cheered when this happened—in the 1980s!**

• Don Waller, author of *The Motown Story* (Scribners, 1985), says his favorite music usage is Richard Gere getting drunk to Smokey Robinson & the Miracles' "The Love I Saw in You Was Just a Mirage" in *American Gigolo*.

• There's a great line in *The Buddy Holly Story*. When the band arrives at the Apollo Theater in New York City, the theater manager, **expecting a black group, slaps his head and says, "If you're the Crickets, I'm Joe Shmuck."** A Cricket played by Charles Martin Smith[5] extends his hand and says, "Pleased to meet you, Mr. Shmuck."[6]

THE SPACE LEFT BLANK ON THE NEXT PAGE IS FOR YOUR SIGHTINGS AND FAVORITES:
WRITE 'EM DOWN!
SEND 'EM TO ME!
WE'LL WRITE ANOTHER BOOK!

[1] *Hollywood Rock* (Harper Perennial, 1994).

[2] Busey should know better, because before getting into movies he was a musician, drumming in the rock band The Carp and, as Teddy Jack Eddy, for Leon Russell. (Oops. Did I call a drummer a musician?)

[3] Also in the shot is the Golden Crest Hotel, where Bob Dylan and Al Kooper stayed in 1965 during Dylan's stand at the Hollywood Bowl. (For more fascinating Los Angeles rock history tidbits *just like these*, be sure and see my book *The L.A. Musical History Tour* [Faber & Faber, 1991]. Or did I mention it already?)

[4] It features Gene Vincent, Little Richard, Fats Domino, the Platters and Eddie Cochran! Even the unknowns—wild sax man Nino Tempo (at the beginning, on full-length prints) and lounge-rockers Johnny Olenn and Eddie Fontaine—are great! It is unfathomable how Hollywood producer-director Frank Tashlin chose so many right-on rock & rollers when so many lame ones were in other movies.

[5] Though he played the Cricket's bassist in the movie, he did not portray actual Cricket bassist Joe B. Mauldin, but rather a generic Cricket of no historicity. No actual Crickets were portrayed in the movie.

[6] *Shmuck* is Yiddish slang for "prick," as in the sentence, "Those shmucks at TNT cut this scene out of the movie!"

1964 Phil Spector De-Planes

In a 1964 *New York Herald-Tribune-New York* magazine profile later reprinted in his book *The Kandy-Kolored Tangerine-Flaked Streamlined Baby*, Tom Wolfe captured a not uncharacteristic moment in the life of 23-year-old record producer Phil Spector. Phil, on a plane full of record industry people as it taxied down the runway, decided **the plane was going to crash**. **"This plane's not going to make it,"** he said. "Just open the door and let me off. I'll walk back."

In fact, he was let off, after long and tense negotiations with the pilot and the Federal Aviation Administration. His record industry companions left, too, slapping his back and exhorting, "Phil, baby, you saved my life." His luggage was searched. He was an exotic-looking troublemaker in long, flowing hair, Italian suede coat, tight pants and pointed-toe shoes, and the airlines wanted **to make sure he wasn't going to blow up the plane!**

Phil Spector, then or now, can inspire those sorts of reactions.

The story in the *New York* magazine was titled "The Tycoon of Teen," because that's what he was, **a self-made millionaire** who got that way *producing hit records—teen records, "little symphonies for the kids,"* he called them. The string of hits was impressive, starting, really, with "He's a Rebel," through "And Then He Kissed Me," "Da Doo Ron Ron," "Be My Baby," and ending, really, with "You've Lost That Lovin' Feeling." By then it was

Phil Spector, 1969

164

1964 and the British tide was too strong to fight. Spector's teen-angst operas were too reminiscent of the early '60s of "Soldier Boy," "Leader of the Pack" and "Johnny Angel."

So he hibernated for a while, then reemerged with the Beatles. The Beatles idolized Phil, as did the Rolling Stones and other big British bands, and hired him to embellish their last album. Many people to this day complain that Phil ruined the songs "Long and Winding Road" and "Let It Be" by adding strings and lush instrumentation.

Balderdash. If he "ruined" any Beatles albums, why would George and John have him produce their post-Beatles hits?

Phil was as important as the Beatles.

Phil Spector was God.

Time now to explain the Spector style, otherwise known as "the Wall of Sound." Some people know him only for his Beatles years, others for his later association with the Ramones, and still others for one feisty night in 1989 at the Rock & Roll Hall of Fame.

What *you* need to know is the sound, the dense, complex, mystically hypnotic sound with the soft, crashing drums. It's on "Be My Baby": When those first drumbeats come in, it's a call to action, a command to stride with pride, with power. It's the beat of the street like no one had ever captured before. That record turned a lot of people on, including Brian Wilson. He has said, "I was driving in my car with a girl when this record came on. I heard the first beat, I said, Yeah, I heard the verse, I said OK, then I heard that chorus singing 'Be my baby,' and I pulled the car over and said, **'Wait a minute, what is THAT?' It blew my mind, man. Blew me away."**

"Be My Baby" established the Spector sound, or perhaps it should be the Spector Sound 2: The first records, "Uptown," "Da Doo Ron Ron" and "And Then He Kissed

Me" were dense, powerful records too, but with "Be My Baby" came the introduction of spaces and isolated instruments. The new Wall of Sound hit its zenith in 1964 with the Righteous Brothers' "You've Lost That Lovin' Feeling." It was Spector's first Wall of Sound venture with male singers, and when he played the finished product for the songwriting team of Barry Mann and Cynthia Weil they thought it was playing at a slow speed, the voice was so deep. "Lovin' Feeling" was a masterpiece, as attested by its ubiquity today.[1] Fully four minutes long, maestro Spector listed it on the record at 3:05 so deejays wouldn't automatically toss it out; he would have liked to make it shorter to conform to radio standards, but he couldn't do it artistically.

The last shot in the first (or second) Spector era came in 1966 with "River Deep, Mountain High." Spector signed Ike & Tina Turner, but then recorded Tina while Ike just stood around—somewhat galling for Ike, whose stature in rock & roll prehistory equals Spector's.[2] What he created was **a mountain of sound, a soaring, galloping, rubber-bass, crashing-drum, chanting, wailing, everything-plus-the-kitchen-sink** effort that moved the world, but only a little. Despite loud and enthusiastic praise from George Harrison, who as a Beatle in 1966 carried a lot of weight, the record sank from sight after a small time on the charts.[3]

The first Spector era was over, and the world was less rich for it.

---

[1] The Righteous Brothers jumped their contract with Spector in 1965, reportedly to try and reduce the enormous cost of his productions (which was charged to them), and purloined his sound, somewhat, for their first Verve single, "Soul & Inspiration." They faded from view soon afterward, only to make more comebacks than any other band in history. Spector sued Verve's parent company, MGM Records, and received a handsome settlement.

[2] Ike Turner may be best known as the quiet partner of Ike & Tina, or as the madman who beat her for no reason (Ike reportedly received a payment up front not to protest his portrayal in the film *What's Love Got To Do with It*), but to historians he is known as the giant who pioneered rock & roll in the early 1950s with

electric guitar-driven rhythm & blues. Ike's 1951 recording of "Rocket 88"—he wrote, produced and arranged it, and his band, the Kings of Rhythm, played on it—is widely acknowledged as the first rock & roll record. But the record label, Chess, credited it to his singer, Jackie Brenston, so Turner was pushed aside, like he was at the Spector session, at his moment of glory. Canvassing the South as a talent scout, Ike cut records with Howlin' Wolf, Bobby Bland, B.B. King and many others and leased them to Sun and Chess and other labels.

[3] It did well in England, however, prompting Spector to quip, "Maybe Benedict Arnold wasn't such a bad guy after all."

1983 Once "Jilted" by Johnny Rotten and Sid Vicious, Chrissie Hynde Has Child with Kinks' Ray Davies

In John Lydon's book of first-person accounts of the Sex Pistols, *Rotten: No Irish, No Blacks, No Dogs* (St. Martin's Press, 1994), Chrissie Hynde reveals that when she was living in London in 1976, she was scheduled to marry her close friend Johnny Rotten[1] in order to be permitted to stay in the country. It was just a visa thing, **but Rotten chickened out and volunteered Vicious** as a replacement. Vicious at first rejected the idea, then said OK, and finally didn't do it either. (Hynde then drops that part of the narrative and never tells how she got to remain in England.)

Hynde led a rock & roll life. She grew up in Akron, Ohio, and was in a band, Sat. Sun. Mat., at Kent State University with future Devo guy Mark Mothersbaugh. Between 1974 and 1978 she hopped back and forth between France, London and Akron seeking a musical situation that suited her. (She was hired by Malcolm McLaren to play guitar for a band, then was dismissed: The band became the Damned.) In 1978 she formed the Pretenders, which took England by storm,[2] and by 1980 they were world-beaters.

In 1982 she commingled musical and personal desires with the Kinks' Ray Davies; they produced a daughter, born in 1983. (They tried to get married, but a London registrar refused to issue them the license because they fought too much in his presence.) **In 1984 she married Jim Kerr from the band Simple Minds,** and they had a daughter also. They have since divorced.

[1] Hynde and Rotten both did housecleaning before attaining rock stardom (though she had the plum job of cleaning Keith Richards' house). Some other rock mopper-uppers were Billy Swan and Kris Kristofferson, both of whom were janitors at CBS Studios in Nashville before making records.

[2] Hynde wasn't the first Iron Belt rockin' lady to embrace England and become successful there. Leather-clad Detroiter Suzi Quatro immigrated there in the early 1970s and became Britain's most popular female rocker, setting the stage for Joan Jett in the '80s. (Unlike Hynde, Quatro's fame did not extend to the U.S., where her biggest impact was guest shots as Leather Tuscadero on TV's *Happy Days*. Her U.K. fame, however, remains intact, as evidenced by her 1993 appearance on the popular *Absolutely Fabulous* TV series.)

1958 Jerry Lee Lewis Marries 13-Year-Old Cousin

In May 1958 Jerry Lee Lewis was at the height of his rock & roll career. Less than a year after his sensational TV debut on the *Steve Allen Show* catapulted "Whole Lotta Shakin' Goin' on" to the top of the charts, the piano-pounding wildman from Ferriday, Louisiana, was considered heir to Elvis' vacated throne. (Presley was drafted into the Army in mid-1957. It's been reported that the night before his induction, he went into Sun Studios in Memphis—once the record label he recorded for, now the home of the next rock-comet—and told Jerry Lee Lewis, "It's yours, take it," passing the King's crown to—the Jester!) But during Jerry Lee's premiere tour of England, all hell broke loose.

Jerry Lee Lewis was a hard-living man from the git-go. Always part child and part adult, he was first married at 14—legal in Louisiana—and then a second time a little later.

In 1957, when he moved in with his bassist and second cousin J.W. Brown, 21-year-old Lewis fell in love with Brown's 13-year-old daughter, Myra Gale. (Myra Gale's bewilderment and unpreparedness for this are conveyed in her book,

Jerry & Myra

Great Balls of Fire.) They courted on the sly, and then married in late 1957, not revealing it to her parents, with whom they both were living! (Shades, sort of, of Woody Allen, though it is certain *nobody* would've considered Jerry Lee a father figure.) Their secret was kept until his debut concert tour of England. The English press, always more viperish and snippy than America's, was already up in arms over rock & roll and had their gunsights set on young Lewis when he arrived at Heathrow Airport. Eyeing the entourage, an enterprising reporter pulled Myra Gale aside and asked who she was. Myra, too naive to lie or simply say she was the bassist's daughter, **revealed she was Mrs. Jerry Lee Lewis, and that she was 13**. The English papers seized on this, and by all reports some people booed him at his concerts.[1] His tour was canceled and he was hounded out of the country.

Back in America his professional life collapsed. The press here moralized about the scandalous marriage **(Jerry Lee's response was as honest as Myra's: "Heck, I plumb *married* the gal, didn't I?")** and Lewis found his bookings canceled, his records not being played (it didn't help that the current release had the words "high school" in the title, though at that time his wife was too young to be in high school) and his former friends such as onetime booster Dick Clark turning his back on him.

It led to 10 years of being an outcast, but Jerry Lee never stopped rocking.

[1] Though not *all* concertgoers. Many were screaming for Jerry Lee to rock!

1965 Bob Dylan Booed at Newport

The annual Newport folk music festival was a huge event in Newport, Rhode Island. The cream of folkdom came, and happy crowds gathered. They were bound in their love for acoustic folk music, and in 1965 Bob Dylan spoiled their fun by playing his new electric folk-rock.

The spoilage really wasn't his. Two days before his appearance, the acoustic-instrument barrier had been broken by the Paul Butterfield Blues Band—shades of bringing drums to the Grand Ole Opry!—who used electric instruments and drums, and there had been a hell of a row getting them there. The purists argued that this was a gathering for nonelectric folk, and if you wanted electrically amped music you could find it easily elsewhere. But avant-gardists, or maybe just troublemakers, countered that electrification and rock & roll was the new folk music and the old-timers had better make way for it (or weren't they heeding the words "don't criticize if you can't understand"?).

Both arguments were valid, but of course folk-rock won out. But this year was the change year, and tempers flared. And the persona of Bob Dylan did nothing to ease them. Dylan had been an acoustic-folkie when he started recording in 1962. In the course of his development as a

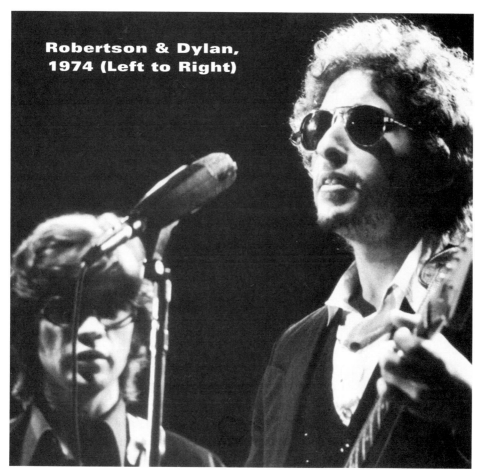

Robertson & Dylan, 1974 (Left to Right)

songwriter, he became an **avatar of the civil rights and progressive movements,** with songs such as "Blowin' in the Wind" and "The Times They Are a-Changin'." But in 1965 he jumped ship. Tired of being the denim-clad folk singer, he did his first rock & roll album and titled it *Bringing It All Back Home*, allegedly to turn the spotlight back on America in the midst of the British Invasion. The songs were lacking in social commentary but rife with wordplay, and *driven by a new, consciously loose feeling* that would mark his music through his subsequent career.

At this point he played Newport. When they invited him, he was a folkie, but when he showed up, he was this guy with a shock of wild hair, a matador-orange shirt and a black leather sportcoat with pointed-toe boots.

It caused a **stir that has yet to die down.**

At that ground-breaking show, he did only three songs, new rock & roll ones, and some people in the audience booed, setting a standard that would dog him. Subsequently, for at least a year, he would split his show into an acoustic part and an electric part. When the second part fired up, folk fans would loudly and dramatically rise and leave the auditorium in protest.[1]

In hindsight, it's not certain that the people booing at Newport disliked Dylan's turn to rock. By testimony from people who were there, this day's show (it was a three-day fest) drew a large crowd to see Dylan, the electric rocker. And when Dylan did a short set (partly because he had rehearsed only three songs with his makeshift band[2]), the crowd became angry and booed. Also, it was reported that the sound mix was bad, so people couldn't hear the music properly.[3]

To palliate the audience, Dylan encored solo with "Mr. Tambourine Man" and the new "It's All Over Now, Baby Blue."

No scientific exit polls were taken asking "Did you boo?" and "Why?" so we'll never really know. It could've all been some kinda misunderstanding.

---

[1] An artist subjecting himself to public excoriation at every show was something new in rock. As an idea, it wouldn't gather a full head of steam until punk rock in 1977, when gobbing and throwing garbage and screaming back at the band became a style.

[2] Guitarist Mike Bloomfield, drummer Sam Lay and bassist Jerome Arnold were recruited from the Paul Butterfield band; Al Kooper and Barry Goldberg rounded out the band. The night before their appearance they rehearsed until dawn.

[3] It would have been worse if folk legend Pete Seeger had had his way. Seeger was reportedly rushing around backstage with wire cutters, trying to stop the show. A festival official said, "I have never seen any trace of violence in Pete, except at that moment." It could be, though, that Seeger saw clearly, and was horrified by, the direction the festival was taking; its final year, 1969, was marred by audience rowdiness during a performance by those old folk favorites, Led Zeppelin.

"Get the Knack" Is Fastest Debut Album to Go Platinum—and the Knack Become Rock's #1 Critically Hated Band

When Knack leader Doug Fieger was 17 and in high school in Detroit, he wrote a letter to record producer Jimmy Miller ("Gimme Some Lovin'," *Blind Faith, Beggar's Banquet, Let It Bleed*) asking him to sign his band, The Sky. Miller came to Detroit, called Fieger and asked him to show him around town so he could see the Motown studios. Fieger did, and then he and his partner, John Corey,[1] played Miller some songs in Fieger's basement. A month later, Sky (their name had been halved by RCA) was in England recording at Olympic Studios with Miller producing, and the Rolling Stones were recording *Sticky Fingers* right next door.

Two albums were released on RCA in 1970 and 1971, but nothing came of them, and Fieger, now living in Los Angeles, worked in local bands (including the Rats, who, as the Sunset Bombers, did an album for Ariola) and took an unfulfilled stab as bassist and vocalist for the Carpenters (Karen had fired the previous guy, her boyfriend, but they made up and Fieger was jettisoned). In 1978 he formed The Knack with Berton Averre, Bruce Gary and Prescott Niles. The Knack developed a look—white shirts, black vests (adapted from another local band, the Heaters)—and played hard around Los Angeles. Their throwback rock & roll was original but **rooted in '50s and Beatles-era sounds, and was a breath of fresh air on a music scene under siege by disco.** Many established rockers, including Tom Petty, Bruce Springsteen and Stephen Stills, saluted them by joining them onstage. Their fever-pitch popularity led to a record company bidding war. Capitol got them and fashioned a Beatles-like promotional campaign that offended most critics.[2]

"We were just a band making music," Fieger recalls. "People dug us. When Capitol released 'My Sharona,' it was the fastest-moving single they'd had since the Beatles![3] But some writers took umbrage to the Beatles comparison, which was engineered by the record company. As a result, we're remembered only by our fans, who number in the millions, but not by rock writers, who have written us out of history!"

A couple of other hits—the Top 10 "Good Girls Don't" and Top 30 "Baby Talks Dirty"—followed, along with two more albums, and then the band drifted apart. A 1991 reunion album had a Top 5 AOR track (AOR being album-oriented rock, non-top 40), "Rocket O' Love," and the inclusion of "My Sharona" on the 1994 *Reality Bites* soundtrack spawned a 32-city summer tour.

As Fieger basks in memories of rock stardom and counts his money (the *Reality Bites* soundtrack sold pretty good), it's not for us to feel sorry for him (How many girls have ever screamed at *you*? With desire, I mean), but the critics' opposition is something to analyze now a couple of decades down the road.

What caused the ferocity of their hatred? What caused a graphic artist from San Francisco (not that anyone from that city's *ever* slagged L.A.), to create a "Knuke the Knack" campaign? What caused **fellow Detroit native Dave Marsh to say of Fieger,** "I'd like to punch him in the face"? What caused rock writer Barney Hoskyns, in a 1994 *Mojo* article, to needlessly say, ***"And of course the Knack sucked."***

Fieger, laughing, says it was three things:

1.   Not being punk. "In 1979, punk was what you had to be to be credible to the typewriter crowd. We were angry and subversive—we said fuck and shit on a million-selling album, we consumed groupies and substances aggressively—but we were pop stars and that was

wrong. [Remember that the now-cherished Abba was reviled then, too.] Never mind that we made music that people liked, we weren't politically correct."

2. Being a little bit punk. "Some people thought the chord shift that sold the record was reminiscent of 'New Wave' without actually being it. In other words, elements of the music were perceived as being borrowed, or stolen, from more deserving acts. It's untrue, incidentally."

3. The darned Beatles thing. "Capitol put it together and we went along. The grandiosity and supposed arrogance of comparing our band with the Fab Four struck us as funny. Some people got the joke, but not the rock crits—our hubris in 'comparing ourselves to the Beatles' was a sacrilege. Of course, no real standard prevailed. Six months after the *LA Times* guy blasted us for *Get the Knack* looking like *Meet the Beatles,* he praised the Clash's *London Calling* cover for its resemblance to the first Elvis Presley album. But they were punk, so it was OK."

Indeed, for a band with a song as big as "My Sharona," the Knack have found little berth in rock-history annals. *The Faber Companion to 20th Century Popular Music* has no listing for the group, despite the presence of lesser one- and no-hit critical favorites. *The New Rolling Stone Encyclopedia of Rock & Roll* includes them, but with a snide tone.

I guess the only place the band's gonna get any respect is in *this* book.

---

[1] Corey, now playing with the Eagles, co-wrote "Garden of Allah" and "The Last Worthless Evening."

[2] That's why they call 'em critics.

[3] Mind you, Capitol's biggest pre-"Sharona" 1970s single was "I Am Woman" in 1972.

1958 Little Richard Forms a Sex Train: Buddy Holly's the Caboose

In the book *The Life and Times of Little Richard* (Harmony, 1984), Little Richard told author Charles White: "Buddy liked Angel. He was a wild boy for the women. One time we were playing at the Paramount Theater and Buddy came into my dressing room when I was *jacking off with Angel sucking my titty. Angel had the fastest tongue in the West. Well, she was doing that to me and Buddy took out his thing.* He was ready, so she opened up her legs and he put it in her. He was having sex with Angel, I was jacking off, and Angel was sucking me, when they introduced his name on stage! He was trying to rush so he could run on stage. He made it, too. He finished and went to the stage still fastening himself up. I'll never forget that. **He came and he went!"**

Little Richard was the architect of rock & roll, a 100% original (well, he copped a little from his contemporary southern bisexual singers Billy Wright and Esquerita) whose music and, as later revealed, lifestyle, shocked the world.

Beginning with the release of "Tutti Frutti" in late 1955, Richard's mark was indelible. Adapted from a dirty rhyme ("Tutti frutti, good booty"—and just guess what that gal named Sue knew what to do) this raw, savage-sounding record shook American culture to its foundation, with its suggestive lyrics, raw, guttural singing and manic, boogie-woogie rock & roll piano never before heard anywhere!

Teenagers marched like to the Pied Piper to snap up "Tutti Frutti" and his follow-up hits, "Rip It Up," "Keep a Knockin',"[1] "Girl Can't Help It," "Ooh My Soul"[2] and his trademark, "Long Tall Sally"[3] until the string was broken. In late 1957 Little Richard abandoned rock & roll for a career in the ministry.[4]

What's possibly **most important about Little Richard was his breaking the radio color barrier.** Until 1956, Nat King Cole and a handful of "nice" black entertainers were heard on white radio but seldom seen on TV. Talented black newcomers were discarded and their songs covered by white artists. The Top 40 of the early 1950s is larded with black-originated music that was usurped by white people: "Tweedle Dee" by Georgia Gibbs (originally by LaVern Baker), "Sh-Boom" by the Crew-Cuts (the Chords), and so forth.

Sometimes originals slipped through, as when the Penguins' "Earth Angel" competed with the cover version by the Crew-Cuts, but none of the breakthrough artists before Little Richard did it with an identity; their versions of the songs were more soulful, but their personalities made little impression. But when you heard Little Richard, you didn't forget it.[5] **His strangled scream contained such joy and release, it was like someone opening your soul.** His sound was unique and foolproof: there was no getting around it, if you wanted the real thing, you had to come to the originator.

His appearance was startling, too. Here was a dark-skinned black man with hair piled high atop his head. He wore bright green suits and clambered over, under and atop his piano. He drove the band's beat like someone stoking a locomotive, and made strange akimbo leg movements, the result of a childhood bout with polio that left him slightly dragging one leg. And if you looked closely and were aware of such things, he had an effeminate manner.

All told, he was as different a being as ever to hit the American entertainment scene. He might as well have been a Martian.

The success of his "Tutti Frutti" can also be attributed to the white cover version of the song. **As we look back through the junkheap of white covers**, we see that only one artist took on the great Little Richard—Pat Boone, and that was like Pete McNeely taking on Mike Tyson, only more weighted toward the champ. Pat Boone's version of "Tutti Frutti," though played incessantly by disc jockeys, was so pale, so sickly, so unsatisfying that it has been forgotten by history and assailed when it's remembered. But Boone should be lauded: His insipidness drove open the floodgates.

Today, Boone says his version of that song was silly.

And of his early penchant for covering black songs, he says, "My producers gave them to me, and I sang them. I'm sorry if this caused hardship to anyone. I know a lot of black songwriters benefited, so at least there's that. I have about as much chance of getting into the Rock & Roll Hall of Fame as getting on Mount Rushmore!"[6]

[1] Though Little Richard claimed authorship, Louis Jordan recorded essentially the same song, with the same title, in 1939.

[2] This song was twice plagiarized, first by Ritchie Valens, whose "Ooh My Head" was originally "Ooh My Soul," and then by Led Zeppelin, whose "Boogie With Stu" cut "sampled" that song. (See "John Fogerty Sued," page 189.)

[3] "Long Tall Sally" is Richard's most oft-covered song, though he's seen little income from it. The story of its genesis down South in 1956 is fantastic. In the Chas. White book, Bumps Blackwell says, "I went to this awful downtown hotel, and there was [disc jockey] Honey Chile with this young girl about 16, 17. Honey Chile said to me, 'Bumps, you got to do something about this girl. She walked all the way from Appaloosa, Mississippi, to sell this song to Richard cos her auntie's sick and she needs money to put her in the hospital.' I said okay, let's hear the song, and this little clean-cut kid, all bows and things, says, 'Well, I don't have a melody yet. I thought maybe you or Richard could do that.' So I said okay, what *have* you got, and she pulls out this piece of paper. It looked like toilet paper with a few words written on it:

Saw Uncle John with Long Tall Sally
They saw Aunt Mary comin'
So they ducked back in the alley.

And she said, 'Aunt Mary is sick. And I'm going to tell her about Uncle John. Cos he was out there with Long Tall Sally, and I saw 'em. They saw Aunt Mary comin' and they ducked back in the alley.'

I said, 'They did, huh? And this is a song?'"

The next day, as a favor to Honey Chile, they cut it, and it became one of the most popular rock & roll songs in history.

(However, for the record, "Long Tall Sally," "Jenny, Jenny" and "Miss Ann" were all written or co-written by Enotris Johnson, who with his wife Ann ran the Tick Tock Inn in Macon, Georgia. The Johnsons "took in" the young Little Richard just before he signed with Specialty. Their relationship is detailed in Timothy White's book *Rock Lives*.)

[4] He renounced materialism maybe too thoroughly, selling all his song royalty income to Specialty Records owner Art Rupe for $10,000. In the early 1980s he sought to get his song rights back, claiming Rupe had made an unfair business deal with him, but he failed.

[5] In his book *Astonish Me* (Viking Press, 1973) author John Lahr relates that his father, actor Bert Lahr, upon hearing "Long Tall Sally" on the radio for the first time, pulled his car off the highway and laughed for 10 minutes.

[6] Just for saying that, they oughtta let him in.

1967   Hendrix Sets Fire to Guitar: Outfoxes the Who at Monterey

American immigrant to England Jimi Hendrix was signed to the Who's managers Lambert & Stamp's Track record label in early 1967. They taught him Pete Townshend's signature windmill guitar move, an "homage" that threatened rather than delighted ***Townshend, who was not in Hendrix's league as a guitar player.***

When both were booked on the Monterey Pop Festival for June 17, 1967, they both knew that their acts were showstoppers—Hendrix for his fierceness and flamboyance, the Who for their guitar- and amp-smashing—and neither wanted to follow the other. That is, each wanted to be the penultimate loud, flamboyant hard rock act. Both acts were virtually unknown in the U.S.[1] and both wanted desperately to be in the spotlight at the very right moment on this possibly historic gig.

They flipped a coin: Hendrix lost, so the Who came out first, which is to say, fourth from last (the Grateful Dead were sandwiched between the Who and Hendrix, and the Mamas and Papas closed the show) and did a fiery, loud, mike-twirling, guitar-busting, amp-smashing finale that left the crowd dazzled.

But they didn't know what Hendrix had up his sleeve. When Jimi had his turn, he delivered an avalanche-sounding set of current hits (covers—he adapted his set to the situation) and finished on *his knees spraying lighter fluid on his guitar, which he set on fire[2] and kicked and wrestled as the feedback and over-amped string-noise built to an unbelievable climax* of distortion and deviltry.

The Who won the bet, but 30 years later, it's Hendrix who's most remembered at Monterey.

---

[1] The Who were slow starters. Though they opened for the Beatles as early as 1964, they began recording later. In March 1967, they made their U.S. debut on Murray the K's '50s-like stage show in Brooklyn, destroying equipment five times a day for two weeks as an opening act (along with the Cream) for the Shirelles, Gerry & the Pacemakers and others. Their second U.S. exposure came as opening act for Herman's Hermits on an extensive 1967 tour: Hermits leader Peter Noone was taken by their furious music, and perhaps humorously—like the Monkees having Hendrix open for them that same summer—forced their loud obnoxiousness on his teenybopper audience.

[2] Supervising this stunt, and worrying like a demon, was Dylan keyboardist and all-around rock guy Al Kooper, who was stage manager.

1988 Roy Orbison's Comeback Shortened by Death

Roy Orbison was a myopic, thin-haired guy with a voice like honeyed thunder. Like Screamin' Jay Hawkins, Tony Williams of the Platters, Jay Black of Jay and the Americans and Freddie Mercury, he was a founder of the operatic wing of rock & roll. **Elvis Presley called him the singer he'd most like to sing like**.

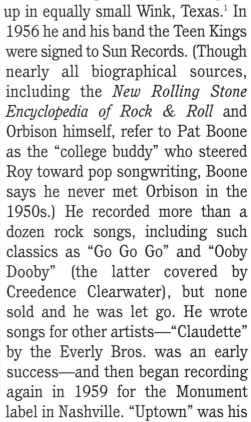

Born in Vernon, Texas, on April 23, 1936, he grew up in equally small Wink, Texas.[1] In 1956 he and his band the Teen Kings were signed to Sun Records. (Though nearly all biographical sources, including the *New Rolling Stone Encyclopedia of Rock & Roll* and Orbison himself, refer to Pat Boone as the "college buddy" who steered Roy toward pop songwriting, Boone says he never met Orbison in the 1950s.) He recorded more than a dozen rock songs, including such classics as "Go Go Go" and "Ooby Dooby" (the latter covered by Creedence Clearwater), but none sold and he was let go. He wrote songs for other artists—"Claudette" by the Everly Bros. was an early success—and then began recording again in 1959 for the Monument label in Nashville. "Uptown" was his first hit in January 1960, followed by "Only the Lonely," a song that set his musical identity as a lovelorn, wounded soul. **In April 1961 he gave full throttle to the operatic strength;** of his singing with the poignant, dramatic "Running Scared" (in this song, he wins the girl), which ends with a wall-scaling wail of triumph previously unheard in the rock world. Other paint-peelers followed, including "Crying," "Leah," "The Crowd," "In Dreams" (perversely revived in the 1986 film *Blue Velvet*), "Falling," "Blue Bayou" (in 1977 an enormous hit for Linda Ronstadt) and the ominously titled penultimate hit, "It's Over."

He became very popular worldwide and did concert tours of Europe. **In 1963 the Beatles were among his opening acts.** He weathered the British Invasion initially through 1964, scoring his biggest hit, the martial, Dave Clark-like, double-drummed "Oh,[2] Pretty Woman,"[3] that summer, but the sales and, frankly, the quality of his songs fell off soon after he switched to MGM Records[4] late in 1965. By the end of the decade he was a well-respected relic of rock history.

Though he never was a country artist, in 1980 he climbed onto the country charts in a duet[5] with hot country gal Emmylou Harris, "That Lovin' You Feelin' Again," which appeared in that much-ballyhooed mess of a rock movie, *Roadie*.

Orbison's life was marked with tragedies. His first wife, Claudette, was killed in a motorcycle accident on June 7, 1966, and his two sons were killed in a fire in 1968. Orbison said that he indeed had faced many hardships in his life but did not consider himself a tragic figure.

In 1987 the Traveling Wilburys, an unlikely over-the-hill-gang formed by Roy, Bob Dylan, George Harrison, Jeff Lynne and Tom Petty,[6] recorded a best-selling album of new songs.

Orbison, the best singer of the lot, was once again on top of the world, both through his Wilburys association and his new album, *Mystery Girl*, when he died suddenly on December 6, 1988. (A single from the album, the

Petty-Lynn-Orbison composition "You Got It," reached the Top 10 in 1989.)

[1] Where today there is an annual Roy Orbison festival.

[2] A song frequently unfindable in song lists, for the "Oh."

[3] This song frustrated lyricists, who pointed to its seeming failure to make satisfactory rhymes, baldly matching "truth" and "you" in one chorus, and "Pretty woman look my way" and "Pretty woman yay yay yay" in another.

[4] He was lured away by MGM's promise of getting him into movies. His debut, and swan song, was the memorable, preposterous 1965 flop *The Fastest Guitar in the West*, in which he fought bad guys with a James Bond-like guitar-gun.

[5] Countryish gals dug Roy. In 1987 k.d. lang recorded "Crying" in a duet with him.

[6] By the time they formed, everyone had forgotten about the Masked Marauders, the bogus supergroup invented by *Rolling Stone* magazine, otherwise press comparisons would've been drawn. The phantom 1971 album, which existed only in a printed review, by the team of Bob Dylan, John Lennon and Mick Jagger was allegedly recorded in northern Canada and was much-sought by rock fans unaware of the magazine's intent of humiliating them. (A San Francisco group, the Cleanliness and Godliness Skiffle Band, rushed into a studio and recorded an album made of titles supplied in the review, and it was released as a Masked Marauders album by Warner Bros. Records. Today, though this album is hard to find, no collector's market has developed for it.) It was just a short while after the Paul-is-dead hoax, and people, apparently, would believe anything.

Harry Nilsson Gets $5 Million from RCA Thanks to Lennon

When Harry Nilsson first started in the music business, he was working at a bank in Los Angeles and writing songs for other people.[1]

But in 1967 his first album, *The Pandemonium Shadow Show*, on RCA Records, caught the attention of all the Beatles,[2] especially John Lennon. His favorable comments, however, stickered onto the album jacket still didn't push the album of soft, cleverly written songs to staggering sales or popularity.[3] Nilsson remained a moderate-selling act whose biggest hits were written by other people. His signature song, "Everybody's Talkin'" (#6, 1969), featured in the film *Midnight Cowboy*, was written by folk singer Fred Neil, and his biggest hit, "Without You" (#1, 1972), was by Pete Ham and Tom Evans of

Badfinger. He had only one big hit of his own composition, the Caribbeanish "Coconut," which reached #8 in 1972.

He was so admired by the Beatles that he was taken into their fold, most particularly by Ringo and John. With Ringo, Nilsson made the movie *Son of Dracula* in 1974, and with Lennon he made the album *Pussy Cats*.

Around that same time, Lennon and Nilsson were raging around Los Angeles (See, "John Lennon Disrupts the Troubadour," page 216), getting into the newspapers as disruptive party animals, not musicians. **During this "lost weekend" (their antics were in the main fueled by alcohol) which lasted a year,** Nilsson's contract with RCA was up for renewal, and in the boldest example of "drafting" ever heard, he got his renewal at the rate of $1 million per album. "Drafting" is a long-distance driving technique wherein the driver of a small car huddles behind a massive truck and, caught in its draft, is carried forward. (It's done in NASCAR racing and in Russia.) Similarly, Nilsson rode on Lennon's draft, at least according to doubtable writer and provocateur Albert Goldman,[4] who reported the following uncheckable incident in his scurrilous book *The Many Lives of John Lennon* (Morrow, 1988).

Nilsson had not been a big record-seller despite his occasional hits. In 1973 he coerced the president of RCA to draw up a contract for **a five-album deal guaranteeing him $1 million per album.** The deal then sat in a drawer for a year, during which time the administration at RCA changed. In 1974, right after the *Pussy Cats* album, Nilsson dragged Lennon into the new president's office and said, in effect, "If you don't sign that contract, I'm leaving the company. But if you do, well, my friend John's recording contract at Apple expires soon, too, so maybe…"

The deal was made, and **RCA lost a bundle.** Nilsson fulfilled a couple of album obligations, then stopped recording for a long, long time. (Lennon quit, too, around this time.)

Goldman describes Nilsson in 1988 as a wealthy man who invested well the money he cadged from RCA. However, his wealth did not last. In 1992 his business manager stole all his money, and it is thought that his anguish over his sudden and unexpected bankruptcy prompted his death in 1994 of a heart attack at age 52.

The business manager got a three-year jail sentence, less than the average second-offender petty thief. In 1995 producers Al Kooper and Danny Kapilian finished and issued the **Nilsson tribute album,** *For the Love of Harry: Everybody Sings Nilsson,* **featuring Brian Wilson, Marshall Crenshaw** and many others, that they had been compiling at the time of Nilsson's death.

[1] "Cuddly Toy," a song the Monkees recorded, brought in good money to the fledgling writer; so did his singing and writing the theme song to the TV show *The Courtship of Eddie's Father*. In 1966 he wrote "Paradise" with Phil Spector, who recorded it with the Ronettes. That recording, possibly the zenith of the quiet-opening, crashing-ending Spector style, was not released at the time, a tragic loss to Spector fans who hungered for his music. The song saw the light of day on a Shangri-Las album in 1966, on a 1972 post-Diana Ross Supremes album produced by Jimmy Webb, and by the Ronettes on a 1976 Spector rarities album issued in England, and on a Warner/Spector single. (It is now available on the box set *Phil Spector Back to Mono* (*1958-1969*), Phil Spector Records/ABKCo 7118-2), and on a single CD, *Best of The Ronettes*, Phil Spector Records/ABKCo 72122.)

[2] They dearly wanted Nilsson on Apple Records, but RCA wouldn't let him go.

[3] In this respect he resembled his good friend, songsmith Randy Newman, whose records similarly drew press and peer-group praise but sold little. In a combination sure to not sell, he recorded an album of Newman songs, *Nilsson Sings Newman*, that crashed like a lead dirigible.

[4] Lennon and Nilsson are dead, but so is Goldman, so it's not only the good that die young. Before the Lennon book, Goldman was widely hated for savaging Elvis Presley in his 1981 biography, *Elvis*. Elvis fans, not normally "activists," rushed to bookstores and defaced copies of this book so they would be sent back to their maker—the same thing they would have done to Goldman, if they'd had the chance. (Phil Spector, upon hearing of Goldman's death, issued a statement saying, in effect, "Are you sure he's dead? Absolutely sure? That's a relief.")

1988 Mike Love's Memorable Moment at the Rock & Roll Hall of Fame

On January 20, 1988, at the third annual Rock & Roll Hall of Fame induction dinner in New York City, the Beach Boys took the stage to take their bows. Singer Mike Love spouted some off-the-cuff remarks to the star-studded audience, including:

"I challenge the Boss to get up onstage and jam."

"We do 180 performances a year. I'd like to see the Mop Tops do that. I'd like to see Mick Jagger get onstage and do 'I Get Around' rather than 'Jumpin' Jack Flash.'"

"I wanna see Billy Joel, see if he can still tickle the ivories."

"I know **Mick Jagger won't be here tonight**. He's gonna have to stay in England. He's always been **too chickenshit to share the stage with the Beach Boys!"**

Later, when Bob Dylan was inducted, he said, "I wanna thank Mike Love...for not mentioning *me*."

The incident was a highlight, so to speak, of an awards show that is held privately. Only when a person speaks spontaneously, like Love did, or calls attention to himself, like Phil Spector did a year later, does it seem

The Beach Boys at their R&R Hall of Fame induction, with Mike Love at far right.

to make headlines.

Construction of the Rock & Roll Hall of Fame building in Cleveland was long seen as a shaggy-dog story, a story that never ends. It was promised to be completed at various dates in the late 1980s and then every year in the 1990s. The massive I.M. Pei-designed structure, crammed full of rock & roll memorabilia and historical information, was finally unveiled at a gala ceremony on September 1, 1995.

The question long raised by Coastal snobs was, **Why Cleveland?,** but it could well have been, Why not? Cleveland has had its share of rock & roll monsters,[1] including founding father Alan Freed, Screamin' Jay Hawkins, the Outsiders, and Eric Carmen and the Raspberries, as well as Pere Ubu, the Cramps, Tin Huey, the Dead Boys and the Waitresses. (And let us not forget nearby Akron, with Chrissie Hynde, Devo and Rachel Sweet.)

Rock & roll didn't just come from the coasts and the big cities—it came from everywhere!

Significantly, the city of Cleveland poured in money toward the construction of the immense edifice, banking on a future infusion of tourist dollars. (Within months of opening it seemed to be paying off: Hotel bookings were up and museum hours were extended.)

New York and Los Angeles didn't need another entertainment monument, Memphis didn't try very hard to snag it and Chicago apparently wasn't interested. So, again, why not Cleveland?

---

[1] He pre-dates rock & roll, but let's mention Benjamin "Bull Moose" Jackson, whose late 1940s "jump" gems included "Why Don't You Haul Off & Love Me" and "Big Ten-Inch," later covered by Aerosmith!

John Fogerty Sued for Plagiarizing His Own Song

In 1985 John Fogerty emerged from a 10-year recording hibernation with a top-selling album, *Centerfield*. That album's biggest hit, ***"The Old Man Down the Road," had musical similarities to "Run Through the Jungle,"*** the Creedence Clearwater song Fogerty had written and produced and sung in 1970 on Fantasy Records. Fantasy owner Saul Zaentz, who had acquired publishing rights to Fogerty's Creedence output in exchange for releasing him from his record contract, sued him for copying "Jungle," which Zaentz controlled.

Fogerty won in 1988, but not before lending credence, perhaps, to the image he was, perhaps, trying to paint on the song "Zanz Kant Danz" (later changes to "Vanz Can't Dance") on the *Centerfield* album: "Vanz can't dance but he'll steal your money." (To be fair, Zaentz plowed money into films with more than a dollop of integrity: *Payday*, *One Flew Over The Cuckoo's Nest* and *Amadeus*.)

The notion **of song stealing has long dogged the music business. It didn't rear its ugly head in rock too often until the 1970s, when these famous cases came down:**

- The estate of Ritchie Valens sued Led Zeppelin for appropriating Valens' "Ooh My Head" in their song "Boogie with Stu." The Zeps were found to have appropriated the music without credit or permission, and remuneration was made. On later editions of *Physical Graffiti*, Boogie with Stu's credits have been changed to add "Mrs. Valenzuela." She died in 1987, and is buried next to her famous son at San Fernando Mission Cemetery in San Fernando, California (Valens may have "borrowed" the song himself. The Lost Tapes [Ace UK, CHP317], a 1990 CD of Valens outtakes, shows that up until the last take, "Ooh My Head" was Little Richard's "Ooh My Soul.")

- Led Zeppelin's *Dazed and Confused* was taken outright from composer Jake Holmes, who was already making a fortune singing commercials and didn't sue. Its first rock & roll expression (Holmes' was a ballad) was by the Yardbirds on their *Live at the Anderson Theater* album on Epic in 1968.

- The writers of the 1962 Chiffons hit, "He's So Fine," sued George Harrison for musicial similarities in his hit "My Sweet Lord."

- John Fogerty was sued by Little Richard for the resemblance between Richard's "Long Tall Sally" and Fogerty's "Travelin' Band."

- When the Beach Boys blithely appropriated Chuck Berry's "Sweet Little Sixteen" for the tune of their "Surfin' USA," they didn't bother to split credit with him (he was in jail—maybe they thought he wouldn't notice), so he subsequently sued them and got back royalties AND sole songwriter credit for the whole tune!

- Bob Dylan successfully challenged Rod Stewart's song "Forever Young" for its similarity to his song of the same name.

- The song "Ghostbusters" resembled Huey Lewis and the News' "I Want a New Drug," and a lawsuit was settled out of court. (The Lewis song was a "temp track" used during the film's production to indicate the type of song the filmmakers wanted.)

In subsequent years such lawsuits clogged the courts, especially those from little-known songwriters whose unheard songs resembled big hits: Michael Jackson, the Bee Gees, Stevie Wonder and others were targets, but most of the suits were rejected; judges and juries sided overwhelmingly with the stars. (In a flagrantly lopsided case in the mid-'80s, New York reggae singer Patrick Alley sued Mick Jagger over Jagger's song "Just Another Night," which strongly resembled Alley's tune of the same name. Jagger was found innocent by a star-struck jury, despite testimony that a former associate of Alley was hired by Jagger just prior to "his" song's emergence.)

The Rock & Roll History of "Jailbait"

Maybe you've never encountered the term *jailbait*. It's an old term for an underage girl: get caught with a girl under 18[1] and face a jail sentence.

If you study the history of rhythm and blues, you'll see references to it, most pointedly in the **Andre Williams song "Jailbait," whose lyrics "Fifteen, sixteen, seventeen—that's jailbait"** and "Seventeen-and-a-half is still jailbait" are variations on the old theme, *"Fifteen'll get you twenty."*

Now let's look at some rockers and their jailbait problems:

- Sad for Texas swamp-pop fans was the 1996 arrest of longtime record producer Huey P. Meaux on child porn and molestation charges. Meaux jumped bail, then was **captured by a bounty hunter in Juarez, Mexico.**

- In the early 1990s Michael Jackson was accused of taking **sexual liberties with underage boys**. Charges were resolved privately, and Jackson is a free man.

- Longtime Stone bassist Bill Wyman had underage girls but no troubles when, at age 50, he married a 16-year-old girl he'd been dating for two years. Incredibly, Wyman's grown son took a fancy to the gal's mother.

- In 1980 Don Henley of the Eagles was caught with *a 16-year-old hooker in his Los Angeles home.* Henley, who admitted that he had a madam send her over but said he didn't know her age, became alarmed when the girl had violent drug reactions (police later found **pot, cocaine and Quaaludes** in his domicile) and called the Fire Department. Henley, still a naif though in his 30s, believed the Fire Department representative who told him he wouldn't call the police. Police came, and Henley was arrested. Instead of being driven out of the country like Roman Polanski, though, Henley was fined and ordered to attend drug counseling. Never normally one to whine, Henley wrote a blistering song, "Dirty Laundry," attacking the press' interest in his private affairs,[2] and continued onto a successful solo, and later re-Eagled, career, unscathed by the now-forgotten incident.

- The morning after Moby Grape's album-release party on June 6, 1967, the band was arrested outside of San Francisco for consorting with underage groupies.

- **Elvis Presley had the smoothest PR of anyone**. In 1960 he installed 14-year-old Priscilla Beaulieu, the daughter of an Army officer he met while stationed in Germany, in his Graceland home. Though he claimed to be raising her as a guardian, he was actually grooming her for marriage, which transpired on her 21st birthday. Though **Priscilla has said she and Elvis did "everything but" penetration before they married,** she didn't say how old she was when the physical contact started.

- Chuck Berry had hooker problems, like Don Henley. In 1959 he took a 14-year-old prostitute from

Yuma, Arizona, to his St. Louis home, and installed her as a hatcheck girl at the nightclub he owned. When he dismissed her with just a bus ticket home, she went to the police, who arrested Berry. **He stayed jailed from 1962 to 1964 for violating the Mann act,** which forbids the transportation of minors across state lines for immoral purposes.

- Jerry Lee Lewis was driven from public life because he married a 13-year-old girl. (See "Jerry Lee Lewis Marries 13-Year-Old Cousin", page 168.)

[1] The age of consent is 16 in England. It has been suggested that when the Beatles first did "I Saw Her Standing There," the opening line was "She was just sixteen, you know what I mean," but it was too blatant, so it was changed to the meaningless "seventeen." (Some people maintain that "sixteen" lacks the extra beat necessary to the song. However, "You know what I mean" reverberates next to the age of consent, while it just lays there next to seventeen, like "She just turned twenty-two, so she could buy liquor.")

[2] Not the first "get your nose out of my business" song. See "Family Affair" in the "Sly Stone Becomes Famous," page 40.

1966 Bobby Fuller: the First Rock & Roll Suicide?

Bobby Fuller was on top of the world in July 1966, or just on the other side. His band, the Bobby Fuller Four, the premiere L.A. club band, had *topped the national charts in mid-1965 with the Buddy Holly sounding (a post-Holly Crickets tune), "I Fought the Law,"*[1] and a hit follow up, Holly's "Love's Made a Fool of You."

Yet on July 18, 1966, his body was found in his car, which was parked in front of his Hollywood apartment. Fuller died of what police ruled a suicide.

People do unlikely things, but Bobby's method of "suicide" was decidedly ghastly: gasoline had been poured down his throat until he drowned. This unpleasant and possibly ceremonious death—his body showed signs of battering—spurred speculation of Mob involvement, a police cover-up or a jealous boyfriend.

Like most celebrity deaths, the given explanation of Fuller's demise had never fully satisfied everyone.

David Bowie did a song, "Rock & Roll Suicide," but he's all right.

Here are some other rock & roll notables who took that way out:

• **Johnny Ace**. On New Years Eve, 1954, the black singer whose first hit, "Pledging My Love," was crossing over into the white record market, shot himself in the head playing Russian roulette. His death is dogged by rumors of Mafia hits, manager's revenge and his own despondency.

• **Joe Meek**. The British producer of "Telstar" by the Tornadoes was an avid fan of Buddy Holly. On February 3, 1967, the eighth anniversary of Holly's death, he killed himself (and his landlady; renters take note).

• **Phil Ochs**. The 1960s folk singer and sometimes rock star wanna be had manic depressive swings that ended when he died in 1976 by hanging. (His brother Michael runs a world-famous photo and record archive service, naturally the world's largest repository of Phil Ochs information.)

• **Richard Manuel**. In 1986, after more than 25 years with The Band as keyboardist and frequent lead voice ("Tears of Rage"), Manuel's ability to perform was undermined by his alcohol and chemical problems. In 1986 he hanged himself after a gig in Winter Haven, Florida.

• **Del Shannon**. The "Runaway" man had recently kicked alcohol and drugs through AA, but not his despondency. On February 8, 1990, he took his life with a shotgun blast at his home outside Los Angeles.

• **Kurt Cobain**. Nirvana played the Husky Union Building at the University of Washington in April, 1989, headlining a "Four Bands for a Buck" concert. They ended a chaotic, hour-long set by destroying the university's PA and inciting a small riot, prompting the venue to "ban Nirvana for life."

Five years later, band leader Kurt Cobain lay dead from a self-inflicted gunshot wound in his lakefront home three miles to the south.

In that brief time Cobain had risen from an impoverished dropout to generational poet to corporate pariah. The kid who spent part of his teenage years sleeping under bridges in his native Aberdeen, Washington had suddenly noticed $100,000 deposits added to his account when he went to withdraw $20 from a cash machine on Melrose Avenue.

In the end his death was not surprising to keen observers. In a rambling suicide note, Cobain lamented that music wasn't "fun" anymore. One shotgun blast brought an entire generation to a stopping point,[2] and it was possibly taken more personally than the Challenger blast: Where were *you* when you heard about Kurt?

Of course, in death Cobain has been an uber-celebrity of the weirdest kind. Church of Kurt Cobain announced it was forming in Portland, Oregon. However, when followers arrived they were told they'd been duped. Earlier, a memorial to Cobain in Aberdeen was scrapped after

Nirvana bassist Krist Novoselic announced he would take the life-sized park sculpture and "Smash it to bits!!"

The garage where Cobain killed himself was demolished in June, 1996.

[1] Versatile ex-Cricket songwriter Sonny Curtis (he penned *The Mary Tyler Moore Show* theme) still performs this song today with the original lyric, "Robbing people with a zip-gun." (Zip-guns were homemade guns used by juvenile delinquents in the '50s.) Bobby Fuller's change to "six-gun" makes the song less specific and removes the time element: His way, it could be a Western song from 100 years ago.

[2] [Anyone seeking real value from the whole thing should simply consider his lyrics, songs and passion. But overanalysis yields that Cobain has joined Morrison (and, to a lesser degree, Jimi) in a discontented martyr society. Struggling against an imperfect world, they eventually fold in one way or another, like us all, but in a *big* way. So the suicide seems to reaffirm our feelings of apathy and discontent, while maybe it *should* reaffirm our appreciation of each other while we're around.—Ed.]

"Hair": a Song Subject, a Broadway Show and a Constant Thorn In Society's Side

Modern actors never get it right when they portray long-haired kids in movies set in the 1960s: Their comfort shows.

'Twasn't like that, McGee. **To have long hair then was like wearing a target, or one of those signs that said "Kick Me."** Non-long haired people felt license to point and giggle, pelt you with things, scream in your face and, if the climate was right, hit you. What you see in pictures of long-haired kids' faces from that era is fear and discomfort.

The Beatles were the first people in modern times to bring long hair to these shores[1] in 1964. It'd been brewing for a couple of years in England. In retrospect, their falling bangs were the shaggy part, with only Ringo sporting a real crop of back hair.

Reaction was swift. **Kids adopted**

Bamboo's lead men from the early '70s display their enviable grasp of hair and fashion.

it, and adult America, by and large, despised them for it.

Almost immediately, other British long-haired groups arrived, most notably the Hullabaloos, whose long, long blond manes shocked both sensibility and reason: first in its inherent offensiveness, and second in "How did they grow it so long so fast? It's only been a style for six months!" The Stones and a thousand other longhairs followed—including the first pony-tailed import, the lumberjacklike Tom Jones—but American groups were slow to follow, because in America being different has always been not only unpopular but unsafe. Bobby Vee combed his hair down in front but kept the sides swept back.[2] Elvis was unmoved. In L.A., the Bobby Fuller Four pulled their hair down one man at a time, and the Standells dropped their Bobby Rydell rolls for Prince Valiant do's. The Beach Boys stood pat, the Four Seasons—please! And TV comedians fell all over themselves scrambling for Beatles wigs.[3]

The first mounted assault on hair barriers was the Monkees TV show in 1966. The producers, insisting the characters have long hair, had to fight furious network execs and outraged advertisers who **feared the subversive, faglike mops of Micky, Davy, Mike and Peter.** This was the Fort Sumter of the long hair movement. After that, hair flowed freely.

Hair songs? Other than cuts like "My Boyfriend Got a Beatle Haircut," the Barbarians, **"Are You a Boy or Are You a Girl?"** and **Sonny Bono's protest "Laugh at Me"** (see "Sonny Bono," page 97), the subject wasn't directly addressed until the Broadway show *Hair* in 1968. But the show was known more for its all-cast nude scene than its title, so, it did nothing to tackle or change things.

Then in 1970 came the anthem of the long hair movement, David Crosby's "Almost Cut My Hair."[4] This

song, in which the proponent contemplates a haircut, *has as its denouement the radical declaration "I'm going to let my freak flag fly."*[5]
What more need be said?

[1] Truth be told, the first long-haired rocker was Jerry Lee Lewis. When he arrived on the scene in 1957, his long, wavy locks were piled high on the back of his dome, and when his head jerked forward, the hair cascaded down like a lion's mane. However, this did not spark a rush of copycat hairdos, for two reasons: one, not everyone's hair could fall forward like that, and two, Lewis was seen as a stark raving madman.

[2] And incidentally, in 1964, Vee made one of the best Beatles' knockoff records, "I'll Make You Mine," replete with Beatles first-wave "woos." It's on par with the Knickerbockers' "Lies."

[3] You could make a case that adult society's utter rejection of this totem of youth culture sowed the seeds for the rebellion of the late '60s.

[4] A significant peek into Crosby's mental processes at the time was not only this album's title, *If I Could Only Remember My Name*, but the title Crosby wanted, *Does Anybody Know Who I Am or Any of My Relatives? So Where's My Cousin? Do You Have Any Papers?*

[5] Copped from Jimi Hendrix's "If 6 Was 9."

Sam Cooke

I Shot the Sheriff: Some Noteworthy Rock Shootings

Rock & roll, like any business, has had its share of violence.

A few were near-misses: **Jerry Lee Lewis playfully winging his bass player** in 1976, a love-starved woman shooting Jackie Wilson in 1961 and **robbers shooting Bob Marley in Jamaica in 1976.**

The fatalities are more numerous and, frankly, too **morbid to list.** These are the three famous ones, and two not-sos.

Sam Cooke was a handsome man with a

beautiful, raspy voice; **singers he influenced include Otis Redding, Al Green and Rod Stewart.** He was near the top in show business when he was killed at a seedy motel in Los Angeles on December 11, 1964.

The circumstances weren't pretty. A married man with kids, he'd taken a girl he met at Martoni's Hollywood restaurant to a motel in south Los Angeles. As he undressed, she fled, and he chased after her, wearing little more than a topcoat. He banged on the manager's door, thinking she was inside. The manager, afraid of the seeming madman, shot him dead.

Conspiracy theories abound, but what's sure is that when he died, a chunk of America's soul died with him.

In 1957 Cooke was an established gospel music star when he took a crack at pop music. The gamble paid off: His first song "You Send Me" was a smash hit. After that he was rarely off the upper reaches of the pop charts with "Havin' a Party," "Chain Gang," "Twistin' the Night Away," "Cupid" and many others.

He might've gone where? Who knows? If only he hadn't gone to that motel.

John Lennon died maybe of naivete. Happy, alert and recording for the first time in five years, **he'd walk the streets of New York "free as a bird," but he left** too many windows of opportunity open. On December 8, 1980, a supposed fan who flew to New York City for the purpose of meeting, or killing, the ex-Beatle, shot and killed him outside Lennon's residence, the Dakota. The man was imprisoned for life, Lennon's widow was inconsolable, his children were deprived of a father and his **fans felt the loss as if an asteroid had collided with the Earth.**

A spot in New York's Central Park has been named Strawberry Fields in Lennon's memory.

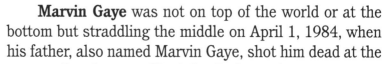

Marvin Gaye was not on top of the world or at the bottom but straddling the middle on April 1, 1984, when his father, also named Marvin Gaye, shot him dead at the Gay (true spelling) family home in Los Angeles. *They were having a family squabble, and Gaye's father, whose mental state was shaky, settled it conclusively.*

Gaye Jr. was plagued with tax problems, marital problems and drug use. He had fled America for Belgium in the late 1970s but returned to record "Sexual Healing," his first hit in many years.

Thanks to his trigger-happy pop, he never got to fully resume his proper place in American music.

Larry Williams had a lot to live for, it would seem, when his life ended in his Hollywood hillside home on January 2, 1980. He had had a modestly successful career as a musician over the past 25 years, and two of his songs had been recorded by the Beatles and one by the Stones, making for a pretty darned good annual songwriting royalty income.

But his death was ruled a suicide for a good reason: He was found dead with a gun in his hand, in a room locked from the inside. Why did people think otherwise? Because he showed no signs and made no announcement of ending his life, and his non-music business associates were on the unsavory side—pimps, prostitutes and drug dealers.

A hit? A rub-out? A genie?

In any case, **a gun done it,** and it was the last of Larry.

John Dolphin ran several record labels in south Los Angeles in the 1950s, but his career was cut short by songwriter Percy Ivy. Ivy was **angry over**

unpaid royalties, and he was not alone: Many people were angry at Dolphin for that and other business reasons. But Ivy took things a step further and shot Dolphin dead in his office.

What's so important about Dolphin to have his story listed alongside the famous people we've mentioned? Just the company he kept that fateful day. Also in the office were two Beverly Hills teenagers presenting Dolphin the rock & roll instrumental they'd recorded. The two teenagers, Sandy Nelson[1] and Bruce Johnston,[2] never got that record on Dolphin's label, but in Johnston's words, "got a hell of an introduction to the record business."

[1] Sandy Nelson's next noticeable gig would be drumming on "To Know Him Is to Love Him" by the Teddy Bears. A year later he had his own hits, "Teen Beat" and "Let There Be Drums," and then he dominated the rock-drum record field through the '60s. He later lost a leg in a motorcycle accident. Other drummers to lose or not have limbs are Rick Allen of Def Leppard, who lost an arm as a result of an auto accident in 1986, and Moulty (Victor Moulton) of the Barbarians, from Boston, who had a hook for a left hand. (The Barbarians had two important hits, 1965's "Are You a Boy or Are You a Girl," and the follow-up, "Moulty," his story of the difficulty of meeting girls when you have only one hand.)

[2] Bruce Johnston next produced Ron "Love You So" Holden for Donna Records, made surf records both as the Ripchords and as Bruce and Terry with partner Terry Melcher, joined the Beach Boys in 1965 as Brian Wilson's stage replacement and, in the late 1970s, wrote "I Write the Songs," which became a huge hit for Barry Manilow.

 Paranoia Runs Amok: the Sunset Strip Riots

In the 1930s an unincorporated[1] area of Sunset Boulevard known as the Sunset Strip was the gambling capital of California. Late in 1938 the gangsters and gamblers were thrown out (and not long afterward Las Vegas was born), but the nightclubs and the jazz joints stayed.

In 1965 things were changing. The Beatles and the Rolling Stones revived the sounds of Chuck Berry on the American Top 40, and television was booming the message to teenagers. In New York Ed Sullivan boosted his ratings with rock & roll acts, but **the most down rock & roll shows emanated from Los Angeles:** *Shindig, Hullabaloo, Where The Action Is, Hollywood a Go Go, Shivaree, Shebang, 9th Street West* and *Lloyd Thaxton's Hop.* Even *American Bandstand* was in town, so L.A. became the most important stop on every band's itinerary. Sunset Boulevard was the creative center of this universe, and the youth of the city flocked to the overspill of clubs accommodating the action. **The Trip,** the Sea Witch, *the Red Velvet,* the London Fog, **the Hullabaloo**, Ciro's (later It's Boss), the Gazzarri's Hollywood Palladium, the Cheetah, P.J.'s, **Gazzarri's,** the **Whisky a Go Go** and Pandora's Box to name some, featured incoming talent. A wide array of local bands, including the *Byrds*, Love, **the Standells,** the Seeds, the Bobby Fuller Four, the Music Machine, the Leaves, Buffalo **Springfield**, **the Doors** and Frank Zappa and the Mothers of Invention set the world on its ear. Brian Wilson created *Pet Sounds* and *Smile* in this atmosphere, and many groups from the Bay Area immigrated, too: the Chocolate Watch Band, the Syndicate of Sound and the Count 5 were welcomed warmly.

Needless to say, ***the Strip was rocking to new sounds during the summer of 1966.*** But local businesses and city administrators didn't get it. Why weren't these kids going to movies? More established jazz clubs were losing business from the kids filling the streets. These kids looked strange in their mod clothes and long hair, so in November 1966, **city barons decided to squeeze them out by enforcing a 10 p.m. curfew on teenagers.** The LAPD and L.A. County Sheriff's Department, whose *vigor in squelching social deviance* was tougher than other cities' police departments (with a low crime rate, they had time and billy clubs on their hands), **enthusiastically wailed on errant kids on the Strip** and at other favored gathering spots (Canter's on Fairfax, for one), leading to the Sunset Strip riots. Kids gathered around Pandora's Box at Sunset and Crescent Heights when news of the club's demolition was announced, and vowed to hold their ground. Armed, helmeted police, rehearsing for political protests to come, laid into unarmed adolescents with zeal. In the melee **windows were broken, buses were destroyed, cars were overturned and people were arrested.**

Stephen Stills witnessed this mayhem and, **sickened,** wrote "For What It's Worth" (see "Don't Let Me Be Misunderstood", page 204). (The movie *Riot on Sunset Strip* is an artificial but still evocative look at the times, featuring the Standells and the Chocolate Watch Band performing at Pandora's Box. You can also get impressions of the times in the B-films *Mondo Mod, Mondo Teeno: The Teenage Rebellion*, *You Are What You Eat* and *Mondo Hollywood*.)

After the fracas, the scene cooled, and a lot of music people headed north to San Francisco. By 1970 the Sunset Strip was a ghost of its former rock & roll prominence. A few clubs lingered, but the scene had vanished. In the late '70s a new local scene flourished, first with the punk rock scene at the Whisky and the Starwood with **X, the Germs, Black Flag and others,** then with the folk- and roots-rock scene with *the Blasters, Los Lobos, the Long Ryders* and others. As the '80s unfolded, bands such as the Knack, 20/20 and the Plimsouls defined a new power-pop scene.

Simultaneously, an enormous Heavy Metal scene developed on the same Strip, spanning the Whisky to the Rainbow. The parade of leather and denim, mascara and hair was awesome, but established bands found the **new club rules bogus: pay-for-play** was the new way (instead of bands being hired by a club, a promoter would rent the hall for a night, charge the band for the privilege of playing there and pay them back from the door profits, if there were any. Cynics say it was fueled by indulgent parents laying out cash for their kids' hard-rock dreams). Though the hair-heads are gone now, pay-for-play is still in practice, so **don't envy your friend if you see his name in lights**: He may have paid for it.

[1] Not officially under Los Angeles city jurisdiction.

Don't Let Me Be Misunderstood: Some Songs That Were Hits for the Wrong Reasons

In early 1967, in the heat of nationwide **tension over the Vietnam War, one song stood out** as an anthem of youth: ***"For What It's Worth" by Buffalo Springfield.*** Its shimmering, eerie guitar opening set a somber tone, and the lyrics, about "something happening here, what it is ain't exactly clear" and "Paranoia strikes deep, into your life it will creep" **touched a nation being ripped apart** by the Vietnam conflict.

But that's not what the song was about. It was a much smaller issue, the manhandling of kids on Los Angeles' Sunset Strip. Cops clobbered them freely on a couple of consecutive weekends late in 1966, and the resulting paranoia and fear (sometimes paranoids are *right*) was reflected in the haunting song. (See "Paranoia Runs Amok," page 202.)

It's not the first time a song got popular for the

wrong reason.

In 1959 pop-vaudevillian producer-songwriters Leiber and Stoller wrote a song, "Charlie Brown," for their group the Coasters (so named for their locale on "the Coast," New York parlance for Los Angeles). Its popularity had to be at least slightly fueled by record buyers familiar with Charlie Brown of the "Peanuts" comic strip.

Then, in 1964 RCA Records cagily released a cut off a corny album of Western songs by Lorne Greene, the father on the *Bonanza* television show, about a gunslinging gambler with a Western name. The song, "Ringo," rocketed up the charts as kids grasped for anything remotely associated with the Beatles, wrongly thinking it was a fable spun around *their* Ringo.

Three years later, another song leaped onto the charts for entirely the wrong reason. **"I Was Kaiser Bill's Batman"** was a British instrumental by Whistling Jack Smith. It had no relevance to Americans, who did not know that a batman is a valet to a British army officer. On the contrary, American record buyers heard the key word and assumed it referred to the still-popular camp TV show *Batman*.

Bruce Springsteen's 1984 record **"Born in the U.S.A."** is often viewed as a **bit of American chauvinism**, with the Boss singing about his beloved native land, but in fact it is about tough times felt by Vietnam vets. (The opening line, "Born down in a dead man's town" is a hint.) The character is **screaming** he was *born in the U.S.A. and a fat lot of good it's done him*.[1]

Like "Louie Louie," another Springsteen song got mileage out of mistaken lyrics. "Blinded by the Light," from his *Greetings from Asbury Park* album, was a big hit for Manfred Mann in 1977 partly because people—snickering boys, one imagines—thought they were hearing the word "douche" when they sang "like a deuce."

Two big Randy Newman songs—I should say THE two big Randy Newman songs—lent themselves to misunderstanding. **"Short People,"** in 1978, was a satire of how unfeeling people can be; there are so many prejudices in the world, why haven't they thought of persecuting people for being short? Of course, the song was taken literally by the selfsame ugly-spirited people it lampooned, and hurt the feelings of some height-challenged Americans to boot. On a reverse note, *"I Love L.A.,"* in 1983, was embraced virtually as a city anthem, its dark intent overlooked. It's bouncy, and it has that chorus shouting "We love it," but what is it saying? You and me, babe, all we gotta do is put the top down and ride? It's **an indictment of empty values**, of looking at the mountains and the trees and **ignoring the bum down on his knees.**

Some songs seem romantic but aren't:

- The Turtles' "Happy Together" is a lament about the singer's wish that he were with the object of his affection. The seeming nonsequitur line "How is the weather," is him changing the subject to keep from crying.

- "Tell It Like It Is" is a favorite slow-dance record in which the singer is telling his girl to hmfff or get off the pot, that he'll find another girl if she won't commit to him.

- Engelbert Humperdinck's "Release Me" is another snuggle favorite, in which the singer says, "I don't love you anymore, I want to go off with someone else."

- **R.E.M.'s "The One I Love" is accepted as a romantic ballad,** when he's actually saying *"I'm glad you're gone."*

But people don't listen to lyrics, do they?

[1] Ronald Reagan, no rock connoisseur (he read about it in a newspaper article by George Will, who didn't get it either), cited Bruce's song as evidence that pride in America was returning.

Janis Joplin Survives Rejection, Becomes Queen of the Blues

Janis Joplin's singing roared defiance to the demons that plagued her: loneliness, rejection and self-doubt. But music wasn't enough, and—fighting fire with fire?—**she picked another demon, heroin, to banish them**. And that was the end of Janis.

She was reared in Port Arthur, Texas, an oil refinery town on the Gulf of Mexico. A loner, she suffered a *tormented adolescence plagued by acne and weight gains.* **In college she gravitated toward arty and beatniklike folk singing** and poetry at the University of Texas at Austin. She sang at coffeehouses (and at Threadgills, a popular restaurant that still honors her memory), but college-town life wasn't her scene. She left after a school poll handed her what must have been the worst news of her life: She had been voted Ugliest Man on Campus.

She traveled to pre-hippie San Francisco to seek kindred souls. After suffering a nervous breakdown—who knows what drugs contributed to it—she returned briefly to Port Arthur and later played in bands around Austin. In 1966 she heard that a San Francisco band, Big Brother and the Holding Company, needed a lead singer, so she flew back there to her destiny. **In 1967 she turned the Monterey Pop Festival on its ear with a torrid, stuttering, gut-busting blues performance** that pushed her promptly to the top of the emerging hippie scene.

She instantly became the psychedelic rock scene's best-known character. Hard-living and hard-loving, she seemed to be making up for all the unhappiness of her teen years and early 20s. She dressed outrageously, swore freely, took lovers, imbibed drugs and swilled Southern Comfort like it was soda. In one highly publicized event, she returned to her Port Arthur high school reunion to rub everyone's face in her fame. And she contributed money to erect a headstone on the grave of Bessie Smith, the great blues singer.[1]

Janis reigned as *queen of the psychedelic blues* in the late 1960s, singing lead on the million-selling *Cheap Thrills* album (1968) with Big Brother, and then on her own on *I Got Dem Ol' Kozmic Blues Again Mama!* (1969). She had just more or less finished the brilliant album, *Pearl* (her nickname), on October 3, 1970, and was set to be married, so it's doubtful she had suicide on her mind when she shot pure heroin into her vein and died at her room at the Landmark Hotel in Hollywood. It's pretty much agreed that she didn't know it was 100 percent stuff—**heroin was normally cut by drug dealers. It was just her bad luck she got an honest one.**

As provided in her will, money was set aside for a big party after her death, with cards on tables proclaiming "the drinks are on Pearl."

[1] Smith was a blues singer of the 1920s and 1930s. She died of injuries suffered September 26, 1937, in a car accident near Clarksdale, Mississippi. (The "classic" story, that she was taken to a white hospital and denied treatment and died en route to a colored hospital, is lately in disfavor.) A touching tribute to Janis' headstone gesture is "A Stone for Bessie Smith," on the long-deleted 1973 Dory Previn album, *Mythical Kings and Iguanas* (Medi-Arts 40-10).

1967   Hendrix Booted from Monkees Tour by DAR (Not)

Jimi Hendrix's performance at the Monterey Pop Festival (see "Hendrix And Who," page 180) was witnessed by Monkees members Micky Dolenz (who had seen Hendrix in London) and Peter Tork. They'd tried, and failed, to get the Monkees on the bill to establish their credibility, but when they saw Hendrix they had another brainstorm: How about Hendrix opening for them on their upcoming tour?

Hendrix's co-manager Mike Jeffery[1] agreed this was a good idea despite co-manager Chas Chandler's[2] reluctance, and Jimi played his first show with the Monkees on July 8, 1967, in Jacksonville, Florida.

Audience response was chilly. Hendrix did 20 or 25 minutes, often with his back to the audience, who weren't interested either. They moved him out of the "death slot" (right before the Monkees, when Monkee anticipation was reaching fever pitch) but that did no good.

Hendrix was pulled off the show, but Chandler and tour promoter Dick Clark needed a pretext, so **publicists concocted a story that the Daughters of the American Revolution (DAR)** (right-wing people were handy bogeymen, or bogeywomen, back then) **objected to Hendrix's sexuality and**

demanded he be sacked.[3]

His last day of Monkee business was July 16, making him a literal "nine-day wonder."[4]

[1] Mike Jeffery was "probably the most mysterious and elusive manager of any big-name act," according to Harry Shapiro and Caesar Glebbeek's authoritative book, *Jimi Hendrix: Electric Gypsy* (Heinemann Ltd., London, 1990). His financial dealings were bizarre, his background was vague (he hinted at government undercover work) and he was never photographed without his shades. When he died in a plane crash in 1973, he was being sued by both the Hendrix estate and the Animals.

[2] Chandler, bass player for the Animals, saw Jimi working as Jimmy James (see "Teenager Randy Wolf," page 131) at the Cafe Wha? in New York and hocked his instruments to finance Jimi's early days in England.

[3] News to both Hendrix and the DAR, but it's widely reported even today that this was the reason for his departure.

[4] A military term for someone who moves up in rank too fast. Familiar to Hendrix, who was in the Army from 1959 until he was discharged in 1961 because of a parachuting injury.

 ## Brian Jones Dies in His Own Swimming Pool

Brian Jones, co-founder and original lead guitarist of the Rolling Stones, had an encyclopedic knowledge of the blues, but he wasn't a songwriter.[1] As Jagger and Richards began to realize the monetary benefits of doing original material, Jones had less and less of a place in the band. The more alienated he became, the more his drug and alcohol intake increased, creating *a vicious circle that culminated in his "quitting" the band.* (There is little doubt that he was actually **pressured into doing so by Jagger.)**

His terse announcement, "The Stones' music is not to my taste anymore"[2] came on June 9, 1969. Due to his numerous drug busts, Jones had now switched to alcohol and his life collapsed around him. Not only had he been booted from the band he founded, but his girlfriend, Anita Pallenberg, had dumped him for bandmate Richards.[3]

Alcohol may well have contributed to Jones' death;

he was found accidentally drowned[4] in his own swimming pool on July 2.[5]

[1] One Jones song now exists. In 1990 Carla Olson (founder of the Textones, recording partner of Gene Clark and Mick Taylor) set a Jones poem, "(Thank You) For Being There??" to music. It appears on the album *True Voices* (The Right Stuff/Capitol), performed by Scottish vocalists Krysia Kristianne and Robin Williamson.

[2] If this had been proffered when *Their Satanic Majesties Request* was released, nobody would have questioned its veracity. (The title is a goof on the phrase "By Her Britannic Majesty's Request," which appears on British passports. An earlier album's title, *Between the Buttons*, was an art director's note as to where the title was to appear; "buttons" were markers on the layout.)

[3] Obviously drug use in paramours was not a hang-up for her.

[4] The incident was ruled "death by misadventure" by the coroner. Like most celebrity deaths, this one is mired in controversy. Suicide was never seriously considered. A.E. Hotchner, in his book *Blown Away: The Rolling Stones and the Death of the 60s* (Simon & Schuster, 1990), spins a yarn about jealous, thieving on-site workers drowning Jones in full view of a dozen witnesses. A Brian Jones biography by Terry Rawlings, *Who Killed Cock Robin*, (Boxtree, UK, 1995), says Stones roadie Tom Keylock got a deathbed confession from Jones employee Frank Thorogood that he indeed killed Jones. Thorogood was reportedly miffed that he had been dismissed, and was jealous of Jones' lifestyle.

[5] Remember "Sympathy for the Devil," the July 5, 1969, Stones concert at Hyde Park, where Jagger wore a dress? It had been planned for the debut of Brian replacement Mick Taylor, but when Jones died on July 2 they switched it to a tribute to him. (If you look up gall in the dictionary, this story might be supplied as the definition. Also known as the "Crocodile Tears for the Devil" concert.)

 ## Jim Morrison Caught with Pants Down, America Terrified

The Doors were the house band at the Whisky a Go Go in Los Angeles before they landed a contract with Elektra Records in 1966.

One night they played their first set as a trio because Jim Morrison didn't show up. Between sets, Robby Krieger, John Densmore and Ray Manzarek went to his room at the Tropicana Motor Hotel to get him. Hearing simpering noises, they broke in and pulled him out from under a bed, where he had been hiding after taking psychedelics.

Back to the Whisky for the second set, Morrison altered, for the first time, their song "The End." As he went into the chant, **"The killer awoke before dawn, he put his boots on,"** the usually **raucous Whisky crowd fell silent, staring open-mouthed** as Morrison screamed about killing his father and fucking his mother.[1] The band was fired on the spot.

Within a year, they were the biggest band in America.

Most of the songs they played then had been written by Morrison in early 1965 during a three-week mescaline binge while living on a friend's roof in Venice, California.[2]

Rock has always meant rebellion, and being the son of a U.S. Navy admiral during the Vietnam war, Jim had a lot to rebel against.

He looked like a Greek God and was possessed of a unique baritone voice, a deep mind and a way with words.[3] He was also, at times, a raving, drug-addled, alcoholic goofball; *in his words, "an intelligent, sensitive human with the soul of a clown,* which always forces me to blow it at the most important moments."

Many of those moments got him into trouble, and he was arrested numerous times both onstage and off, culminating in a Miami concert where he was charged with exposing himself and causing a riot. His trial lasted months. Decency rallies were held in various cities to protest his behavior (and rock & roll in general), and in the end he was found guilty of indecent exposure (later reversed). Although there are hundreds of photos of this concert, none shows him **drawing his rapier,** which leads one to conclude that **it was either a police setup** or, as he felt, *a mass hallucination.*

It's hard now to imagine a time when rock musicians were so feared that society would go to the lengths it did to persecute Morrison. But **at that time rock had a**

power and a social relevance that it does not enjoy today—The Red Hot Chili Peppers perform naked with socks on their John Thomases and nobody protests.

But the Miami incident caused deep problems for the Doors. Where once they had been critical favorites, they now were a parlor joke, and although they recorded some great and lasting records after Miami, while Morrison lived they never again enjoyed the acclaim of the rock press.[4]

He wanted to be a poet, like his hero Arthur Rimbaud, and remembered for his words. Indeed, after his death by heroin overdose in Paris in 1971, the marker on his grave at Pere-Lachaise cemetery[5] said (until it was stolen) "Jim Morrison, Poet."

[1] He always said in interviews that his parents were dead.

[2] In fact, most of the songs on the Doors' first three albums were written in this astonishing period. Jim claimed it was like automatic writing. Among the songs that Morrison didn't write were "Light My Fire" and "Love Me Two Times," their first two big hits. In a rare show of generosity (for a rock band), all their compositions were credited to the Doors as a group. Upon his death, Morrison's estate passed to his wife, Pamela. When she died (probable heroin overdose) in 1974, all his earnings passed to her parents, who subsequently struck a deal to split it with Morrison's parents. The ultimate irony is that two institutions he hated, the military (father) and the school system (father-in-law, a high school principal), ultimately got his money.

[3] He also had a photographic memory and could recall verbatim passages from any book he read.

[4] The Doors became bigger after his death. In the mid-1970s they were rediscovered by a new generation of fans, and the clamor has never let up. But *Rolling Stone* seemed to begrudge him (possibly retaining the "traditional" San Francisco hatred of anything from L.A.) when in the 1980s they ran beneath his cover photo, "He's hot, he's sexy, he's dead."

[5] Even in death he was still causing trouble. Due to graffiti, vandalism and alcohol use at his grave site, when his lease on his grave in Paris expires, it reportedly will not be renewed.

Some Sexual Landmarks

Starting in 1967, the Plaster Casters, a group of strangely **enterprising young women** in Chicago, *took plaster casts of rock stars' balls and penises.* Rock stars lined up eagerly to be so immortalized. The Monkees were first on the list (though Jimi Hendrix's, they say, is, mmmm, "numero uno"). Speaking of Jimi, England picked up on Hendrix's sexual appeal more than libido-phobic America and ran a more liberated *Electric Ladyland* cover (pictured here).

In the Grand Funk song "We're an American Band," they mention **"sweet sweet Connie from Little Rock, she had the whole band and that's a natural fact."**[1] Connie of Little Rock gave oral sex to every band member that passed through town—every member in the "head count" sense, roadies, publicists, van drivers included. *(Supposedly she even did a later famous Arkie governor, too!)*

Rick "Super Freak" James' interest in "restraint" sex led, allegedly, to the point where he and a girlfriend kept a woman captive for two days. He was tried and convicted. Such goings-on make it hard to believe that James started his music career in a squeaky folk-music group in Canada with Neil Young.

In the August 9, 1969 *Rolling Stone*, early rocker Ronnie Hawkins told about visits he and his old band-mate, Band drummer Levon Helm, made to an Arkansas hooker named Odessa: "Levon was always the best fuck-er," he told interviewer Ritchie Yorke. "I remember with Odessa that Levon would go first, and when I went in she would say, 'Mr. Ronnie, you can go ahead, but I think Mr. Levon has gone and taken it all. That Mr. Levon has a strip of meat on him like a horse!" The comments didn't sit well with "Mr. Levon," who was a happily-married family man at the time.

In 1970, **51-year-old Canadian Prime Minister Pierre Trudeau took a 22-year-old wife. Margaret Trudeau's** youth and spriteliness contributed to Pierre's image as a young-thinking chief executive, and probably to his re-elections, but she was terribly independent-minded. She **missed state functions to go to rock & roll shows;** at one she was photographed sitting with her dress up, plainly sans underwear. In 1977 her antics hit a high note when she left Ottawa (and her husband, and her three children, and her wedding anniversary) to see a Rolling Stones show, taking a room adjoining Keith Richards' at the Harbor Castle Hilton. She attended shows with Richards, slept with Mick Jagger and, as the tour continued, switched to Ron Wood. After she switched to Wood, Jagger ungallantly remarked, "I wouldn't go near her with a barge pole." Pierre Trudeau, when asked about his wife's whereabouts, sensibly replied, "None of your damn business."

---

[1] On the original records. Later pressings omitted this passage.

John Lennon Ejected From the Troubadour–Twice

In 1974 John Lennon was on a tear. Separated by distance and, possibly, by formal arrangement from Yoko Ono, he made his home in Los Angeles and often embarked on **nocturnal nightclub visits.** Wherever he went there was a stir, because L.A. or no L.A., *this was John Lennon,* and people got excited. But sometimes the excitement wasn't all that positive.[1]

What's remembered by most casual rock fans is that Lennon went into the Troubadour, the famous L.A. nightclub, with a **Kotex taped to his forehead and disrupted** a show by the Smothers Brothers. He was **thrown out,** along with Harry Nilsson. Those things happened, all right, but that story's a hodgepodge. Actually, *things happened on two different nights.*

On a Saturday night in January, John and his girl-

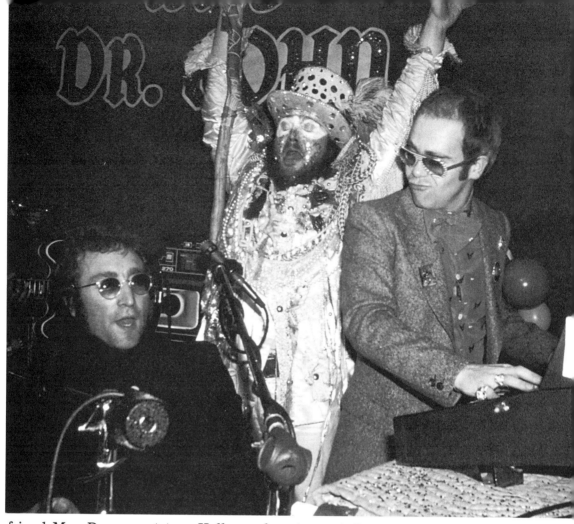

friend May Pang went to a Hollywood restaurant, Lost On Larabee, with drummer Jim Keltner, his wife Cynthia, and guitarist Jesse Ed Davis and his girlfriend. After a few rounds of double brandy Alexanders, Lennon repaired to the bathroom, where he rummaged through a supply cabinet and found a ladies' sanitary napkin, which he affixed, with tape apparently, to his forehead. Returning to his table, the others acted amused by John's childish stunt and had more drinks till the manager suggested the noisy party leave. They went a few blocks west to the Troubadour, where Ann Peebles, then hot with "I Can't Stand the Rain," was playing. Lennon insisted on wearing his new head ornament[2] when they went in, but in the course of the show he made so much noise (including shouting obscenities at the stage) that

"Three Johns" at Troubadour, October, 1973: (Left to Right) Lennon, Dr. and Elton.

the Troubadour management asked them to leave, too.[3]

Two months later, on March 12, 1974, while on a drinking binge with Harry Nilsson,[4] Lennon re-visited the Troubadour along with constant companion Pang. There the two men, already in their cups, made a fuss before **the Smothers Brothers appearance,[5] disturbing fellow A-list section attendees Peter Lawford and others. Then they really went into a monkey show** when the star performers hit the stage, bellowing such brilliant lines as **"Hey Smothers Brothers, fuck a cow."** After several minutes of this, distraught Smothers manager Ken Fritz grabbed Lennon by the shoulder and told him to cool it.[6] Lennon stood up to fight and overturned his table, prompting a phalanx of Troubadour bouncers, reportedly **_led_ by actor Lawford, to swoop down on Lennon, fists flying** and force him out of the room. While outside sheepishly waiting for the valet to get their car, Nilsson tried to swing at photographers, resulting in a famous drunken-rock-star photo that was engraved in the minds of music lovers worldwide.

---

[1] Not all of his Troubadour visits were confrontational. In October 1973, Lennon and Elton John amiably got onstage with Dr. John at his headlining performance there and jammed.

[2] Supposedly he said, "Do you know who I am?" to the waitress, and she said, "You're some asshole with a Kotex on your forehead." In May Pang's book, *Loving John*, Jesse Ed Davis actually does the waitress-needling, with no memorable response from the waitress, who was too swamped with drink orders to hassle with the ex-Beatle.

[3] May Pang's book says they then returned to her West Hollywood apartment, where Lennon, now falling-down drunk, beaned Davis with a Coke bottle so severely that they thought he'd killed him. Davis was OK when the police arrived (one asked Lennon, "Do you think the Beatles will ever get back together?").

[4] Supposedly being "on a drinking binge with Harry Nilsson" was somewhat redundant, because Nilsson was on a perpetual binge. He died in 1994 mainly because nothing could be done to save his drink-ravaged physique. (See "Harry Nilsson Gets $5 Million," page 184.)

[5] Pang's book reports that Lennon and Nilsson chanted and banged out the Ann Peebles song, "I Can't Stand the Rain" before the show, obviously in reference to Lennon's previous disruptive visit to the club.

[6] In 1969 the Smothers Brothers were dumped by CBS-TV for being too "radical"

on their highly rated weekly TV series, and this night was to be their comeback show, their first public appearance in five years. (See "Keith Moon Deafens Stage Explosion," page 118.)

1973 Road Manager Steals Gram Parsons' Body, Attempts to Burn It in the Desert

Gram Parsons is a rare example of a person both famous and obscure. In his lifetime Parsons **neither wrote a hit song nor saw a record he performed on reach the Billboard charts.**[1] His albums never sold well, but they sure moved a lot of people in a deep way.

Since his death at age 26 in 1973, praise for his music has spread like ripples from an asteroid crashing into the sea. Every day, the *circles of his influence extend further.*[2]

He's best known as an inspiration to others. His girlfriend Emmylou Harris went on to substantial fame after her time with him and she continues to sing his praises. Bob Dylan's country-honed *Nashville Skyline* came on the heels of the **Byrds'** Parsons-led *Sweetheart of the Rodeo* and led to the country-rock explosion of the '70s. Elvis Costello recorded an entire album of Parsons songs and the **Eagles'** Bernie Leadon, an ex-bandmate of Parsons from the *Flying Burrito Brothers,* recorded "My Man" a song written about Parsons—

I once knew a man, very talented guy
He'd sing for the people, and people would cry
They knew that his song came from deep down inside
You'd hear it in his voice and see it in his eyes.

And let's not forget that the Stones' "Wild Horses" was written for, and probably about, him.

Born in Winter Haven, Florida, Gram Parsons, came to L.A. in 1967 with his group the International

Submarine Band and recorded an album, *Safe at Home*, that went nowhere. His next job was in the Byrds in 1968 replacing David Crosby. Byrds leader Roger McGuinn was leaning toward country when Parsons joined and virtually let Parsons and Byrd Chris Hillman craft *Sweetheart of the Rodeo*. (Parsons sang lead on many tracks, but his vocals were wiped off when his previous record label threatened suit.[3]) Too daring and too abrupt a style switch for Byrds fans, that album failed utterly (though like the Velvet Underground's poor-selling debut album, it left a trail of believers in its wake). Parsons soon left the Byrds, taking Chris Hillman with him, and founded his avant-garde country band, the Flying Burrito Brothers. Their two albums, *The Gilded Palace of Sin* (1969) and *Burrito Deluxe* (1970), further developed Parsons's "cosmic American music" dream but sank like stones.

For the next **couple of years Parsons hung around with Keith Richards,** assisting on the recording of *Exile on Main Street*; not coincidentally, the country-influenced "Honky Tonk Woman" emerged during that period. In 1972 he returned to L.A. and cut an album, *GP*, for Warner Bros. featuring vocal duets *that introduced that label to Emmylou Harris.* In the spring of 1973, after completing his second Warner album, *Grievous Angel*, he formed a touring band that included ex-Byrds guitarist Clarence White, but the tour was cut short on July 14 by White's hit-and-run death. Despondent at White's funeral, Parsons told his road manager, Phil Kaufman, to burn his body when he died at Cap Rock at Joshua Tree National Monument.

On September 19, 1973, Parsons died of a drug overdose at the Joshua Tree Inn in the California desert. **Kaufman, honoring his pact with Parsons, stole his body from the airport**[4] as it was to be shipped to New Orleans for burial, and trucked it to Cap Rock. There, Kaufman has said (in his book, *Road Manager Deluxe*, White Boucke, 1993), he and friend Michael Martin put gasoline in the casket and a joint in Gram's mouth and blew everything sky-high…thus releasing at least some of Parson's ashes into the desert air. Park authorities immediately spotted the fireball and retrieved the charred and scattered remains, which were moved to New Orleans for burial.

[1] But he saw at least one substantial royalty check, from Joan Baez singing his song "Drug Store Truck Drivin' Man," on the Woodstock soundtrack.

[2] *Hickory Wind* is the name of Ben Fong-Torres' book about Parsons' life. And Coal Porters singer Sid Griffin (formerly of the Long Ryders) assembled a book of Parsons quotes and remembrances titled *Gram Parsons, A Musical Biography* (Sierra Books, 1985).

[3] A Byrds box set released in the 1990s reinstated those vocals.

[4] The GTOs held a fund raising concert for Phil Kaufman at his North Hollywood home after his arrest. Music was provided by Bobby "Boris" Pickett and the Modern Lovers (among others).

Battling Brothers: Everlys Lead the Pack, Kinks a Close Second

The magic of the Everly Brothers was their **harmony, a tight-knit, family-bred musical con-**

fluence that astonished and inspired every rock & roll fan who heard it.[1] Personally, they harmonized as best they could, considering the fact that they were as firmly attached to each other as Siamese twins.

On July 14, 1973, they severed that tie at a show at Knotts Berry Farm amusement park in Los Angeles. Booked to do three shows that night, Don performed so wobbly and, perhaps, intoxicatedly during the first set that brother **Phil, nominally the quiet brother, smashed his guitar on the floor and stomped off,** instantly launching their solo careers.[2] (Don did the remaining two shows alone.) Individually the brothers enjoyed middling success for the ensuing 10 years. Phil's song, "The Air That I Breathe," was a hit for the Hollies, and both he and Don recorded several solo albums. They reunited in 1983 at an emotional, packed-house performance at London's Royal Albert Hall.

Known **more for their battles than for their harmonies** are brothers *Ray and Dave Davies of the Kinks.* As lead singer, elder brother Ray is the better known, while Dave, whose lead guitar riffs fueled several of their biggest hits, is the background player.

Their tussles span their career: *a ticket to a New York Kinks concert in the past 30 years was a potential double-deal. You might get both a concert and a full-scale fistfight, with bottles thrown and equipment overturned.* On the 1993 Kinks album *Phobia*, on Sony, Ray & Dave Davies sing a song called "Hatred (A Duet)," which includes the lyrics "Hatred, it's the only thing that keeps us together."

That covers the '50s and '60s, sort of. The '70s I dunno, unless you count the battles the Beach Boys brothers encountered trying to get Brian Wilson back on

On the wrong side of the road again, the Blasters in England, 1982: Dave Alvin on the right and Phil Alvin on left.

track. In the '80s the most noted battling brothers were Dave and Phil Alvin of the **Blasters.** Phil, the elder, held sway over the band through impeccable logic and threats, but his younger brother, the group's songwriter, was not easily swayed. Their battles in recording studios and on the *Today* show are well known and doubtless had a hand in Dave's decision to go solo in 1985.

On record, more brothers got along than didn't, at least for public consumption. Did the Isley Brothers fight? Johnny and Edgar Winter? David and Jimmy Ruffin? Don and David Was? (Oops, not really brothers. Don Was is Don Fagenson and David Was is David Weiss. But they're "Detroit brothers.".) (Kinda like the Doobie Brothers kicking out central writer-singer Tom Johnston.) the Kalin Twins? Tom and John Fogerty? (Oops again. They fought, and Tom quit, tired of being second fiddle—well, second guitar—to his younger brother.) the Ritchie Family? the Cowsills? **the Neville Brothers?** the Jackson Five? **the Osmonds?** the Ramone family? the Walker Brothers? (Triple oops. They weren't brothers either. Or even Walkers. And they split up.) the Brothers Johnson? Gunnar and Matthew Nelson? the Smothers Brothers? (THEY didn't fight, but they fought with John Lennon; see "Lennon Ejected from Troubadour," page 216.) *The Righteous Brothers were not related, but they fought.* In the 1990s Oasis has continued the sibling rivalry tradition: brothers Noel and Liam fought so badly their 1996 tour had to be cancelled.

Sisters? Surely Nancy and Ann Wilson had some fights, but none were Heart-breakers. **Sister Sledge were sisters,** and so were two members of Fanny. And don't forget the Peterson sisters in the Bangles; did they battle? **Aretha Franklin's sister Erma sang the original version of "Piece of My Heart,"** which Janis Joplin covered, but she and 'Retha never were an act. The Wilson sisters in Wilson Phillips parted ways; rancor?

Brother-sister acts are rare. Nino Tempo and April Stevens come to mind, as do the Carpenters, and Inez and Charlie Foxx ("Mockingbird"). As far as we know, no fisticuffs ever ensued in their shows. But one brother-sister act that was nipped in the bud, *to the lifelong regret of their fans, was the 1950s teenage rockabilly duo the Collins Kids.* Popular on TV but not on record (they had no hits), Larry (Lawrence) and Lorrie (Lawrencine—ooh, that's country) Collins were riding a steady rocket when 16-year-old Lorrie got married in 1958.[3] They reunited in 1993 in answer to the overwhelming clamor from rockabilly fans in England and throughout Europe.

[1] Beatles John and Paul were briefly named the Nurk Twins, after the Everlys. Let us not forget Paul's not-so-cryptic mention of "Phil and Don" in "Let Him In." Dave Edmunds and Nick Lowe and Rockpile released an EP of Everly covers in 1978.

[2] Warren Zevon, who was the Everlys' piano player for several years prior to their breakup, wrote a song about them, "Frank and Jesse James," on his self-titled Elektra/Asylum album in 1976.

[3] Lorrie was engaged to Ricky Nelson in 1957, but according to Nelson biographer Joel Selvin, dad Ozzie Nelson broke up the romance for the exact reason Ricky loved the Collins Kids: They were true hillbillies, Okies who migrated to L.A. Oz had grander things in store for young Eric (Ricky's given name).

Gay-Rock

Gays have always worked in popular music. Much of the best popular music of the 20th century came from gay songsmiths, including *Noel Coward and Cole Porter.* In the rock music field, though, they stayed hidden until the 1970s. Little Richard's bent, now apparent, was viewed as "theatrical" in the 1950s, and non-rocker Johnny Mathis' was whispered about but never broached.[1]

There were other blips on the screen, too. In 1966 the Stones appeared in drag for the single sleeve of "Have You Seen Your Mother Baby Standing in the Shadows," but it was hardly a homosexual statement, just British boys dressing up. (Dressing as women for a video would finally kill Queen in America. See "Freddie Mercury of Queen" page 81.) And, of course, **Jagger appeared in a dress**[2] **at their famous Hyde Park** concert in 1969. There was a teasing sexual ambiguity running through the Kinks'[3] 1970 song **"Lola,"** which **was not resolved in the final verse, "I'm glad**

I'm a man and so's Lola."

David Bowie finally broke the rock barrier in 1970 when he was pictured in a dress on the (U.K.) album cover for *The Man Who Sold the World*. In 1973, during his ***Ziggy Stardust phase, Bowie announced his bisexuality.*** Also in 1973, Lou Reed confronted homosexuality in **"Walk on the Wild Side."** [4]

Elton John's career took a nosedive, however, after admitting in a 1976 interview in Rolling Stone that he was bisexual. Two years passed between his moribund *Blue Moves* album, late 1976, and his comeback album, *A Single Man*, late 1978. Surely his November 1977 "retirement" did as much damage as his admission of gayness, but in the long run it did no harm, as he resumed Top 30 album sales in the 1980s.

In the late **1970s disco music, like Broadway, had a strong gay component, epitomized in cross-dressing Sylvester,** who never scored a big hit but left a big imprint on that scene. The Village People, four gay men and a straight lead singer, never *explained* the gay subtexts in their songs "Y.M.C.A." and "In the Navy," so many Americans remained clueless. And, of course, Queen's Freddie Mercury was blatantly gay but somehow it didn't register with his straight audience.

In the mid-1980s a huge wave of gayness washed over from England. The Tom Robinson Band, Culture Club's **Boy George,** Frankie Goes to Hollywood, the **Bronski Beat** and other new bands leaped out from MTV and radio in record numbers. On American shores, Bob Mould of **Husker Du,** who left that band in 1988 to pursue a solo career, came out.

By the 1990s it was no huge deal for k.d. lang to quietly confirm that she was what she seemed, a lesbian; ditto Melissa Etheridge, and the Indigo Girls. Several others have chimed in, too, including Pete Townshend and Michael Stipe. Unregenerate rockers such as Axl Rose (see "Another Manson Related Death", page 70) still lashed out at gays from time to time, but the Moral Majority/Pat Buchanan homophobic camp never seriously affected gay rockers.

[1] In the early 1950s torch singer Johnnie Ray, whose soulful singing style is often cited as setting the stage for Elvis Presley, was involved in several homosexual scandals but somehow weathered them. (For Ray's full story, read Jonny Whiteside's fascinating Ray bio, *Cry* [Barricade Books, 1993].)

[2] Jagger's heterosexuality is so unassailable that his poutiness and limp-wristed-ness was always dismissed as a sham, and Angie Bowie's "revelation" that she caught David in bed with him has been ignored. (The explanation: she had to sell books.)

[3] Straight performers widely effected gay mannerisms at the height of glam-rock: The New York Dolls, who wore dresses but otherwise acted like thugs, come to mind. Not all gays liked it. In the British *1985 Rock Year Book*, writer Jon Savage, celebrating the flood of gay musicians, chided the Sweet, whom he unkindly called "bricklayers," for wearing "rent-boy" makeup and lisping on "Ballroom Blitz" to promote heterosexual lust!

[4] In 1973, RCA, the conservative record label that in the 1950s had refused to show Elvis Presley covers on their inner-sleeve advertising, found itself the stronghold of gay rock with Bowie, Reed, and, if you considered "Lola" meaning-ful, the Kinks.

Sex Pistols Kill Their Career with U.S. Tour

In the '70s people paid $300 to go to a seminar where they were denied bathroom access, called ass-holes and told they'd been defrauded.

Sensing perhaps that this same ethic might apply to rock & roll, London promoter and anarchist-capitalist Malcolm McLaren *assembled a bunch of raga-muffins in a band that could not play music and presented them to the world as the next big thing.*

He was right.

Armed at first only with a penchant for insulting people, in late 1975 the Sex Pistols—lead singer Johnny Rotten, bassist Glen Matlock, guitarist Steve Jones and drummer Paul Cook—grew into a musical force that shook the world. Their musicianship was secondary to their passion, and their **passion was applied to their anger. They were pissed off about a lot of things,** and they quickly learned a lot of people felt the same way. That energy was harnessed by manager McLaren, who milked the situation masterfully for as long as it lasted. His outright sham worked until, like the Frankenstein monster, his creation raged out of his control.

The Pistols' *punk rock was a punch in the face to a music scene dominated by churchy groups like Emerson, Lake and Palmer,* country-rockers the Eagles and Linda Ronstadt and the dire specter of disco. Their music was hard-edged, fast and malevolent, and the lyrics simplistic, sarcastic and way over the top. (Songs about anarchy and royalty bashing were intentionally arch and over-reaching. Others, with subjects like "your baby is ugly" and "I'd like to spend a holiday in a concentration camp" were clearer clues to the con.) When lead singer Rotten emptied his nose onstage, it inspired, if that be the word, members of the audience to spit at him,[1] a "tradition" that followed them to the end. In the spring of 1976 they were splashed across the front pages in England as "Is this what the world's come to?" Like the plant in *Little Shop of Horrors* that craved blood, they fed on the controversy and thrived.

The Pistols' antagonism was real enough. **Rotten** was chosen by McLaren for the *malignant aura he exuded* hanging around McLaren's shop, Sex, in London. His ratty voice[2] conveyed it magnificently: **The transparent rage sent chills through both believers and non believers.**

In short time, the Sex Pistols became the rallying point for the disaffected youth of England and, to a lesser extent, of America.[3]

British record companies battled to sign them. In November 1976 EMI won, and promptly released the apocalyptic single "Anarchy in the U.K." A month later **EMI dropped them as too offensive, musically and personally,** after the band members swore on a TV interview. Next, A&M Records picked them up and paid them a bundle but held onto them for only a week.[4] Virgin Records finally landed them for long-term but released only the **near-sacrilegious "God Save the Queen"** (timed to ensure maximum outrage in England, it coincided with the national celebration of Queen Elizabeth's 25th year on the throne and featured the timeless rhyme, "God save the Queen she ain't a human bein'") and the album *Never Mind the Bollocks, Here's the Sex Pistols.*[5]

But by mid-1977 the ritual hostility that greeted a Sex Pistols concert had turned from mere absurdity to ugliness. People showed up just to pummel other people and spit on the band. Their tour of America in late fall 1977 was their swan song.[6] They intentionally booked into cities and places that were wrong for them—country music clubs, shopping malls, ballrooms and former strip bars. While people in big cities yearned to see them, people in the South and West ignored them or came to beat the shit out of them.

They had their own problems, too. Replacement

Rotten

bassist Sid Vicious (the first, Glen Matlock, was *fired reportedly after it was discovered he owned some Beatles records)* was a massively maladjusted kid who took readily to heroin; it caused him to kill, and then killed him.[7] He would routinely **slice his own flesh at concerts;** on the American tour he sliced his hand open at a truckstop and bled into his breakfast.

Like The Band (whom they probably had never heard of but surely would have hated), they chose Winterland in San Francisco for their last performance, on January 14, 1978. Malevolence hung in the air that night. Local punk bands opened the show, and L.A.-based "performance artist for a night" Richard Meltzer gave, at McLaren's insistence, a scabrous, insulting introductory monologue that matched the Pistols for ugliness of tone. The band was greeted by a volley of spit and gave back in kind. When they left, that was the last of the Sex Pistols.

Rotten, tired of being McLaren's puppet, quit the band after their final U.S. show. Resuming his given name John Lydon, he formed Public Image Ltd., which made records and toured through the '80s. Vicious died in 1979. Jones, Cook and Matlock went on to join several punk and pop bands of no distinction.

Proof of the lingering insincerity bannered in McLaren's documentary on the Sex Pistols, *The Great Rock & Roll Swindle*, was the band's seeming eagerness to re-form and tour without even rehearsing.

---

[1] Several punk-era performers, including Billy Idol of Generation X, developed conjunctivitis, an inflammation of the eyes from tainted saliva hurled at them.

[2] Rotten's screeching, bansheelike wailing over the band's loud, cluttered, anarchic backing sounded like a descent into Hell.

[3] It is also believed that the (American) Ramones' speed-rock, which hit America and England in 1976, was the real base for the punk-rock movement.

[4] EMI paid a massive 40,000 British pounds (more than $100,000 in U.S. dollars) for them, and A&M paid 150,000 British pounds (more than $300,000). This constitutes the only known instance of a band screwing a record company.

[5] *Bollocks* is a dirty word in England, translated roughly as "balls."

[6] Like the Velvet Underground, Iggy Pop, Big Star, X and other cult-audience bands, the Sex Pistols' primary influence on American music was their inspiration to nascent bands. Their album did not go gold here until 1989; the antimonarchy, pro-anarchy stance of their songs caused a huge stir in England, but none here. (For their U.S. concerts they altered "Anarchy in the U.K." to "Anarchy in the U.S.A." but no one cared.)

[7] He stabbed girlfriend Nancy Spungen to death on October 12, 1978, and died of heroin overdose on February 1, 1979. (The 1986 movie of their life, *Sid and Nancy*, featured Courtney Love.)

Poor Otis, Dead and Gone by Paul Body

Otis Redding was on his way to superstardom when he ended up in a frozen Wisconsin lake. Like Buddy Holly, Ritchie Valens and Eddie Cochran before him, he was, as Mick Jagger would say, *just a shot away.* The Big O started off as a Little Richard clone with a bit of Sam Cooke thrown into the mix. He ended up almost inventing a whole new thing: heartbreak in 6/8 time. *His voice could tear your heart out when he sang "These Arms of Mine" and "Change Gonna Come."*

He was huge in the barbershops of South Central L.A. and in the soul food palaces across the United States, but he wanted more. After a few years of solid rock on the soul stations, he wanted to cross over. He wanted some of that Beatles money. So in the summer of '67, he played the **Monterey Pop Festival.** Looking like a fullback in his electric-green suit, **he conquered the Love Crowd. That is what he called the hippies;** they had been seeing soul watered down and when they saw Otis, they were seeing the Chitlin Circuit through a haze of patchouli oil.

The Big O hung around Sausalito after the festival and ended up with the idea for "Sittin' on the Dock of the Bay." After an appearance on *Upbeat* with his backing band, the Bar-Kays of "Soulfinger" fame, they boarded his private plane and plunged into a frozen Wisconsin lake.

There was one survivor, but the Big O's luck had run out, and he died strapped in his seat. It was December 10, 1967, exactly three years after his hero Sam Cooke was gunned down in that L.A. motel.

Ironic, but luckily for his fans, he had left behind **a beautiful recording of "Dock of the Bay," and it went to number one** on the charts in early 1968. So Otis did cross over. Now he is in the Rock & Roll Hall of Fame; there is a piece of his plane, a crumpled-up part with his name on it. Talk about bad taste. They should have tried to get his electric-green suit, the one he wore at the Monterey Pop Festival.

ADDITIONAL BIBLIOGRAPHY

Amburn, Ellis, *Buddy Holly: A Biography*, St. Martins, 1995

Anderson, Christopher, *Mick Jagger Unauthorized*, Delacorte, 1993

Balzac, Honore de, *Lost Illusions*, 1847

Bono, Sonny, *And the Beat Goes On*, Pocket Books, 1991

Brown, James, with Tucker, Bruce, *James Brown: The Godfather Of Soul*, Thunder's Mouth, 1986

Cole, Richard, with Trubo, Richard, *Stairway To Heaven*, Harper Collins

Crosby, David, and Gottlieb, Carl, *Long Time Gone*, Doubleday

Friedman, Myra, *Buried Alive: the Biography of Janis Joplin*, Bantam, 1974

Goldman, Albert, *The Lives of John Lennon*, Morrow, 1988

Goldrosen, John, *Remembering Buddy*, Viking Penguin, 1986

Hadleigh, Boze, *The Vinyl Closet: Gays In the Music World*, Los Hombres Press, 1991

Hardy, Phil, and Laing, Dave, *The Faber Companion to 20th-Century Popular Music*, Faber & Faber (U.K.), 1990

Hoskyns, Barney, *Across the Great Divide - The Band and America*, Hyperion, 1993

Jancik, Wayne, *One-Hit Wonders*, Billboard, 1990

Jones, Allan, *Rock Yearbook 1985*, St. Martins, 1984

Marsh, Dave and Stein, Kevin, *Book of Rock Lists*, Dell, 1981

Marsh, Dave, *Born To Run: The Bruce Springsteen Story*, Dell, 1981

Marsh, Dave, and Bernard, James, *The New Book of

Rock Lists, Fireside, 1994

New Rolling Stone Encyclopedia of Rock & Roll, Fireside, 1995

Rogers, Don, *Dance Halls, Armories and Teen Fairs*, Music Archive, 1988

Ryan, Thomas, *American Hit Radio*, Prima Publishing, 1996

Sander, Ellen, *The Case of The Cock-Sure Groupies*, Realist, November 1968

Selvin, Joel, *Summer Of Love*, Dutton, 1994

Shannon, Bob, and Javna, John, *Behind the Hits: Inside Stories of Classic Pop and Rock & Roll*, Warner, 1986

Shapiro, Henry, and Glebbeek, Caesar, *Jimi Hendrix, Electric Gypsy*, Heinemann (U.K.), 1990

Spungen, Deborah, *And I Don't Want to Live This Life*, Villard, 1983

Stallings, Penny, *Rock 'n' Roll Confidential*, Little Brown, 1984

Sugerman, Danny, *Appetite for Destruction*, St. Martins, 1992

Tobler, John, *This Day in Rock*, Carlton (UK), 1993

Tobler, John, *The Rock 'n' Roll Years*, Crescent, 1990

Walser, Robt., *Running with the Devil: Power, Gender, & Madness in Heavy Metal Music*, Hanover: Wesleyan University Press, 1993

Whitburn, Joel, *Joel Whitburn's Top Pop Singles*, 1955-1990, Record Research, 1991

White, Timothy, *Rock Lives*, Henry Holt

Wilson, Brian, with Gold, Todd, *Wouldn't It Be Nice*, Harper Collins, 1991

Wolfe, Tom, *The Kandy Kolored Tangerine Flake Streamline Baby*, Pocket Books, 1966

INDEX

ABOUT THE AUTHOR

Art Fein started life at a very young age in Chicago, Illinois, and left when he was accepted at the University of Colorado sometime after the Paleozoic Era. Moving to Los Angeles at the turn of a decade, he worked peripathetically for a variety of record companies and newspapers, including *Variety*. In 1980 he left the comfort of hand-to-mouth freelance work for the more meager paying life of band management, semi-steering the careers of the Blasters, the Cramps, and then the Blasters again. (Along the way he co-produced the B's first couple of Slash albums.) In 1983 he assembled the album *L.A. Rockabilly* for Rhino Records (often difficult to find because its full title was *Art Fein Presents L.A. Rockabilly*), the first album appearance for Los Lobos and (solo) Dave Alvin, and the last for several others. In 1991 his first book, *The L.A. Musical History Tour* was issued by Faber & Faber of Boston, to critical huzzahs and even some sales. Whilst waiting to finish *The Greatest Rock & Roll Stories* for Rhino/GPG, he also contributed to Marshall Crenshaw's informative book *Hollywood Rock*, and wrote a book about Hanoi Rocks that was only printed in Japanese.

Fein's screen credits are as slender as he is: *Eating Raoul* was filmed in his apartment; he was music supervisor for the CBS-TV series *Tour of Duty*, as well as for several films; and he continues to host *Art Fein's Poker Party*, the public access TV show where he's interviewed Brian Wilson, Southern Culture on the Skids, Timothy Carey, Bull Moose Jackson, the Legendary Stardust Cowboy, Screamin' Jay Hawkins, Ted Hawkins—and *you* may be next.

He lovingly dedicates this book to the girls in his life: his wife Jennifer, his daughter Jessie, and Jessie's grandmothers.

Art Fein, Hollywood, California 1996

Art in 1973 (right) with some friends.